W9-BNC-065

Syntax, Speech & Hearing

APPLIED LINGUISTICS
FOR TEACHERS OF CHILDREN
WITH LANGUAGE AND HEARING DISABILITIES

Syntax, Speech & Hearing

APPLIED LINGUISTICS FOR TEACHERS OF CHILDREN WITH LANGUAGE AND HEARING DISABILITIES

Alice H. Streng

Professor Emeritus
Department of Exceptional Children
The University of Wisconsin-Milwaukee

GRUNE & STRATTON
New York and London

Library of Congress Cataloging in Publication Data
Streng, Alice H
Syntax, speech, and hearing.
Bibliography: p.
1. English language—Study and teaching (Higher)
2. English language—Grammar, Generative. 3. Deaf
—Education—English language. I. Title.
PE1066.S8 425 72-1072
ISBN 0-8089-0756-5

Grune & Stratton, Inc.
111 Fifth Avenue
New York, New York 10003

Library of Congress Catalog Card Number 72-1072
International Standard Book Number 0-8089-0756-5
Printed in the United States of America

To Verna

my tutor, my mentor, my colleague, my friend

Contents

Trees

Tables

Acknowledgments

To Professor Verna Newsome, my colleague at the University of Wisconsin-Milwaukee, who awakened my interest in modern linguistics and who guided and generously aided me throughout the writing of this book, I am most grateful.

To my students at the University of Wisconsin-Milwaukee and the University of Cincinnati who tested the original lessons and offered constructive suggestions for their improvement, I offer my sincere thanks. If they look closely they may find their names scattered throughout the book.

And finally, to my friend, Marian Quinn, Director of Hearing and Vision Services, Catholic Charities, Chicago, who provided the means for the production of the manuscript and to Marguerite Maguire who typed it, I am very much indebted. Without their help, it might not have materialized.

A. H. S.

Introduction

Language that is learned naturally through the ear develops so spontaneously, so effortlessly, and so early in life that one seldom stops to think about the process as a remarkable human feat. But when it is considered from the standpoint of children who have difficulty in their initial language learning, it unveils itself as a very complicated intellectual task.

One of the most evident conditions that prevent the natural learning of language is lack of hearing present at birth or acquired at a very young age. Other conditions that could deter the acquisition of language include faulty auditory perception, inability to relate spoken or graphic symbols to referents, inability to recall symbols, and very low intellectual capacity. Whatever the cause of linguistic deviance, the children who do not learn language naturally will need the guidance of teachers in acquiring an understanding of and proficiency in using language.

Anyone who aspires to teach English to children with language-learning problems will be a better tutor if he understands the manner in which language normally develops. Beyond that, he must be thoroughly grounded in the grammar, or syntax, of English. It would be quite unusual for an instructor in physics not to have a thorough theoretical knowledge of his subject, but it is not unusual to find teachers of language-handicapped children who are not adequately prepared for their task. The ability of a person to communicate his thoughts clearly in the spoken and written forms of language does not guarantee that he can teach children his own skills. He needs a thorough and detailed knowledge of how his language operates. This book is designed to present to teachers the minimum essentials of English grammar that are necessary for them to understand in order to guide children toward competent use of English. No single book could possibly include all the fine details of the grammar of a language. Therefore, only those aspects which are elementary and basic and which seem relevant to teaching children with language deficiencies have been included in this text.

Perhaps you have already been introduced to the new grammars used in linguistic study since the 1960's. One of these is transformational-generative grammar (Chomsky, 1957). Since a great deal of linguistic research has been based on the theoretical concepts propounded by transformationalists and since this approach presents very clearly and concisely the details of our language in a way not available in the older grammars, this text will be heavily slanted toward transformational grammar. Research in linguistics—especially in syntax—continues, and as linguists delve deeper and deeper into the subject, more information will be available to teachers. Because transformational grammar is only one way of looking at the structure of language, references will be made to aspects of language study not strictly related to the transformational point of view. Even though not all the questions about syntax have been answered by the new grammars, compared with the old prescriptive grammar they offer a freshness and clarity we have not enjoyed in the past.

Transformational-generative grammar uses much of the terminology of the old, but it adds a new dimension by stating rules essential to the understanding of English syntax in a precise manner. It suggests that each language has a basic sentence pattern from which all sentences can be generated by transforming the basic sentence: that is, by rearranging sentence word order, combining sentences, or deleting words and groups of words according to specific rules. Psycholinguists tell us that it is probably the fact that transformations are based on a single pattern that makes it possible to learn language. It would be quite impossible to remember thousands of discrete sentences that were unrelated to each other, but it is possible to generalize and internalize the rules that generate structurally related and at the same time structurally correct sentences. Normally, children do this by the time they are four years old if they have all the sensory and neurological requisites for acquiring language.

Rule learning is an inherent human ability, nicely illustrated by normal initial language learning. From a welter of sounds presented in no special order or under any special conditions, a young child discovers the rules of his language inductively. Nobody ever tells him that he should use a noun instead of an adjective or that "a noun is the name of a person, place or thing" while he is learning language, yet the child begins to categorize certain words and to incorporate them in the correct places in sentences. In short, he inductively formulates his own rules about grammar.

Children who must learn language in a more directed or structured manner because they cannot learn it naturally must not be burdened by definitions and rules *about* language. They may make faulty generalizations about the rules they are trying to formulate and may need the guidance of a teacher as they proceed to master them. Most children go through this stage before they gain proficiency in language. Handicapped children should also have this privilege.

Although the words *rule* and *rules* are widely used throughout the book, the rules referred to are for teachers, not for children. Children are not to be taught grammar; they are to be guided in *learning language* which has little or no relationship to learning rules or definitions about language. Sometimes it may be necessary to use the special vocabulary of grammar when discussing language with, for instance, older hearing-impaired children, but in general it is to be avoided. Instead, children are to be given opportunity to hear and see correctly formulated sentences and to be encouraged to make finer and finer approximations to correct forms. Teachers must be able to analyze the rules a particular child is using, compare his rules with the correct ones, and pick out salient points for clarification to aid him in reformulating his concepts about usage. Therefore, theoretical knowledge of grammar is a prior necessity for the teacher. Here and there, throughout this text, practical applications of theory to teaching are given. Appendix B contains further information that should help teachers in applying the theoretical aspects discussed.

Language, through its grammar and vocabulary, furnishes a means whereby one person's thoughts may be shared with another. There is no question that meanings are conveyed by the arrangement of words, but, beyond that, meaning also resides in the vocabulary we use. Grammarians tend to ignore the lexical aspects of the sentence, but teachers cannot. Communication requires meanings shared at both the syntactic and semantic levels. Therefore, teachers of language must guide children in acquiring a meaningful vocabularly to be used in correctly structured sentences. This is a big order for the learner, but if teachers present lexical meanings in known structures and new structures with known vocabulary, the child's very difficult task may be made a bit easier. Throughout this book, therefore, some attention is given to the importance of meaning beyond the grammatical in teaching new structures.

When you have mastered the contents of this book, you will only have begun to understand the vagaries of English, but you will nonetheless have a firm foundation for learning more about it and a factual framework for applying your knowledge in teaching language.

A.H.S.

LESSON 1

English— An Analytic, Ordered Language

ABSTRACT

- English gradually discarded many of its inflectional endings or regularized them.
- Rules governing word order must be mastered by the learner of English.

Grammarians tell us that the English we speak today differs considerably from English as it was spoken and written in its earliest form. English began its history as a Germanic dialect, but it was influenced along the way by the highly inflected Latin language which used endings to signify grammatical meaning. In Old English, the relationship of words in sentences was expressed by word endings, whereas in today's English the relationship depends on the order of words in a sentence and on the use of auxiliary verbs and prepositions. This characterizes English as an analytic language.

The next two sentences illustrate how meaning is influenced by word order in modern English:

> The man killed the wolf.
>
> The wolf killed the man.

In Old English it made no difference which word came first, second, or third in this kind of sentence, for the accusative object could be identified by the form of the article before it. Each of the following sentences means that the man killed the wolf:

> Ð e mann sloh ð one wulf.
>
> Ð one wulf se mann sloh.
>
> Ð one wulf sloh se mann.
>
> sloh se mann ð one wulf.

English gradually discarded or regularized many of its word endings, changed its pronunciation, and settled on word order as one of the main characteristics of its syntax.

While English-speaking children today may not be as burdened as Russian or German children are in learning and remembering countless word endings, they must comprehend the many rules of word order which English uses in the construction of its sentences. An entire string of words must be organized according to specific rules in order to carry meaning. Moreover, the word groups or constituents within the strings must have their own internal organization and order to make them sound like English.

EXERCISE

Look at the following strings of words in order to discover the importance of word order in the English language. Do these strings sound like English to you? Say these strings aloud as they are printed and then restate them in English word order. Underline the parts which seem out of order to you. Place an asterisk before the printed form of each of these sentences below to remind you that they are non-English sentences. The asterisk is the symbol used to denote this kind of sentence. Then write the corrected sentence in the blank:

1. we the satellite saw

____

2. we have our first satellite seen

____

3. did you where see the satellite

____

4. it traveled last night for an hour overhead

____

Answers:

To be underlined: 1. saw 2. seen 3. did you 4. last night, overhead

Corrected form:

1. We saw the satellite.
2. We have seen our first satellite.
3. Where did you see the satellite?
4. Last night it traveled overhead for an hour.

EXERCISE

Try arranging the following six words in four different ways and note how their order influences the meaning of the resulting sentences:

didn't eat hunters lion the the

1. ______________________________
2. ______________________________
3. ______________________________
4. ______________________________

(Write your sentences in the above spaces.)

Answers:

1. The hunters didn't eat the lion.
2. The lion didn't eat the hunters.
3. Didn't the lion eat the hunters?
4. Didn't the hunters eat the lion?

Since English has retained only a relatively few inflected forms to signal gramatical meanings, word order becomes critical for the learner of our language. Hearing-impaired children seem to find the temporal or sequential ordering of words quite a bit more difficult than children who hear. The only way that they and other children with language learning difficulties can master this skill is to practice again and again certain prescribed word orders in meaningful situations.

A good portion of the remainder of this book will be devoted to clarifying some of the important rules governing English word order about which many native speakers are quite unaware. Teachers must comprehend these rules in order to guide children in using them. Children need to sense the rules, but not to learn the rules as an intellectual exercise.

LESSON 2

What Is a Sentence?

ABSTRACT

- In order to derive meaning from a speaker's utterances, we must understand the vocabulary he uses.
- Relationships of the words in a sentence convey meaning.
- Function words bind form words together.
- Inflectional endings convey grammatical meaning.
- Differently constructed sentences can convey similar meanings.
- A single string of words may convey several different meanings.
- Semantic meaning and grammatical meaning must be taught almost simultaneously to children with hearing impairment.
- A sentence has both structure (constituents) and order (arrangement).

While someone is talking, notice how you judge when he has used a sentence and when he has not. A drop in pitch usually signals the end of a sentence. Strangely enough, many people never finish their sentences but still we have no great difficulty in understanding them. Unless we are familiar with the vocabulary that a speaker uses, we cannot understand or derive meaning from his utterance. Beyond the sound patterns that carry meaning and the lexical meanings that reside in the vocabulary we use, we have to know the relationships of the words in the sentence.

EXERCISE

In the following sentence, you will be able to recognize groups of words as belonging together. Choose the fewest words that form a group. Write these phrases in the spaces provided.

Alice Cogswell became the first pupil at the American Asylum for the Deaf and Dumb in Hartford, Connecticut, in 1817.

1. __________
2. __________
3. __________
4. __________
5. __________

Answers:

1. Alice Cogswell
2. became the first pupil
3. at the American Asylum for the Deaf and Dumb
4. in Hartford, Connecticut
5. in 1817

You had no trouble in arriving at these groupings, did you? You were guided by the verb and the preposition *at* and *in* which introduced the phrases. The use of nonsense words in sentences highlights this ability of yours.

EXERCISE

Divide the following sentence into phrases following the example given in the previous exercise:

The brins at the grik snerled the weches gerling the treff.

1. __________
2. __________
3. __________
4. __________

Answers:

1. The brins
2. at the grik
3. snerled the weches
4. gerling the treff

Your clue to the grammaticality of the above sentence is derived not from the words, which you do not understand, but from those words which function to bind the principal words together and by the inflectional endings, *-ed, -s, -es,* and *-ing.* You will note that a substitution of meaningful words will make this nonsense sentence a bona fide English sentence:

The teachers at the school watched the boys climbing the fence.

As a sophisticated user of language, you know more about sentences than you think you do. Consider this sentence:

de l'Epee standardized the sign language.

You were easily able to decide *who* did *what.* Your skill in deciding who the doer is and what the action performed is depends on your ability, subconsciously, to recognize a difference in the functions of the parts of the sentence. A person must be able to recognize a noun or a verb in the context of a phrase or sentence when he hears or sees one. Since verbs take many shapes and forms, it is often difficult for non-speakers of a language to recognize them and to master their use.

We are also able to recognize the similarity in meaning of two differently worded sentences. For example, contrast the following sentence with the example given above:

The sign language was standardized by de l'Epee.

The two sentences have substantially the same meaning, although the word order has been changed. Sentences can be transformed to have a different surface structure and yet maintain similarity in meaning. These two sentences are further examples of this phenomenon:

A war of words is going on between manualists and oralists.

There is a war of words going on between manualists and oralists.

Transformational grammar helps us, among other things, to understand how we may vary expression and yet maintain basic meaning.

Native users of English are also able to detect ambiguities, conditions in which a single string of words may have two different meanings, as:

Gallaudet's home

If you heard a drop of the voice at the end of the phrase, you could interpret it as a sentence, "*Gallaudet is home.*" If you saw it as a caption under a picture of a house, you would interpret it as a phrase. With no clue at all, you would have difficulty in deciding what the string meant. In this case, confusion in meaning stems from lack of punctuation. Here is another example of ambiguity:

Alice C. likes fish.

Does Alice C. like fish in the water or on her plate? The confusion here stems from the multiple referents residing in the words themselves.

EXERCISE

Cite several ways in which this sentence could be interpreted:

Visiting directors could be worrisome.

1. ____________________
2. ____________________
3. ____________________

Answers:

1. Visiting directors could find their task worrisome.
2. Visiting directors could be worrisome to those they are visiting.
3. Visiting directors could be worrisome to those who visit them.

A hearing-impaired child may not easily become adept at understanding how words are grouped, but it is very necessary that he do so if he is to derive meaning from a sentence. "Read" language is especially demanding of this knowledge. For instance, the next sentence, which is not really ambiguous, might be very difficult for a hearing-impaired child to decode if he could not group the words properly.

The light on the squad car turned.

More than likely he would tell you that the squad car turned if he were asked, "What turned?" We must teach, almost simultaneously, multiple semantic and grammatical connotations of vocabulary and the signals used in grouping words. The deaf child must learn variant meanings of words and various ways of expressing the same idea using several different structures. It is a big order, but not an impossible one if he is given a chance to make alternate choices and to discover ways we use to construct sentences.

Have you decided what a sentence is? You know that it is a string of words. You know that it has structure and order. Beyond that, it would be difficult to give a simple definition of a sentence. The concept of a sentence is a very complicated one. Nevertheless, the sentence is the meat of the language. Throughout this book, we will further develop the idea of the rules which go to making up English sentences.

LESSON 3

Deep and Surface Structure

ABSTRACT

- All sentences have both a deep and a surface structure.
- The form we use to communicate meaning, the form we see in writing, or the form we hear spoken, is the surface structure.
- The surface structure, generally, is made up of one or more transformations of the deep structure.
- Transformations result from combining simpler sentences, rearranging the order of words, and adding or deleting parts of sentences.
- All transformations are made according to specific rules.

All sentences have both a deep and a surface structure. Meaning is conveyed by the deep structure of the sentence. The form we hear or see in print, the form we use to communicate its meaning is found in its surface structure.

EXERCISE

In the following three sentences, you will soon discover that their deeper meaning resides in sentences which are simpler than the form they take here.

1. Thomas Hopkins Gallaudet was a conscientious student.
2. What Gallaudet worried about was his grades.
3. The solution to his problem was to study day and night.

Now, in the spaces to the right, write your answers to the questions. Use complete sentences.

4. Who was a student? ______________________________

5. Who was conscientious? ______________________________

6. What worried Gallaudet? ______________________________

7. What did he do to solve his problem? ______________________________

Answers:

4. Thomas Hopkins Gallaudet was a student.
5. Thomas Hopkins Gallaudet was conscientious.
6. His grades worried Gallaudet.
7. He studied day and night.

The meaning of sentences 1, 2, and 3 in the preceding exercise are condensed in your responses to questions 4 through 7. You will note that your sentences are short, simple, direct statements. The deep structure of the original sentence is contained in your responses to the questions. The surface structure found in sentences 1, 2, and 3 actually resulted from transforming these deep structures into more complicated strings of words. Transformations result from combining simpler sentences, rearranging the order of words, and adding to or deleting parts of sentences. All transformations are made according to specific rules that we shall be studying. Most of the sentences we speak or write are transformations of simple, direct, positive statements.

EXERCISE

Rewrite the following two simple sentences in as many ways as you can without destroying their basic meaning. You may combine the sentences, delete parts, add or rearrange words as you write your transformed sentences.

1. Gallaudet attended Yale.
2. Gallaudet studied law there.

1. ______________________________

2. ______________________________

3. ______________________________

4. ______________________________

5. ______________________________

6. ______________________________

7. ______________________________

8. ______________________________

9. ______________________________

10. ______________________________

Answers:

1. Gallaudet attended Yale and studied law there.
2. Gallaudet attended Yale where he studied law.
3. Gallaudet studied law at Yale.
4. While attending Yale, Gallaudet studied law.
5. Gallaudet studied law when he attended Yale.
6. What Gallaudet studied at Yale was law.
7. What Gallaudet studied while attending Yale was law.
8. At Yale, Gallaudet studied law.
9. Law was what Gallaudet studied while he attended Yale.
10. Gallaudet, while attending Yale, studied law.

Perhaps you have written even more sentences than those presented here. This exercise suggests that there are innumerable ways of combining simple sentences to form the more interesting, more sophisticated ones we use to communicate our thoughts and ideas to others.

EXERCISE

Summarize this lesson by answering these questions.

1. What is surface structure?

____

____

2. What is the relationship of deep structure to surface structure?

---

3. From what do transformations result?

Answers:

1. The form we use to communicate its meaning is the surface structure of a sentence.
2. Surface structure is the result of transformations applied to the deep structure of a sentence.
3. Transformations result from combining simpler sentences, rearranging the order of words, and adding to or deleting parts of sentences according to specific rules. (See Introduction.)

LESSON 4

The Bases of Sentences: Noun Phrases, Auxiliaries, and Verb Phrases

ABSTRACT

- A noun phrase (NP), an auxiliary (Aux), and a verb phrase (VP) are fundamental parts of every sentence.
- A noun phrase (NP) may consist of:

  1. a noun alone
  2. a determiner (Det) and a noun
  3. a determiner, a noun, and a clause or phrase
  4. a personal pronoun
  5. a nondefinite pronoun
  6. a clause

- An auxiliary (Aux) may consist of:

  1. a modal: *can, could, may, might, shall, should, will, would, must*
  2. a non-modal consisting of a form of *have, be,* or *do*
  3. syntactic tense: present or past
  4. a modal or non-modal followed by *not* and preceding the verb
  5. the question constituent

- A verb phrase (VP) may consist of:

  1. a full verb alone used as the main verb (MV)
  2. a modal plus a verb
  3. a non-modal auxiliary plus a verb
  4. groups of words containing a verb plus a noun, adjective, or adverb
  5. a verb with its auxiliary plus an optional adverb (Adv) which may be a single word, a phrase, or a clause

- → means *may be written as* or *consists of*.
- There are two linguistic tenses in English, the present and the past.

Every sentence is made up of three fundamental elements or constituents: a *noun phrase* (NP), an *auxiliary* (Aux), and a *verb phrase* (VP).

A noun phrase (NP) may consist of:

1. a noun (N) alone: *Ann, measles,* as in:

   Ann has *measles.*

2. a determiner (Det) and a noun: *a girl, an orange, the book, some milk, my teacher, these toys,* as in:

   The girls drank *some milk.*

3. a determiner, a noun, and a clause or phrase, as in:

   a. *The knowledge that Helen was blind and deaf* was shocking. (Det + N + clause)

   b. *A child who is deaf and blind* is severely handicapped. (Det + N + clause)

   c. *Helen, a bright and active child,* was deaf and blind. (N + phrase)

4. a personal pronoun: *I, me, you, he, him, she, her, it, we, us, they, them,* as in:

   They saw *us.*

5. a nondefinite pronoun: *anybody, somebody, something, one, everyone, anyone, someone,* as in:

   Everyone is welcome.

6. a clause, as in:

   What she said is true.

EXERCISE

Underline the determiners in these sentences.

1. The doll is Helen's.
2. These dolls are not for sale.
3. Where did you put my doll?
4. I saw a doll in the window.
5. Here are some dolls you may want.
6. Dolls are her favorite toys.

Answers: 1. the 2. these 3. my 4. a, the 5. some 6. her

Every noun phrase can support a sentence that has been transformed into a clause and, as such, it will become part of the NP. The italicized words in the sentence below are the NPs in the sentence.

The day that teacher arrived was *a day that the Kellers never forgot.*

EXERCISE

Underline the NPs in the following sentences.

1. The woman who taught Helen was very dedicated.
2. The two became inseparable.
3. The fact that Helen was deaf and blind created problems.
4. Helen typed the essays which she composed.

Answers:

1. The woman who taught Helen
2. The two
3. The fact that Helen was deaf and blind, problems
4. Helen, the essays which she composed

An auxiliary (Aux) may consist of:

1. a modal: *can, could, may, might, shall, should, will, would, must,* as in:

   Helen *can (could)* read.
   She *may (might)* come.
   She *will (would)* try.

2. a non-modal form consisting of a form of *have, be,* or *do* (used with a full verb), as in:

   She *is (was)* playing.
   She *has (had)* practiced.
   She *does (did)* try hard.

3. syntactic tense: present or past, as in:

   present:
   Helen *can* read.
   She *is* studying.
   She tries.

past:

Helen *could* read.
She *was* studying.
She tri*ed*.

4. the negator *not* placed after the *Aux* and before the verb in the verb phrase, as in:

   Teacher *will not* scold.
   She *has not* finished.

5. the question (Ques) constituent, as in:

   Is Helen going?
   Can Helen go?
   Must Helen go?
   Did Helen go?

Modals and non-modal auxiliaries are familiarly known to deaf children as helping verbs. Lessons 16 and 17 will discuss the auxiliaries in detail.

EXERCISE

Underline the modal auxiliaries in these sentences.

1. Where will Helen find her kitten?
2. She can read now.
3. She could swim well.
4. They may take Helen to Boston.
5. Helen would come to her teacher with dozens of questions every day.

Answers: 1. will 2. can 3. could 4. may 5. would

The concept of linguistic tense may be new to many people, since most of us equate *tense* with *time*, as past time, present time, or future time. Linguists divorce clock time and calendar time from their definition of tense. To them, there are but two tenses, the present and the past, neither one of which may have any relationship to our notions of time. *Tense* is an obligatory element in all verb phrases and is inherent in every verb or verb phrase that appears in a sentence. In later lessons we will explain how English expresses various time relationships, but in this lesson we want only to introduce the new concept of *tense* as a grammatical element.

A verb phrase (VP) may consist of:

1. a verb alone, or a main verb (MV), as in:

   Helen *screams.*
   Teacher *waited.*

2. a modal plus a verb, as in:

   They *must work.*

3. a non-modal, or a form of *have, be,* or *do,* plus an MV, as in:

   Mr. Keller *has arrived.*
   He *is waving.*
   Helen *did not feed* the puppy.

4. groups of words containing an MV (with or without its auxiliary) plus a noun (N), adjective (Adj), adverb (Adv), or infinitive, as in:

   Miss Sullivan *taught Helen.* (MV + N)
   Helen *became studious.* (MV + Adj)
   She *ran away.* (MV + Adv)
   She *seemed to know.* (MV + infinitive)

5. a verb (with the auxiliaries and complements listed in Items 2, 3, and 4 above) plus an optional adverb or adverbs, in the form of single words, phrases, or clauses, as in:

   Helen *came here.* (Adv)
   She *advanced shyly.* (Adv)
   She *took his hand in hers.* (phrase)
   They *walked along the path.* (phrase)
   The Kellers *greeted their guests as they arrived.* (clause)
   The guests *talked while they gathered for dinner.* (clause)

The verb phrase in English is a complicated structure and poses many learning hazards for children with hearing impairments. In fact, standard English verb phrases may not be mastered even by native speakers, especially if they come from homes where a foreign language is spoken or where dialects differ from standard English. Try out your knowledge of verb phrases by doing the next exercise.

EXERCISE

Underline the verb phrases in these sentences.

1. Helen's distracted parents were without hope.
2. Dr. Samuel Gridley Howe had trained Laura Bridgeman to sew.

3. Alexander Graham Bell advised Mr. and Mrs. Keller to see Mr. Anagnos.
4. He will find a tutor for Helen.
5. Helen could read Braille by the time she was eight.

Answers:

1. were without hope
2. had trained Laura Bridgeman to sew.
3. advised Mr. and Mrs. Keller to see Mr. Anagnos
4. will find a tutor for Helen
5. could read Braille by the time she was eight

This chapter has covered a great deal of material that will be developed in detail in chapters to follow. Its main purpose is to introduce the sentence constituents, *NP*, *Aux* and *VP*, so that you can begin to identify them in the sentences you speak and write. Unless a child gains the concept that these three elements make up a sentence, he will be unable to form sentences. This means that he must be exposed to sentences early in life in which the constituents are used in their simplest forms first. He will eventually sense these constituents, but he should not be expected to identify them any more than you did when you were learning language.

LESSON 5

Two Basic Sentence Patterns

ABSTRACT

- One basic sentence pattern consists of NP + Aux + V_i.
- < > indicates a specific feature of a word.
- Intransitive verbs <— transitive> (V_i) can stand alone in a sentence since they do not require a noun or an adjective to complete their meaning.
- A sentence tree shows the relationship of NP, Aux, and VP.
- A basic sentence is one which is active, declarative, positive, and simple.
- The second basic sentence pattern consists of NP + Aux + V_t + NP.
- English verbs in the active voice that carry the transitive feature <+ transitive> require that a noun phrase follow them in the sentence to complete their meaning.
- Some verbs carry both the <+ transitive> and the <—transitive> feature.
- A limited number of transitive verbs in English may be followed by two NPs, the first of which is an indirect object, the second, the direct object.
- A sentence structure carrying two NPs following a <+ transitive> verb can be stated with or without the feature <+ to> or <+ for>.
- Deletion of the <+ to> or <+ for> requires the use of the indirect object transformation.
- The indirect object transformation cannot be applied if the direct object is a pronoun.
- Sentences based on patterns I and II have the option of having an adverb or adverbs added to them.
- An optional adverb is written as (Adv), the parentheses indicating that the adverb is optional.

In Lesson 4, we learned that every sentence contains a noun phrase (NP), an auxiliary (Aux), and a verb phrase (VP). Some verbs can stand alone in a verb phrase. They carry the feature *intransitive* <— transitive> since they do not require a noun or an adjective to complete their meaning. Examples of intransitive <—transitive> verbs are *run, cry, go, come,* and *fall.* We can construct simple sentences with only an initial NP and an intransitive verb (V_i):

The girls ran.

Sandy fell.

She cried.

Some children came.

Some went.

The formula for the basic sentence pattern represented by these simple sentences can be written:

$NP + Aux + V_i$

We have also learned that part of the Aux is tense. When there is no modal or non-modal auxiliary to carry the tense, it becomes part of the main verb itself. This feature, along with others, can be graphically shown in diagrams called *sentence trees.* Tree 1 illustrates a sentence following the pattern, $NP + Aux + V_i$. *S* stands for *sentence, NP* for *noun phrase, Aux* for the *auxiliary,* and *VP* for *verb phrase.* A sentence tree also shows the relationships of these constituents to each other.

Sentence Tree 1: The girls ran.

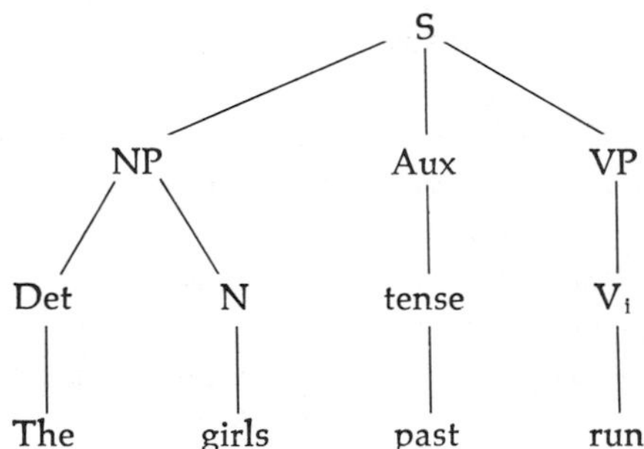

The resulting string of words, *The girls + past + run,* is known as a *terminal string.* From this terminal string we can construct the sentence: *The girls ran.* This is a basic sentence since it is unembellished in any way. All basic sentences are simple, active, declarative, and positive.

EXERCISE

Complete the following sentence trees.

Sandy fell.

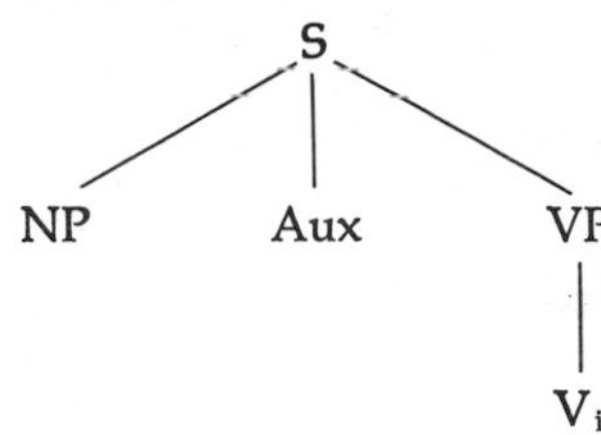

She cried.

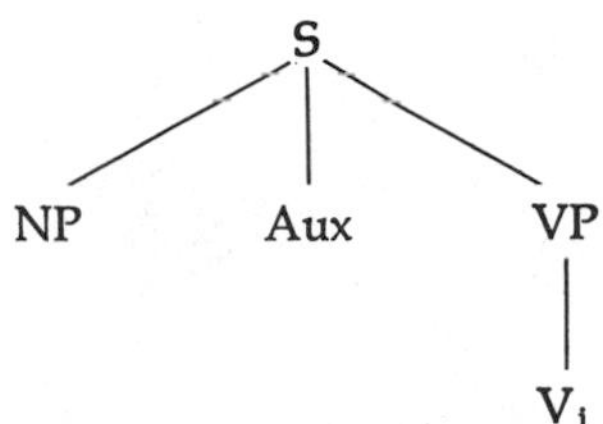

Some children came.

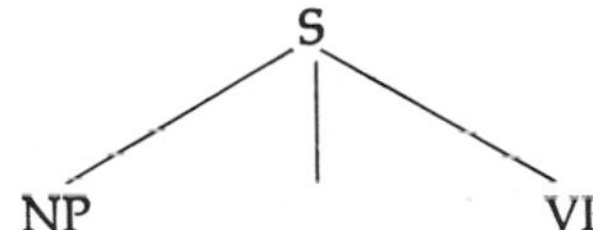

Some children went.

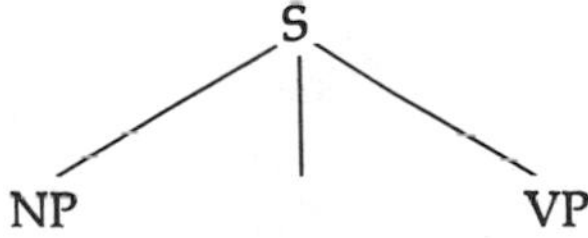

Answers: Check your answers against the example given in Sentence Tree 1.

A great many English verbs carry the transitive feature <+ transitive> which means that they require an NP to follow them in the sentence in order to complete their meaning. The formula for this most commonly used sentence pattern in English may be written:

$$NP + Aux + V_t + NP$$

Sentence Trees 2 and 3 illustrate two basic sentences based on this pattern.

Sentence Tree 2: The boys played ball.

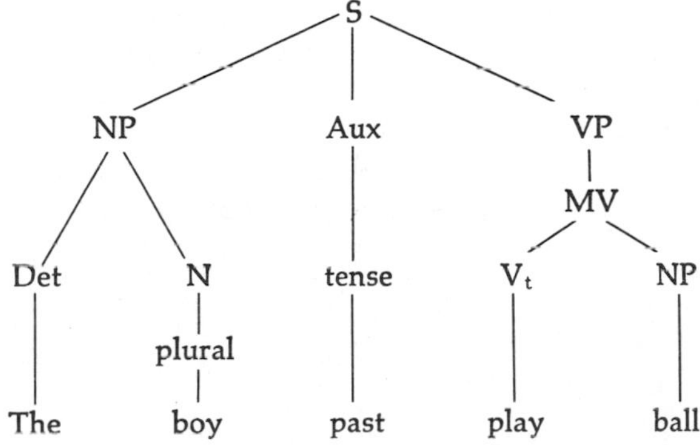

Sentence Tree 3: The girls watched them.

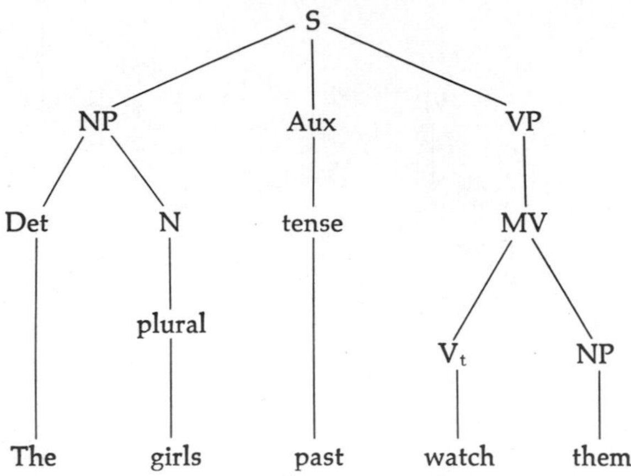

EXERCISE

Complete the following sentence trees with terminal strings.

The children made a mural.

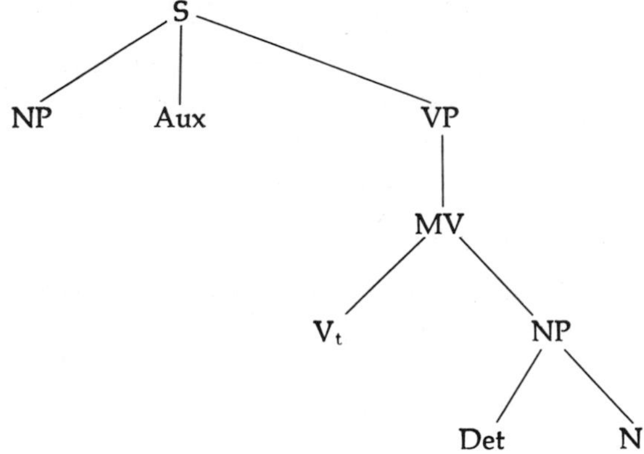

They decorated the classroom.

S

NP VP

Answers: Checks your trees against Sentence Trees 2 and 3 to determine your accuracy in completing the exercise.

EXERCISE

Write the basic sentences for these terminal strings.

1. The + quarterback + past + pass + the + ball

---

2. Jerry + present + like + football

---

3. He + past + watch + the + game

---

4. His + team + past + win

---

5. We + past + cheer

Answers:

1. The quarterback passed the ball.
2. Jerry likes football.
3. He watched the game.
4. His team won.
5. We cheered.

Some verbs may carry both the <+ transitive> and <— transitive> features. For instance, we may say:

The girls ran. <— transitive>

The girls ran a race. <+ transitive>

The woman washed. <— transitive>

The woman washed her hair. <+ transitive>

The rioters shouted. <— transitive)

The rioters shouted obscenities. <+ transitive>

Children with language learning disabilities must understand that some verbs carry both features.

A limited number of transitive verbs in English may be followed by two NPs, the first of which is an indirect object (Ind O), the second, the direct object (DO). Verbs used with NP + V_t + NP + NP include:

ask	buy	get	hand	pay	send	tell
award	deny	give	make	read	show	throw
bring	find	grant	offer	sell	teach	wish

Examples of NP + V_t + NP + NP:

The teachers gave *the students homework.*

The girls sent *their friends invitations.*

The boy bought *his girl a corsage.*

Mrs. Jones made *Marilyn a formal.*

These sentences originally carried a feature <+ to> or <+ for> in their deep structure. We can state the same ideas in sentences using prepositional phrases beginning with *to* or *for:*

The teachers gave homework *to the students.*

The girls sent invitations *to their friends.*

The boy bought a corsage *for his girl.*

Mrs. Jones made a formal *for Marilyn.*

The nouns following *to* and *for* become the indirect objects in the transformed sentences, NP + V_t + NP + NP.

If the direct object is a pronoun, the indirect object transformation (T/Ind O) cannot be applied.

We can say: T/Ind O: The girl sent Bill an invitation.

She sent it to him.

We cannot say: *She sent him it.

*She sent Bill it.

We can say: T/Ind O: Father bought the boys skates.

Father bough them for the boys.

EXERCISE

Write sentences using the preceding list of verbs and the patterns:

A. NP + V_t + NP + *to* or *for* + NP

B. NP + V_t + (NP) + NP

1. A. (buy) ______________________________

   B. ______________________________

2. A. (give) ______________________________

   B. ______________________________

3. A. (make) ______________________________

   B. ______________________________

4. A. (pay) ______________________________

   B. ______________________________

5. A. (read) ______________________________

   B. ______________________________

Answers:

While the sentences written for this exercise will vary, the following examples correspond to the patterns:

A	B
1. I bought a pie for myself.	1. I bought myself a pie.
2. John gave the pie to Mary.	2. John gave Mary the pie.
3. Mary made a pie for John.	3. Mary made John a pie.
4. Mary paid a dollar to John.	4. Mary paid John a dollar.
5. Mary read a story to John.	5. Mary read John a story.

Children will be introduced to sentence patterns I and II in meaningful situations. Teachers will always use sentences when communicating with children, but they will at first accept partial sentences from the children. When they see that children are trying to use a particular pattern, they can guide and direct children to better approximations until they gain mastery over the pattern. For instance, teaching the indirect object transformation has been accomplished with children as young as five years of age.

The following exercise was found highly motivating to children since it gave them power over their environment (Krug, 1967). In order to participate in this practice children must recognize in print (1) their names, (2) a limited vocabulary of nouns in the school environment, (3) color and number words, (4) adjectives of size and shape. They must have been introduced to the request patterns and be familiar with the verbs *give, bring, get,* and *show.* A slot chart, printed flash cards, and objects to be manipulated are provided. The teacher demonstrates each of the following carefully controlled steps, in which the flash cards are inserted into the slot chart, read by the children, and responded to according to the message received. The children then act as teachers and practice each step before proceeding to the next.

1. *Mary*/Beth/Bill, give me the book.
2. Mary, give me the *book*/colors/doll/the headphones.
3. Mary, give *Bill*/Beth the book.
4. Mary, *give*/get/bring me the book.
5. Mary, give/get/bring Beth/Bill the book/the colors/the headphones.

Steps 6, 7, 8, and so on incorporate permutations of all the combinations that involve color + noun, number + noun, adjective of size (big, small) as direct objects, and *him* and *her* as indirect objects. For example, Mary, give Beth the pencil. Give her the colors.

Children may verbalize their activities on completion of each performance, using the past tense of the verbs, thus gaining control over the oral as well as the written form of this pattern.

English sentences based on the two basic patterns described in this lesson have the option of having an adverb or adverbs added to them. The adverb becomes part of the verb phrase (VP), but it does not change the basic pattern. We merely expand the pattern by adding + *(Adv)* to it. The parentheses is read as *optional*. Examples:

The deer moved *swiftly*.

The train arrived *soon*.

She dropped her gloves *there*.

Henceforth, we shall omit the Aux in the patterns, but it should be understood that Aux is a mandatory part of every sentence. The simplified patterns can be written as follows:

Pattern I: NP + V_i + (Adv)

Pattern II: NP + V_t + NP + (Adv)

EXERCISE

Write the sentence patterns for these sentences.

1. He fought a good fight. ____________________
2. He fought bravely. ____________________
3. The girls shouted excitedly. ____________________

4. They played ball. ____________

5. The girls sang beautifully. ____________

6. The children watched the acrobat. ____________

7. They laughted heartily. ____________

8. They listened attentively. ____________

9. The children read their books quietly. ____________

Answers:

1. NP + V_t + NP
2. NP + V_i + (Adv)
3. NP + V_i + (Adv)
4. NP + V_t + NP
5. NP + V_i + (Adv)
6. NP + V_t + NP
7. NP + V_i + (Adv)
8. NP + V_i + (Adv)
9. NP + V_t + NP + (Adv)

The following sentences contain more than one adverb:

The class went there quickly.

The boys watched the game in the schoolyard after school.

In the first sentence, above, we have added two adverbs, *there* and *quickly*. The adverb *there* answers the question, "Where did the class go?", while *quickly* answers the question, "How did the class go?". In the second sentence, the words that answer the question, "Where did the boys watch the game?", are called *adverbial phrases*. Phrases which begin with prepositions, as these do, are *prepositional adverbial phrases*.

EXERCISE

1. Underline the adverbs and adverbial phrases in these sentences.
2. Indicate what question each answers.
3. Indicate whether the sentence pattern is A or B.

A. NP + V_i + (Adv)
B. NP + V_t + NP + (Adv)

Example:

A The girls ran around the playground. where

_______ 1. They played for a long time. _______________

_______ 2. They sat on the stairs. _______________

_______ 3. They rested for a while. _______________

_______ 4. The boys played football in the park. _______________

_______ 5. They practiced their signals yesterday. _______________

_______ 6. They watched the coach attentively. _______________

_______ 7. The coach praised their efforts highly. _______________

Answers:

1. A, for a long time, how long
2. A, on the stairs, where
3. A, for a while, how long
4. B, in the park, where
5. B, yesterday, when
6. B, attentively, how
7. B, highly, how

Children with language deficiency will have to associate the key question words: *how, how long, where,* and *when,* with the adverbial elements in sentences and learn their order of appearance in the sentences. Adverbs and related items will be discussed more fully in Lessons 34 and 36.

LESSON 6

Three Simple Sentence Transformations

ABSTRACT

- A tree diagram divides the sentence into its constituent parts or into its phrase structures.
- The double arrow, =>, is read "is transformed to."
- The T/yes-no transformation is applied when a question can be answered with either *yes* or *no*.
- The T/yes-no transformation changes the word order of the sentence.
- The T/neg transformation is applied by introducing the negator, *not*.
- The T/contr transformation is applied to form a contraction of a modal or a non-modal Aux with *not*.
- Sentences resulting from transformations are surface structures.

A sentence tree is a diagram which shows rather clearly the relationship of the basic ingredients of a sentence, the *NP*, the *Aux*, and the *VP*. It divides the sentence into its constituent parts or its phrase structure. While it is possible to indicate each separate feature and constituent in every NP, Aux, or VP in a tree diagram, we will usually include only those elements which are relevant to the discussion at hand. Do not become confused if we include a modal and leave out tense, leave out a modal and include tense, or include a noun and leave out the determiner. The purpose of the omissions, where they occur, is simplification. In the tree for *Helen Keller could talk,* we will leave out tense in the Aux, but you know it is there.

Sentence Tree 4: Helen Keller could talk.

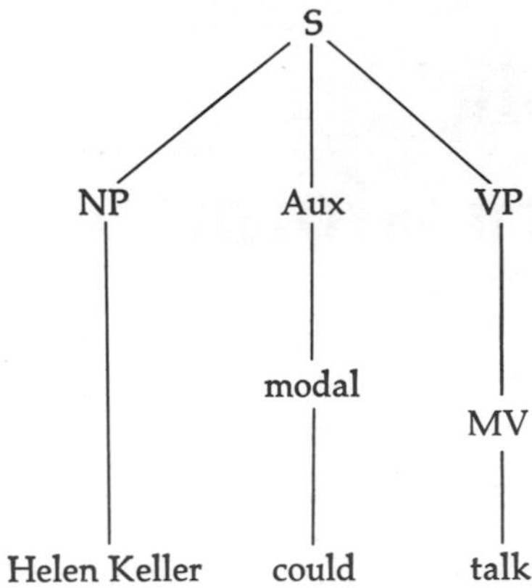

In this sentence, *Helen Keller* is in the position of the noun phrase (NP), the auxiliary (Aux), *could* precedes the main verb (MV), talk.

Suppose we wish to ask a question which can be answered by either *yes* or *no*. We will use the same constituents of the sentence in Tree 4, but we will move the auxiliary to the beginning of the sentence. This is called the *T/yes-no transformation,* the *T* standing for the word, *transformation.*

Sentence Tree 5A: Could Helen Keller talk?

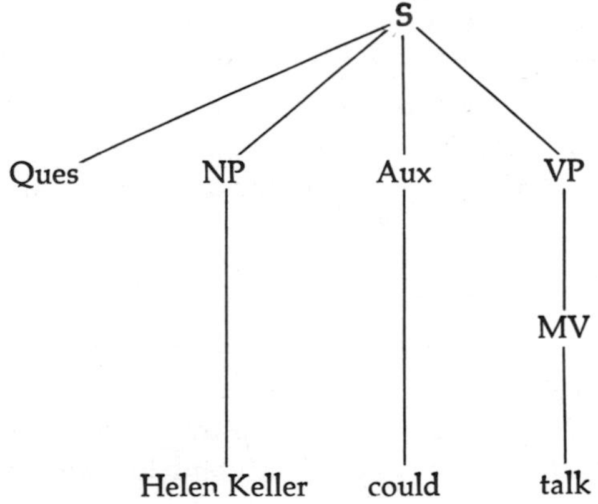

The deep structure of this sentence, like every other declarative sentence, contains the constituent, *question,* which specifies that the interrogative transformation will apply here. The Aux, *could,* is moved to the beginning of the sentence.

Sentence Tree 5B: Could Helen Keller talk?

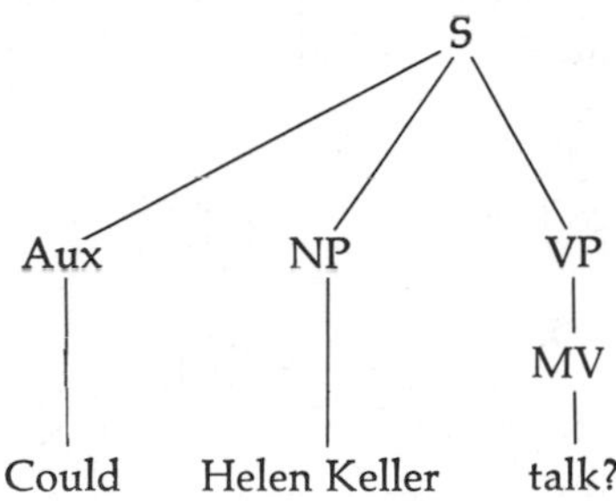

You will notice that this process changes the word order of the deep structure so as to generate a new structure. We have applied a T/yes-no transformation to this sentence. We can also demonstrate the T/yes-no transformation process by rewriting the phrase structure of the sentence to incorporate the rule that shifts the auxiliary to the beginning of the sentence:

T/yes-no: Helen Keller could talk. => Could Helen Keller talk?

Ques + NP + Aux + MV => Aux + NP + MV

NP → Helen Keller

Aux → could

MV → talk

You will recall that a single arrow, →, is translated, "may be rewritten as" or "consists of." The double arrow, =>, is translated as "may be transformed to."

Children who hear ask countless questions to satisfy their curiosity, while teachers ask countless questions to test children's knowledge. They sometimes forget that the child's real reason for asking questions is to get desired and unknown information. When a hearing-impaired child realizes that he can get such information by raising an eyebrow or his shoulders, by a gesture or by a word, the teacher would do well to capitalize on the situation by phrasing the question for the child, accepting one word at first and later a more complete pattern. Encouraging children to ask questions spontaneously by providing question-raising situations will teach the value and use of questions. Guessing games may help stabilize the patterns, but will not clarify the *why* or *when* of asking questions. Used together, they may speed up the very desirable ability of children to use question forms.

The *yes-no* question is a basic pattern for all other questions, and if a child masters this pattern, he should have little difficulty in generalizing other questions beginning with *what, where, when, why,* and *how.*

If we choose to make a negative sentence of the basic sentence, we would apply the negative transformation, T/neg, to it by introducing the negator, *not*, after the Aux in the tree diagram to indicate that the sentence is semantically negative.

Sentence Tree 6A: Helen Keller could not talk.

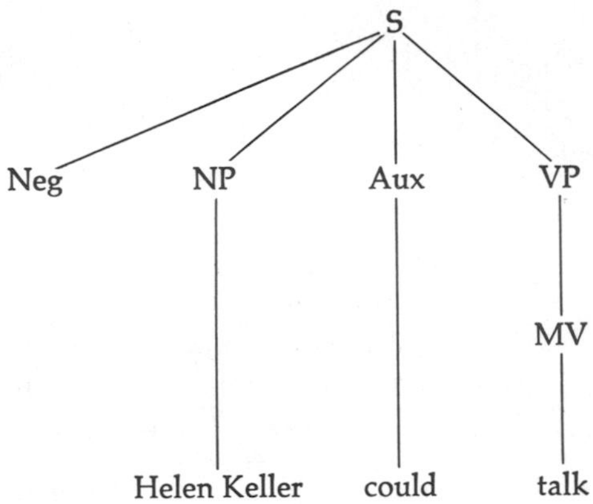

Sentence Tree 6B: Helen Keller could not talk.

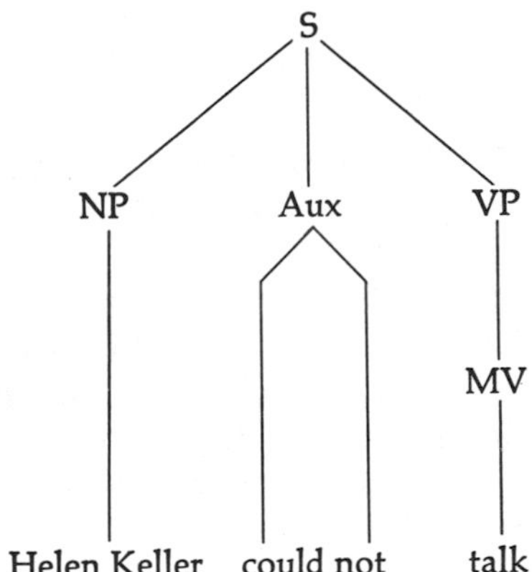

If we wished to make a contraction out of the *could* + *not*, we would generate a new constitutent, *couldn't*, by using the contraction transformation, T/contr. The sentence would then read: *Helen Keller couldn't talk.*

Sentences resulting from the transformations are *surface structures* developed from the underlying grammatical structure which represents the deep structure of the transformed sentences. So far, we have observed that a transformation may rearrange constituents or introduce new ones. These are very elementary transformations.

EXERCISE

Apply the T/yes-no transformation to the following sentences using tree diagrams. Use another piece of paper to draw as many trees as you need in order to master the transformations. First draw the tree for the basic sentence and then for the transformation. Your final strings will illustrate the basic sentences and the related questions.

Example: Helen will learn Braille.

Sentence Tree A

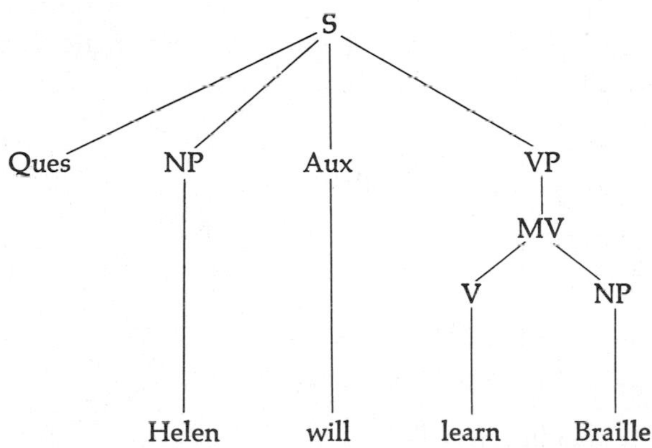

Sentence Tree B

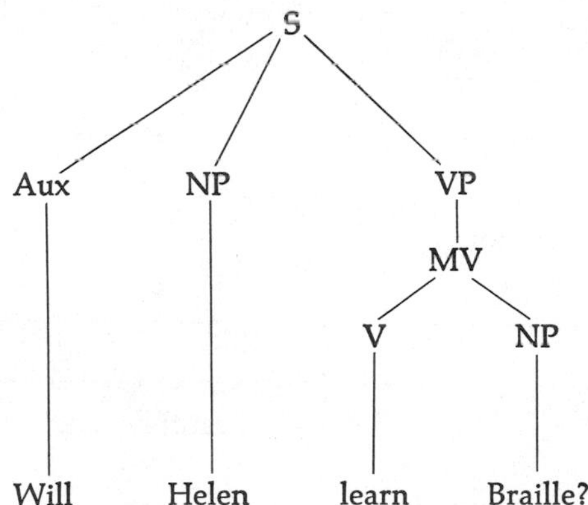

1. Teacher may leave town.
2. Father will watch Helen.
3. Helen can dress the doll.
4. Helen must drink her milk.
5. Helen has touched the leaf.

Answers:

Consult the example given in this lesson to check the accuracy of the sentence trees you have drawn.

EXERCISE

I. Apply the T/neg and the T/contr transformations to the following sentences using these phrase structure rules:

NP + Aux + MV + NP =>

NP + Aux + neg MV + NP =>

NP + Aux + T/neg contr + MV + NP

Examples:

Teacher could hear Helen. =>

Teacher could not hear Helen. =>

Teacher couldn't hear Helen.

1. Teacher should praise Helen.

____

____

2. Helen could remember their names.

____

____

3. Teacher must scold Helen.

____

____

4. Mother has prepared dinner for Helen and Teacher.

____

____

5. Father will come home tonight.

___

___

II. What have you discovered about the contraction of will + not?

___

___

Answers:

1. Teacher should not praise Helen. Teacher shouldn't praise Helen.
2. Helen could not remember their names. Helen couldn't remember their names.
3. Teacher must not scold Helen. Teacher musn't scold Helen.
4. Mother has not prepared dinner for Helen and Teacher. Mother hasn't prepared dinner for Helen and Teacher.
5. Father will not come home tonight. Father won't come home tonight.

II. The contraction of will + not changes the form of both the Aux and the negative to *won't*.

___

The negative transformation is one of the most frequently used and needed in communication. While T/neg has a fairly simple structure, it has several underlying semantic connotations: *non-existence,* as in "John isn't here today;" *refusal,* as in "John won't drink his milk;" and *denial,* as in "I didn't push John." Developmentally, hearing children first use the negator *no* to express refusal and denial as in "No want milk" or "No hit kitty" and *no more* for non-existence as in "No more milk." By the time they are two or three, they use the negator *not* in appropriate situations. It seems more reasonable to introduce the negator *not* into the language patterns of hearing- and language-deficient children than *no,* which would eventually have to be replaced by *not.*

When we use negation in speech, we generally use the contraction transformation also. We say *"I can't/won't/shouldn't/oughtn't* go" rather than the more stilted uncontracted forms. Contractions may obscure meanings in lipread language because the *n't* of the negator is absorbed into the auxillary as an invisible movement. The written form must accompany the spoken form whenever possible to clarify meaning. Children will copy what they see, and if the full form is used by the teachers, they too will use it. Their language will sound stilted and remain so throughout their lives.

LESSON 7

WH-Questions and PRO Forms

ABSTRACT

- Yes-no questions can be asked only in relationship to an entire sentence.
- WH-questions relate to only part of a sentence.
- WH-words are: *who, what, where, why, how,* and *when.*
- *Who* and *what* represent noun phrases (NPs) in a sentence.
- *Where, why, how,* and *when* represent adverbs (Adv) in sentences.
- The T/yes-no transformation must be applied to a sentence before the T/WH-question transformation can be applied, except for the question, "Who . . .?"
- The PRO-forms are: *Somebody, Something, Somewhere, Sometime, Somehow,* and *For Some Reason.*
- PRO-forms may be replaced in a sentence by WH-words.
- Suggestions for eliciting questions from children are described.

Yes-no questions ask about an entire statement. If we wished to ask a yes-no question about the sentence "Helen was there yesterday," our question would contain the same words as the statement, but in a different order: "Was Helen there yesterday?"

If we wished to ask about only a part of the sentence, we would begin the question with a WH-word as *who, where,* and *when:*

Who was there yesterday? Answer: NP $\rightarrow$ Helen

Where was Helen yesterday? Answer: $Adv_p \rightarrow$ there

When was Helen there? Answer: $Adv_t \rightarrow$ yesterday

These questions are answered by only one part of the sentence above, the noun phrase (NP), the adverb of place (Adv_p), and the adverb of time (Adv_t).

Who and *what* are interrogative pronouns and represent noun phrases in sentences. *Where, why, how,* and *when* are interrogative adverbs and stand for adverbs or adverbial phrases in sentences.

The interrogative transformation that produces a WH-question requires that the T/yes-no transformation be applied to the terminal string before the T/WH-question is applied:

> The candy is Somewhere. ==>
>
> Is the candy Somewhere? ==>
>
> Where is the candy?

Sentence Tree 7 illustrates how this is accomplished for the sentence whose surface structure is: *What will Helen wear?*

Sentence Tree 7A: What will Helen wear?

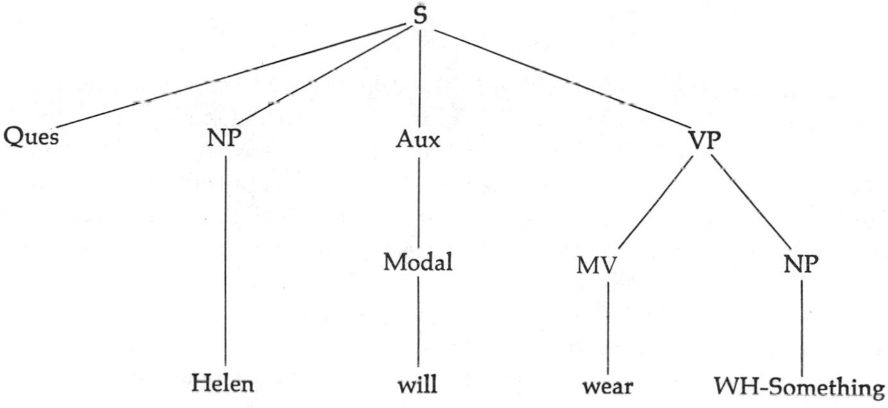

Sentence Tree 7B: What will Helen wear?

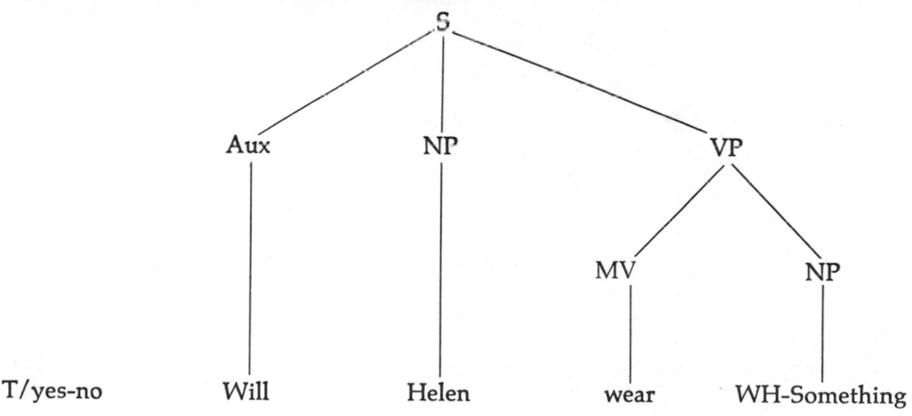

Sentence Tree 7C: What will Helen wear?

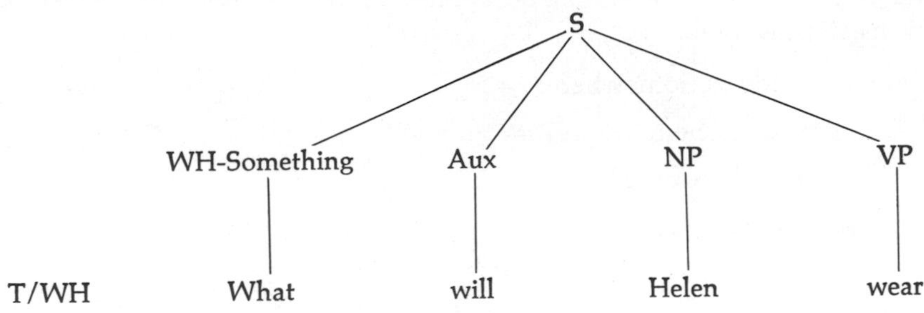

In the question, "Who will go?" the two required transformations are actually employed, but because the T/WH is applied to the subject of the sentence, the total effect is to replace the subject of the sentence with WH-Someone and to retain the order of the verb phrase found in the deep structure of the sentence. Questions employing *who* are the easiest ones for deaf children to use since they follow the word order of the basic patterns from which they are derived. But little children are usually interested not in *who did what* but rather *what happened to whom* and *why*. As a result, their curiosity is seldom satisfied by teaching them the easiest pattern.

The next set of trees illustrates the derivation of the question using an interrogative adverb of time.

Sentence Tree 8A: When can Helen Keller visit Niagara Falls?

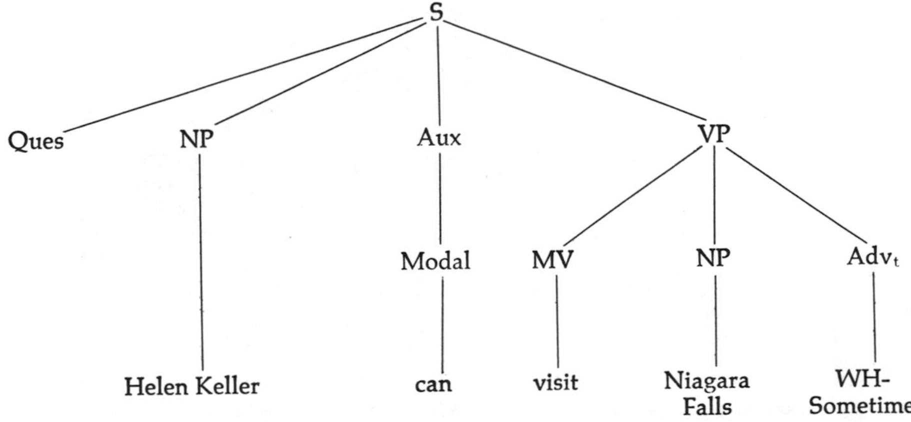

Sentence Tree 8B: When can Helen Keller visit Niagara Falls?

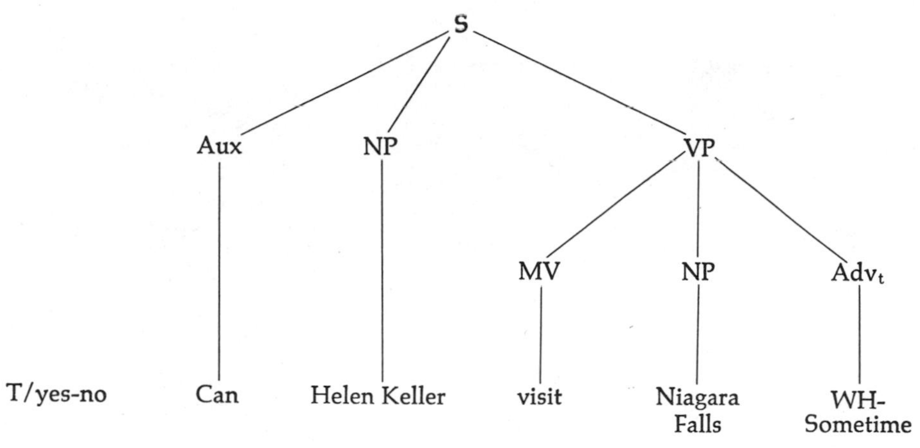

Sentence Tree 8C: When can Helen Keller visit Niagara Falls?

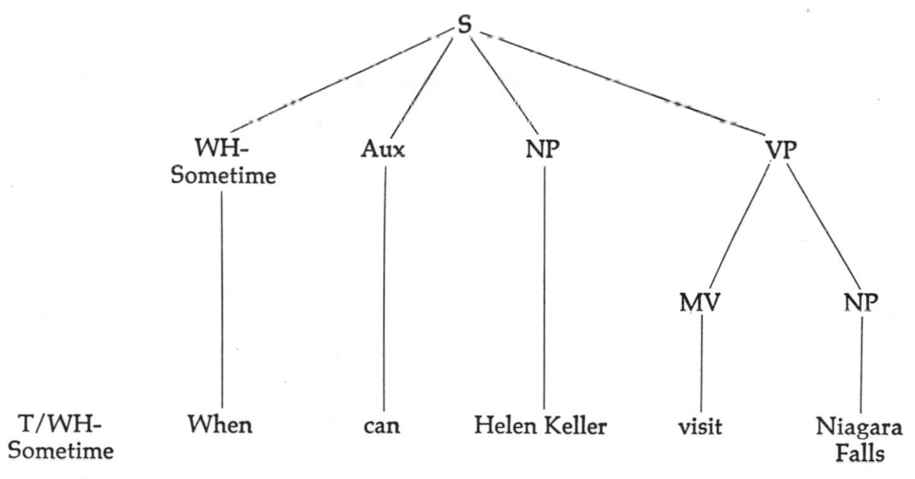

Sentence Tree 9 illustrates the question using an interrogative adverb of place.

Sentence Tree 9A: Where should they go?

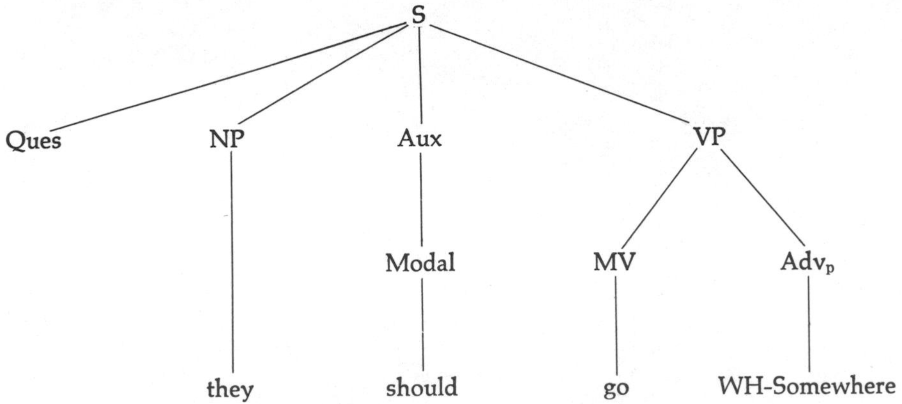

Sentence Tree 9B: Where should they go?

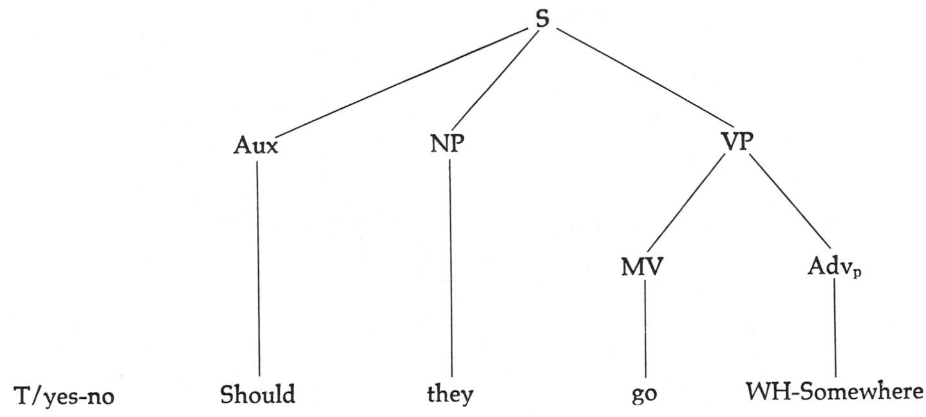

Sentence Tree 9C: Where should they go?

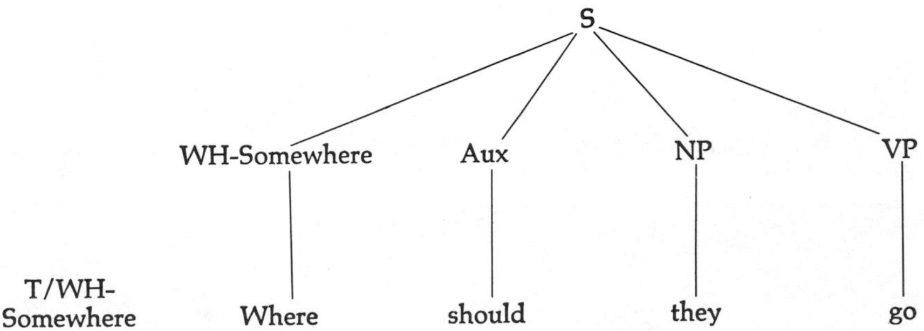

A PRO-form, a word that stands in for another, is a useful device for completing a string of grammatical elements which may omit some parts essential to a sentence. You observed the use of PRO-forms in the preceding sentence trees. *Something, Somebody, Somewhere, Sometime, Somehow,* and *For Some Reason* are rather indefinite words which some linguists call PRO-forms. *Something* and *Somebody* stand for nouns while *Somewhere, Sometime, Somehow,* and *For Some Reason* refer to adverbs:

$PRO_N \rightarrow$ Something, Somebody

$PRO_{ADV} \rightarrow$ Somewhere, Sometime, Somehow, and For Some Reason

In the sentences:

We will visit *Something* next Sunday.

We may go to the zoo *Sometime.*

the PRO-forms give the clues for the questions we may wish to ask in order to find out actually *what* we will visit and *when* we may go to the zoo.

The concept of the PRO-form is very important for deaf children in learning to ask questions. Here is a list of PRO-forms which are replaced in the surface structure of sentences by WH-words:

Somebody → who
Something → what
Somewhere → where
Sometime → when
Somehow → how
For Some Reason → why

EXERCISE

Write the WH-words for these forms.

1. Something __________
2. Somewhere __________
3. Sometime __________
4. For Some Reason __________
5. Somehow __________
6. Somebody __________

Answers: 1. what 2. where 3. when 4. why 5. how 6. who

EXERCISE

Perform the transformations necessary to produce a WH-question.

1. Miss Yale's picture is WH-Somewhere.

____

____

2. You can find WH-Something in the library.

____

____

3. You can find the picture of Miss Yale WH-Somewhere.

____

____

4. We will visit WH-Something next year.

____

____

5. We will visit Clarke School WH-Sometime.

____

____

Answers:

1. T/yes-no: Is Miss Yale's picture Somewhere?
   T/WH: Where is Miss Yale's picture?
2. T/yes-no: Can you find Something in the library?
   T/WH: What can you find in the library?
3. T/yes-no: Can you find the picture of Miss Yale Somewhere?
   T/WH: Where can you find the picture of Miss Yale?
4. T/yes-no: Will we visit Something next year?
   T/WH: What will we visit next year?
5. T/yes-no: Will we visit Clarke School Sometime?
   T/WH: When will we visit Clarke School?

Children who must learn language in a mode different from the natural one frequently find asking questions a difficult task. Besides having to learn new patterns of ordering words in the question sentence, they must also have acquired concepts of space and time, and of causal and other complex relationships which in turn are related to the interrogatives *where, when, why,* and *how.*

The Fitzgerald Key (Fitzgerald, 1926, 1956), widely used in schools for the hearing-impaired, is a device which may be found useful in helping children see the relationships between such time elements as *yesterday, last week,* and *in a little while* and place relationships as *here, there,* and *on the chair.*

Teachers will also find the use of PRO-forms helpful in stimulating children to ask questions. The following dialogue between a seven-year-old deaf youngster and his teacher illustrates their use in conjunction with the interrogatives *where, when,* and *how.* This exercise assumes that the child is thoroughly familiar with the meaning of the interrogatives which were introduced earlier one at a time.

T: We will go *Somewhere.*
You don't know *where* we will go.
Can you ask me *where* we will go?

C: *Where* we will go? NO! Where will we go?

T: Good!
We will go to the zoo.
We will go to the zoo *Sometime* soon.
You don't know *when* we will go to the zoo.
Can you ask me *when* we will go to the zoo?

C: *When* we will go to the zoo?

T: *When* will we go to the zoo? (Teacher rephrases child's question.)

C: *When* will we go to the zoo? (Child uses correct form.)

T: We will go to the zoo next Tuesday.
You don't know *how* we will go to the zoo.
Can you ask me *how* we will go to the zoo?

C: How we will. . . .How we. . . .How will we go to the zoo? (Teacher nods approval.)

T: We will go to the zoo in my car.

Children require practice with similar question patterns over and over again. Guessing games based on hidden objects or an adapted "Twenty Questions" game may help stabilize these patterns, but they will not teach the use of spontaneous questioning by the children. This results from providing and capitalizing on actual situations which stimulate children to ask questions for information.

LESSON 8

Word Affixes

ABSTRACT

- In general, there are two kinds of words in English:

    1. form class words, such as nouns, verbs, adjectives, and adverbs, and
    2. structure words, such as prepositions, conjunctions, negators, determiners, intensifiers, and question words, which bind the form class words together in a sentence.

- An inflectional suffix is an ending added to a form class word which marks a change in grammatical significance. Case, number, tense, person, and voice are indicated by inflectional suffixes.
- An inflectional suffix cannot be added to a structure word.
- A morpheme is any part of a word which carries meaning, either lexical or grammatical.
- Derivational affixes are additions to the beginning or end of a form word which may change:

    1. its form class, as from a noun to an adjective or a verb to a noun, or
    2. its lexical meaning.

- After an inflectional suffix has been added to a form class word, no derivational suffix may be added to it.

Most words in the dictionary belong to one or more of the four form classes, *nouns, verbs, adjectives,* or *adverbs.* Their forms may be changed by the addition of suffixes and prefixes. They constitute the major part of our vocabulary. There is another limited number of words, perhaps 200 or so, whose forms do not change. They are the structure words which bind the form class words together in phrases and sentences. They include such categories as prepositions, conjunctions, negators, determiners, intensifiers, and question words.

EXERCISE

In the following sentence, underline the form class words which carry the meaning load of the sentence.

> In May, 1815, Gallaudet embarked on his long voyage to England in a slow-sailing ship, and didn't reach his destination until June 25.

Answers: May, Gallaudet, embarked, long, voyage, England, slow-sailing, ship, reach, destination, June

Note: The numerals, 1815 and 25, could also be included as form class words since they are symbols standing for words.

By and large, all words carry both lexical meaning and grammatical meaning, with the burden for signalling grammatical meaning falling largely on the structure words. Nevertheless, many structure words, such as prepositions, have multiple lexical meanings. Notice, in the above exercise, how *in* is used in the two phrases, *in a slow-sailing ship* and *in May, 1815*. The first *in* introduces the idea of place, and the second, that of time.

The form class words which carry much of the meaning content of a message also carry grammatical significance. We can add inflectional suffixes to them to change their grammatical meanings. An inflectional suffix is that change of form in words which marks case, gender, and number in nouns, and tense, person, and voice in verbs. Here are the important inflectional suffixes:

> the -*s* or -*es* added to a noun to form a plural
>
> the -*'s* added to a singular noun to form the possessive (the apostrophe alone is usually added to plural nouns ending in -*s*)
>
> the -*ed* added to a verb to form the past tense
>
> the -*s* added to a verb stem to form the third person singular of the present tense
>
> the -*ing* added to verbs to form the present participle
>
> the -*en* represents the past participle form, whatever it may be

For instance, in the preceding exercise, *embark* becomes *embarked* in order to indicate the past tense. *Sail,* combined with *slow,* has become *sailing* and modifies the noun *ship*. These structural changes affect grammatical meaning but not lexical meaning. In the sentences below, -*s* is attached to the noun *boy* and the verb *work*. In the first sentence, the -*s* is a morpheme designating the plural. In the second sentence, the -*s* is a morpheme which signals the third person singular of the present tense.

The boy*s* work.

The boy work*s*.

A morpheme is any part of a word which carries meaning. The inflectional ending *-s* in the word *boys* carries grammatical meaning, while *boy* carries the lexical meaning. Both are morphemes.

We can also add -'s or -s' to nouns to indicate the possessive or genitive forms, as in *the boy's attitude*, or, *the boys' attitude.*

Besides the present tense morpheme, *-s,* which is added to the third person singular, inflectional signals for verbs include the past tense morpheme, *-ed,* as in *worked,* and its variant form *-t,* as in *slept,* as well as vowel changes in the stem of some verbs as in *eat, ate.* Two other inflectional endings peculiar to verbs are the *-ing* form attached to the verb stem to form the present participle as in *drive, driving,* and the *-en* morpheme added to the stem of some verbs to form the past participle as in *driven.* Some verbs add *-ed* instead of *-en* to form the past participle as in *reach, reached.* Some verbs add neither *-en* or *-ed* as in *cut, cut.* In this text, *-en* will be used as a symbol to represent any past participle form of a verb, whatever it may be.

Structure words do not change their form. We cannot add inflectional suffixes to structure words as we can to major form class words. For instance, we cannot say, **thes,* **nots,* **notted,* or **tos.*

EXERCISE

As a test of your understanding of inflectional suffixes, mark the words that carry inflectional endings with a check.

1.	______	practical	6.	______	boxes
2.	______	disappoints	7.	______	girl's
3.	______	ladies	8.	______	oxen
4.	______	actually	9.	______	unfortunate
5.	______	traveling	10.	______	curtained

Answers: 2, 3, 5, 6, 7, 8, 10

Form class words may also have derivational affixes as well as inflectional suffixes attached to them. These may or may not change the lexical meaning of the word, but they usually change the word from one set to another, as from a noun to an adjective. If we add the prefix *en-* to the adjective *rich,* we form the verb *enrich.* If we add the suffix *-ly* to *rich,* we change it from an adjective to an adverb. If we add *un-* to the adjective *true,* the word remains an adjective, but its meaning is changed. By the addition of suffixes, the noun *critic* may become the verb *criticize,* or the adjective *critical.* We may add several derivational suffixes to words. To the adjective *special,* which consists of a bound morpheme *spec-* plus the suffix *-al,* we may add *-ize* to form the verb *specialize,* and then add *-ation* to form the noun *specialization.* We cannot add any more derivational suffixes after we add the inflectional suffix. The inflectional suffix terminates any word, as in *specializations.*

The particular suffixes which mark nouns, adjectives, and adverbs will be discussed in coming lessons. Only a few mark verbs, as *-ify* in *classify* and *codify, -ize* in *neutralize,* and *-ate* in *pulsate.*

In the normal process of learning language, children do not think of the words they use as nouns, verbs, adjectives, or adverbs, but rather sense the functions of these form classes. Young children with language disorders should not be burdened with the task of identifying the words in their vocabularies as parts of speech. However, a frequently used sign for a verb in the written form is the double underline. It aids children in recognizing the necessity of including a verb in every basic sentence.

The inflectional suffixes of nouns as well as verbs must be learned in conjunction with situations and experiences which explain their meaning. Plurals require a child to have number concepts; possessives require the concept of ownership; past tense endings require concept of time. Each of these concepts must be dealt with at a meaning level as well as a syntactical one, and each aspect practiced in appropriate sentences.

A study of derivational suffixes and prefixes is essential for the expansion of vocabulary. After children have acquired a vocabulary of several hundred words, including such items as the verb, *wind,* and the adjective, *happy,* it is time to begin this study. The words *unwind* and *unhappy* may be introduced when the occasion warrants. The prefix *un* takes on the meaning of an opposite or negative aspect and may be generalized to other words as in *uncover* and *unafraid.* Vocabulary study of this type begun fairly early in a child's school life somewhat alleviates the burden of learning thousands of new words later for purposes of reading. It gives children self-help skills in unlocking the meanings of a great many words.

EXERCISE

Mark the words which carry an inflectional ending with an *I,* those with a derivational ending with a *D.*

1.	_______	applicable	6.	_______	determining
2.	_______	indented	7.	_______	exposes
3.	_______	intricate	8.	_______	frozen
4.	_______	extension	9.	_______	princess
5.	_______	hortative	10.	_______	prince's

Answers: Inflectional: 2, 6, 7, 8, 10; Derivational: 1, 3, 4, 5, 9

LESSON 9

Noun Features

ABSTRACT

- Each noun has sound features represented in writing by its spelling.
- Each noun has lexical meaning.
- Each noun has syntactic aspects expressed by the presence or absence of the following features:

  1. <+ common> <— common>
  2. <+ concrete> <— concrete>
  3. <+ count> <— count>
  4. <+ human> <— human>
  5. <+ animate> <— animate>
  6. <+ singular> <— singular>

- A noun may be a member of several of the subsets itemized above.
- The subsets to which a noun belongs restrict its use in combination with other words in the sentence.

Form words, such as nouns, verbs, adjectives, and adverbs, have certain distinctive features. First, each word has its sound features represented in writing by its spelling. Second, each word has a semantic component, or lexical meaning, represented by the definitions found in a dictionary. Third, the syntactic aspect of each word is expressed by the presence or absence of certain features that add to its meaning. This lesson will introduce some noun features.

You are familiar with the terms *common noun* and *proper noun,* such as the words *girl* and *Sheila. Chair, book,* and *glass* have the feature <+common> while *Jim, Mt. McKinley,* and *Newsweek* have the feature <— common>.

Another feature of nouns is their concreteness <+ concrete> or abstractness <—concrete>, as represented by *boy* and *energy.* You can point your finger at concrete objects, such as a *rock*, a *crater*, or some *dust*, but not at anything as abstract as *energy*, *religion*, or *satisfaction*.

Some nouns represent countable things such as *apples*, *beads*, and *elephants*. We cannot count *milk*, *cement*, or *sand*. While it is possible to talk about *sands*, *cements*, or *milks*, we usually do not. If a noun has the feature <+ count>, we use certain determiners with it and others if its feature is <— count>. We can say *an apple* or *many apples*, but we must say *some milk* and *much milk* for <— count> nouns.

Nouns may also carry the feature of humanness <+ human> in contrast to the non-human <— human> feature. This feature places restrictions on the kinds of verbs or pronoun referents which can co-occur with these nouns. We cannot say:

> *The ball remembered the money.
>
> *The boy wound itself.

In fairy tales, the <+ human> feature is sometimes conferred upon nonhuman things, and so in children's books, we may read sentences like:

> The little airplane danced a happy jig.
>
> He said, "I'll show that big jet what I can do."

and consider them perfectly legitimate.

Animateness is inherent in the feature <+ human>. However, nouns which do not carry the <+ human> feature may be animate. *Bees*, *bugs*, and *bears* are alive but not human, and carry the <+ animate> feature.

We must also know whether a noun is singular or plural. Nouns with the <+ singular> feature require that the inflectional ending *-s* be added to the verb stem in the present tense, as in:

> The baby eats solid food.
>
> The babies eat four times a day.

Nouns may belong to any number of subsets by virtue of the features they carry. Table 1 indicates the characteristics of the entries for *boy*, *ball*, *Jim*, *milk*, *dogs*, and *mischief*.

Table 1. Characteristics of Lexical Entries (Specific Nouns)

	LEXICAL ENTRIES					
Feature	*boy*	*ball*	*Jim*	*milk*	*dogs*	*mischief*
common	+	+	−	+	+	+
concrete	+	+	+	+	+	−
count	+	+	+	−	+	−
human	+	−	+	−	−	−
animate	+*	−	+*	−	+	−
singular	+	+	+	+	−	+

*Inherent in human feature.

EXERCISE

I. After studying Table 1, write out the characteristics of each of the following nouns.

Example: boy + common + concrete + count + human + singular

1. zeal ________________________________
2. dime ________________________________
3. money ________________________________
4. mother ________________________________
5. kitten ________________________________

II. To which word do you not usually add an -s for its plural form? _____

III. To which can you not point your finger? ________________

VI. With which do you use the determiner *many*? ________________

V. What determiner do you use with non-count nouns, *much* or *many*?

____

VI. What are the noun features that you learned in this lesson? ________

____

____

Answers:

I. <+ common>: 1, 2, 3, 4, 5
<+ concrete>: 2, 3, 4, 5
<+ count>: 2, 4, 5
<+ human>: 4
<+ animate>: 4, 5
<+ singular>: 1, 2, 3, 4, 5
II. zeal
III. zeal
IV. dime, mother, kitten
V. much
VI. common, concrete, count, human, animate, singular

In transformational grammar, a great deal has to be known about the words we use, for classification plays a very important role in transformation rules. Vocabulary study for hearing-impaired children must contain at least some of this information if the children are to deal with the lexicon intelligently, as the lexicon, or dictionary, contains information about word features.

LESSON 10

The English Verb: Principal Parts

ABSTRACT

- English verbs may be roughly divided into two groups:

  1. "full" verbs which have principal parts and are inflected, and
  2. the copula *be*.

- The full verbs *have* and *do* and the copula *be*, when used as auxiliaries, retain their inflected forms as follows:

  have: has, had, having
  do: does, did, done, doing
  be: am, is, are, was, were, been, being

- The infinitive form of a verb, the stem, is frequently preceded by *to*.
- Some verbs add *-ed*, some *-t*, and some change the stem vowel to form the past tense.

Perhaps the most complicated aspect of English is its verb system. Anyone who masters this complicated system has a very good chance of mastering the language. The child with a hearing impairment must first learn to identify certain words as being verbs, to recognize their function in a sentence, and to associate the multiple forms which each verb assumes. Then he must understand the concept of tense as it is related to temporal events and to other aspects of existence. This requires an inferred knowledge of the rules governing the use of auxiliaries and inflectional endings in the many verb phrases that English employs.

English verbs may be roughly divided into two groups:

1. "full" verbs which have principal parts and are inflected, and
2. the copula *be*.

"Full" verbs such as *cut, invent, teach,* and *show* have from three to five forms, as in:

cut, cuts, cutting

invent, invents, invented, inventing

teach, teaches, taught, teaching

show, shows, showed (shown), showing

Linguists place the copula *be* in a separate category. It has eight forms: *be, am, is, are, was, were, been, being.* It also functions differently from the "full" verbs in transformations. The full verbs, *have* and *do,* and the copula *be,* when used as auxiliaries retain their inflected forms, as in:

Mabel *doesn't* go to school.

She *has* had a private tutor for two years.

She *is* learning to read.

When we list the principal parts of a full verb, we begin with the simplest form, its base, the form that is used to construct the infinitive. When it is necessary to identify this simple form for young children, we usually speak of it as "the name of the verb," and write it, as in:

( ) hop

the parentheses indicating an optional *to* to form the infinitive. Observe in Table 2 how verb forms are developed from the base. The spelling and pronunciation of the various forms must be learned by all children. Your attention is only drawn to this matter here. We shall not go into details about it in this book. You are urged to use the introduction to the dictionary and other references to help you learn and teach the rules of spelling.

Table 2. Principal Parts of Verbs

Base	*Third Person Singular Present Tense*	*Past Tense* (–ed Form)	*Past Participle* (–en Form)	*Present Participle* (–ing Form)
(to) hop	hops	hopped	hopped	hopping
(to) try	tries	tried	tried	trying
(to) watch	watches	watched	watched	watching
(to) run	runs	ran	run	running
(to) eat	eats	ate	eaten	eating

Verbs that form their parts in a similar manner can be grouped for purposes of teaching. There are many verbs that add *-ed* to form the past tense, some add *-t,* and others change vowels to form the past tense (refer to Appendix A for these groupings). Useful as such groupings may be for older children, it is very difficult for young children to understand these generalizations because their vocabularies are not large enough to make groups. The whole matter of spelling changes often remains incomprehensible to a child, and, consequently, each verb must be learned as a discrete set through usage. To illustrate the difficulty of generalizing how the principal parts of verbs are formed, note the following examples. Compare *ring* and *bring, bring* and *buy, sell* and *shell:*

ring	rings	rang	rung	ringing
bring	brings	brought	brought	bringing
buy	buys	bought	bought	buying
sell	sells	sold	sold	selling
shell	shells	shelled	shelled	shelling

EXERCISE

Fill in the headings and write the principal parts of these verbs.

PRINCIPAL PARTS OF VERBS

Base

1. (to) feel
2. (to) dress
3. (to) catch
4. (to) look
5. (to) shop
6. (to) wait
7. (to) lean
8. (to) comb
9. (to) boil
10. (to) offend

Answers:

Headings: Third Person Singular Present Tense, Past Tense, Past Participle, Present Participle

1. feels, felt, felt, feeling
2. dresses, dressed, dressed, dressing
3. catches, caught, caught, catching
4. looks, looked, looked, looking
5. shops, shopped, shopped, shopping
6. waits, waited, waited, waiting
7. leans, leaned, leaned, leaning
8. combs, combed, combed, combing
9. boils, boiled, boiled, boiling
10. offends, offended, offended, offending

Children may need help in remembering the principle parts of an increasing number of verbs they are expected to use. To refresh their memories a dictionary of verbs may be built with them and serve as a self-help reference.

Six or more flash cards (4 inches $\times$ 12 inches) are spirally bound for each verb, the first card containing the base form of the verb, the second, the past tense form, and so on. Each form is added only as the children understand its meaning and use. In the illustration below the dashes allow for insertion of items such as auxiliaries, negatives, or nouns in questions.

go	went	did-go	-going	do-go does-go	-gone

Independence in usage is the final goal. This requires a great deal of practice by the children with increasing emphasis being placed on self-correction.

LESSON 11

The Simple Present and Past Tenses of Verbs

ABSTRACT

- Tense is a grammatical signalling device.
- Clock or calendar time does not determine linguistic or grammatical tense.
- There are only two grammatical tenses in English: present and past.
- Past time can be expressed by the use of past tense forms.
- Simple present tense using finite forms of action verbs often implies frequently occurring activity rather than a statement of what is occurring at the moment.
- A finite< + finite> verb is that form which can stand alone as the main verb in an independent clause.
- A non-finite verb <— finite> may be used with an auxiliary. The auxiliary carries the tense.
- A single verb phrase (VP) may include finite and non-finite verb forms.
- Children with impaired hearing must learn how to express past, present, and future clock and calendar time by using a variety of verb phrases.
- Children must learn to use modals to express varying degrees of possibility, truth, and desire.

In this lesson we shall explore grammatical tense and some of the features associated with it. In English there are only two tenses: present tense and past tense. Linguists limit the meaning of tense to that of a grammatical signalling device, and, therefore, the concept of tense as time, which we learned in the old grammars, should be disregarded. It will be important not to confuse our notions of time such as past, present, and future clock or calendar time with linguistic or grammatical tense. Notional time and grammatical tense have only tenuous relationships.

EXERCISE

1. How many linguistic tenses are there? ______________________
2. What are they? ______________________ and ______________________
3. Is the "future tense" a linguistic tense? ______________________
4. Is the "past tense" a linguistic tense? ______________________
5. Is the "present tense" a linguistic tense? ______________________

Answers: 1. two 2. present, past 3. no 4. yes 5. yes

Let us first consider tense as it relates to the finite form of verbs. A finite form <+ finite) is one that can stand alone as the main verb in a sentence. It is never preceded by an auxiliary. In the following sentences, you will easily be able to identify the present and past tenses of the finite form of the verb *choose:*

> Alexander Graham Bell *chose* Mr. Watson to assist him.
>
> The school *chooses* new teachers every fall.
>
> *Alexander Graham Bell *chosen* Mr. Watson to assist him.
>
> *The school *choosing* new teachers every fall.
>
> *The children *to choose* their partners.

The last three sentences are non-grammatical because a non-finite <— finite> form of the verb *choose* was used.

Non finite forms may be used with auxiliaries, as in:

> Alexander Graham Bell *had chosen* Mr. Watson to assist him.
>
> The principal *was choosing* teachers for his new program.
>
> The principal *is choosing* students for special classes.
>
> The principal *has chosen* the faculty members.

In these examples, the auxiliaries carry the tense. *Had* and *was* are past tense forms, and *is* and *has* are present tense forms. We will discuss auxiliaries in more detail in subsequent lessons.

Non-finite forms may also be linked in verb phrases with a finite form of a full verb, as in:

> Mary *wants to choose* her birthday present today.
>
> Jane *wanted to choose* a new dress for the party.

EXERCISE

Underline the <+ finite> forms of the verbs in the sentences below with two lines, and the non-finite <— finite> forms with one line.

1. The Bells precipitated long discussions about the value of Visible Speech.
2. Audiences responded enthusiastically to their demonstrations held in Scotland.
3. One night the audience stood and cheered after Alec gave a good performance.
4. They are swayed by the demonstrations.
5. The Bells moved to Canada, leaving behind an excellent reputation.

Answers:

Finite:			Non-finite:		
	1.	precipitated		2.	held
	2.	responded		4.	swayed
	3.	stood, cheered, gave		5.	leaving
	4.	moved			

Even though we can speak about only two linguistic tenses, the past and the present, we cannot neglect to discuss notional time in this text. Children with hearing impairments must learn how to express past, present, and future clock and calendar time by using a wide variety of phrases which are characteristic of our language.

Beyond that, they must understand and be able to express certain attitudes of possibility, doubt, degrees of truth and wishing by use of phrases containing modal auxiliaries where little or no time relationship exists. It is extremely important that we understand the forms of verbs required to express these notional ideas so that we can clarify them for the children we teach.

Children, eventually, should understand that time passes, that "before now" is past, and that certain adverbs like *yesterday* and certain phrases like *last week* pattern with past tense. Past tense forms ordinarily express past time. The simple past tense expressed by a finite verb commonly indicates that an action or an event occurred at some definite stated time in the past. The past is a relatively simple tense to teach to children with hearing impairments because its form does not change with the subject of the sentence. We say:

I / you / he / she / it / we / you / they / chose.

In a paragraph, a definite time is usually stated in the first sentence:

> *In 1871*, Alexander Melville Bell sent his son to The Boston School for Deaf Mutes. There, Alexander Graham Bell taught Visible Speech to the faculty. Bell spent two months in Boston.

The past is also used to relate events as continuing throughout a period of the past but not continuing until the present, as in:

In those days, everyone traveled by train or coach.

The long journeys wearied the travelers.

EXERCISE

Underline each simple past tense form of the finite verb with two lines:

Example:

Bell learned Visible Speech from his father.

1. All his life, Bell had been interested in sound.
2. His father taught corrective speech in Scotland.
3. He also invented a cuneiform-like set of symbols descriptive of tongue positions.
4. He trained Alex to assist him.
5. He would write passages in Visible Speech.
6. Alex read these symbols easily and fluently.
7. Today, Visible Speech has been supplanted by the International Phonetic Alphabet.

Answers: 2. taught 3. invented 4. trained 6. read

The simple present tense using finite forms of verbs implies frequently recurring activity or generaliation rather than a statement of what is happening at the moment. We must be careful not to associate the simple present with the adverb *now* when presenting the use of this tense to children with hearing impairments. The adverb *now* does apply when the copula *be* is used in the present tense. For instance:

He is here now.

She is elated now.

We are studying physics together now.

Now would not be appropriate in the following sentences since we are talking about activities which recur or are habitual:

Class begins at 9:00 a.m. on Mondays and Wednesdays.

We do experiments with sound in the lab.

The simple present tense may also apply to generalizations:

Sound waves travel 1100 feet per second.

The inner ear generates electrical potentials.

The simple present tense may even refer to future time:

We leave for the Museum of Science and Industry tomorrow at noon.

The bus arrives there at 12:30 p.m., and we leave for home at five.

EXERCISE

Underline each simple present tense of the finite verbs in these sentences with two lines, and in the space at the right, indicate the meaning expressed by the tense: R = recurrence including habitual; G = generalization; F = future time

Example:

We take a test every day. R

1. The ear converts mechanical energy to electrical energy. ______
2. Sometimes we strike a tuning fork to produce sound. ______
3. Every week we do a new experiment. ______
4. We nearly always enjoy our lab experiments. ______
5. Sound waves travel in all directions from the source. ______
6. The teacher lectures once a week. ______
7. We take our final examination next week. ______

Answers:

1. converts, G
2. strike, R
3. do, R
4. enjoy, R
5. travel, G
6. lectures, R
7. take, F

EXERCISE

Write the verb for.

Examples:

present + play He plays.
present + play They play.

1. present + choose He__________
2. present + precipitate He__________
3. present + respond He__________
4. present + stand He__________
5. past + cheer He__________
6. past + move He__________
7. present + send He__________
8. present + teach He__________
9. past + spend He__________
10. past + travel He__________
11. present + go They__________
12. present + weary They__________
13. past + learn They__________
14. present + invent They__________
15. past + read They__________
16. present + study They__________
17. past + begin They__________
18. present + generate They__________
19. present + arrive They__________
20. past + strike They__________

Answers:

1. chooses
2. precipitates
3. responds
4. stands
5. cheered
6. moved
7. sends
8. teaches
9. spent
10. traveled
11. go
12. weary
13. learned
14. invent
15. read
16. study
17. began
18. generate
19. arrive
20. struck

EXERCISE

Sentences like the ones below appear in children's books. Explain what these sentences mean to you. Discuss them with your colleagues, your classmates, or your profesor. Can you find pictures for these sentences?

1. The dog runs.
2. The children play.
3. The balloon goes up, up, up.
4. Dogs run.
5. Children play.

Answers:

If you said you could find pictures for these sentences your answer would not agree with mine, for I could never find illustrations for them. It would be quite impossible to take a picture of a generality or an habitual activity. It would be possible to illustrate the sentence, "The dog is running." Pictures of actions are usually interpreted verbally as somebody or something *doing* something. Find some action pictures and test yourself as to what you would say in describing them.

LESSON 12

The T/do and T/neg Transformations for Finite Verbs

ABSTRACT

- English chooses the verb *do* to provide an auxiliary in the surface structure of sentences containing finite verbs in order to create a *yes-no* question. This is called the T/do transformation.
- The T/do transformation becomes an obligatory transformation before T/neg can be applied.
- The T/neg transformation is applied to finite forms of verbs when it is desired that a negative sentence be constructed.

One of the most important transformations in English is closely associated with the simple past and present tenses of verbs. This is the T/do transformation. In Lesson 6, we noted that in order to ask a question, we merely changed the order of words in the string, transposing the modal auxiliary to the beginning of the sentence. The modal contained the tense:

NP + Aux + V => Aux + NP + V

Recall the example in Lesson 6. We will first write the terminal string of the basic sentence *Helen could talk,* and apply the T/yes-no transformaiton:

Helen + past + can + talk =>

past + can + Helen + talk =>

Could + Helen + talk

Suppose we wish to make a yes-no question of the sentence:

The family moved.

It immediately becomes obvious that there is no auxiliary other than tense to reverse with the subject. Yet we cannot and do not say:

*Moved the family?

Therefore, it is necessary to provide a moveable auxiliary in the surface structure of the sentence in order to create a question. English chooses the verb *do* to accomplish this transformation. *Do* has no semantic meaning whatsoever when it is used as an auxiliary. It is a verb empty of meaning in this situation. It merely signals tense and fulfills the requirement that a moveable auxiliary be present to transform a string containing a finite verb into a question.

We will write the string of grammatical structures underlying the sentence, *The family moved*, in Sentence Tree 10.

Sentence Tree 10: The family moved.

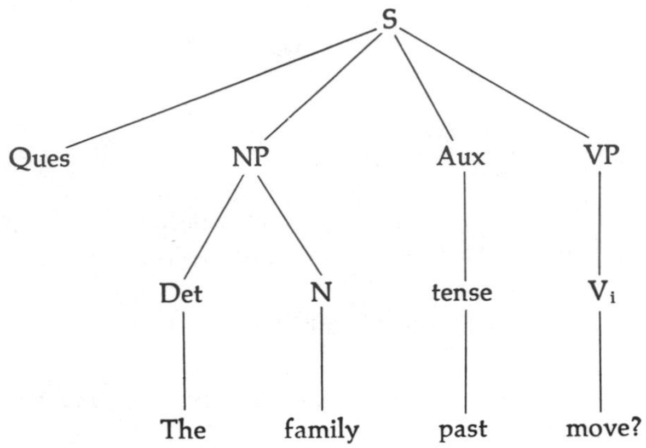

We now rewrite the string to include the auxiliary *do* before we apply the T/yes-no question transformation:

The + family + past + move ==>

T/do: The + family + past + do + move ==>

T/yes-no: past + do + the + family + move →

Did the family move?

If no moveable Aux exists in the verb phrase, T/do is obligatory before we can apply T/yes-no. One more example should clarify this transformation:

Sentence Tree 11: The Bells like Canada.

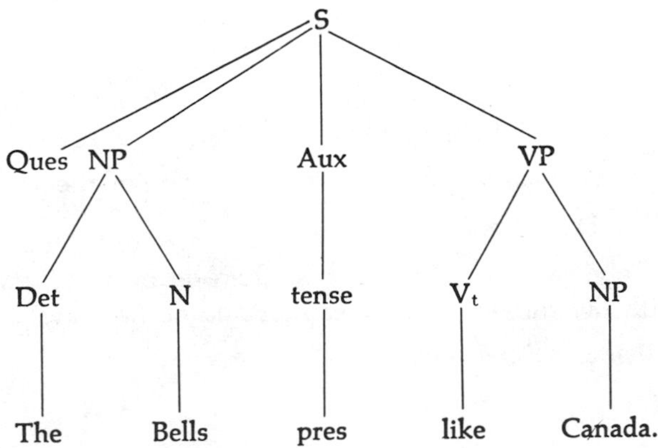

We will now apply the T/do transformation before we apply the T/yes-no transformation to this string:

The + Bells + pres + like + Canada =>

T/do: The + Bells + pres + do + like + Canada =>

T/yes-no: pres + do + the + Bells + like + Canada →

Do the Bells like Canada?

Children with impaired hearing find this transformation most difficult to understand and master. It requires a knowledge not only of the forms of the verb *do* but also of the base form of the verb that follows. This means that a great deal of associative learning of verb forms must take place before recall becomes automatic and use becomes functional.

EXERCISE

Write the terminal strings and apply the necessary transformations to create yes-no questions for each of the following sentences:

Example:

Alec adores Mabel. →

Alec + pres + adore + Mabel =>

T/do: Alec + pres + do + adore + Mabel =>

T/yes-no: pres + do + Alec + adore + Mabel →

Does Alec adore Mabel?

Remember that → means "may be rewritten as" or "consists of," while the => means "transform to."

1. Alec married Mabel.

2. Mabel adored Alec.

3. They visit Scotland every year.

4. They enjoyed their honeymoon.

5. Bell explained his inventions.

6. They like visitors.

7. They have a daughter.

8. They welcomed guests.

Answers:

Check your answers against the example given at the beginning of this exercise.

When the T/neg transformation is applied to finite forms of verbs, past or present, T/do becomes an obligatory transformation before T/neg can be applied. We will apply T/do + T/neg to the terminal string underlying the following sentence:

The Bells celebrated their anniversary.

the + Bells + past + celebrate + their + anniversary ==>

T/do: the + Bells + past + do + celebrate their anniversary ==>

T/neg: the + Bells + past + do + not + celebrate their anniversary. →

The Bells did not celebrated their anniversary. ==>

T/contr may now be optionally applied to produce:

The Bells didn't celebrate their anniversary.

Deaf children also find this transformation difficult because it involves the complexities of T/do. Besides, it is quite difficult to see and differentiate *did* or *didn't* on the lips, so children cannot learn it merely from lipreading. This transformation must be clarified in ways which assure an understanding of how it operates.

EXERCISE

Apply the T/neg to these sentences:

Example 1:

Mabel held the baby.

Mabel + past + hold + the baby ==>

T/do: Mabel + past + do + hold + the baby ==>

T/neg: Mabel + past + do + not + hold + the baby. →

Mabel did not hold the baby.

Example 2:

Alec rocks the baby.

Alec + pres + rock + the baby ==>

T/do: Alec + pres + do + rock + the baby ==>

T/neg: Alec + pres + do + not + rock + the baby—>

Alec does not rock the baby.

1. Elsie took a step.

2. She fell.

3. She cries.

4. She smiles.

5. Baby shook the rattle.

Answers:

Check your answers by comparing them with the examples at the beginning of this exercise.

The surface structures we use in communicating usually contain one, two, three, or more transformations. We are not aware of them as we speak. The children we teach will not know that they are using transformations, but their teachers will. Children will practice transformations in sentences that relate to meaningful experiences. Since T/do and T/neg are very frequently used transformations, children should be given the opportunity to use them early in their language learning. T/do in the past tense would be most useful in talking about past activities, as in:

> Helen did not (didn't) come to school today. She is sick.
>
> Bob did not (didn't) ride his bike to school today. He had a flat tire.
> Did you see my new coat?

T/do, present tense, would be appropriate for expressions concerning likes, dislikes, desires and needs as in:

> I do not(don't) like tomatoes.
>
> Do you like Amy? I love Amy.
>
> Do you need this paintbrush?

LESSON 13

The Copula Be

ABSTRACT

- In this text, the copula *be* will be classified as a special kind of verb.
- In this lesson, we will complete the five basic sentence patterns by examining Patterns III, IV, and V.
- These patterns contain the copula *be,* and are completed by a different structure in each pattern:

    III. NP + be + NP
    IV. NP + be + Adj
    V. NP + be + Adverb of Place

- Other copulative, or linking verbs, pattern in a manner similar to *be:*

    1. *Remain* and *become* fit into Pattern III.
    2. *Seem, appear, taste, feel, remain,* and *become* fit into Pattern IV.

- *Be* becomes the auxiliary in the T/yes-no transformation. It moves to the beginning of the sentence.
- T/contr cannot be applied to *am* when the first NP in the pattern is *I.*
- Negative contractions may take two forms for the second and third persons. The contraction may be applied either to the pronoun or to the verb as in: *You aren't funny. You're not funny.*
- *Be* may be used as an auxiliary in the progressive aspect of verbs, retaining its eight forms as it combines with the *ing* form of full verbs.
- The T/there transformation may be performed on the pattern, NP + be + Adv_p, if the NP contains a non-definite determiner, such as: *a, (an), some, few,* or *no determiner* (Ø) at all, as in: *A man is at the door; There is a man at at the door. Crumbs are on the floor; There are crumbs on the floor.*
- Ø is read as "zero determiner," and is used to indicate a legitimate omission of a determiner in a noun phrase.
- If the subject of the sentence, the first NP, contains any form of a personal pronoun, a proper noun, or a noun with a definite determiner, such as: *each, every, this,* or *that,* the T/there transformation cannot be applied.

Some linguists classify the copula *be* as a verb, while others suggest it has the characteristics of a structure word because it has no semantic connotations as do words like *run, rectify,* or *adore.* In this book, we will refer to it as a special kind of verb, the *copula,* which means that it has a connecting or linking function in a sentence. *Be* appears in sentences in the position ordinarily occupied by a verb, and thus performs the function of a verb in several sentence patterns. It is only verb in its class.

The copula *be* is one of the most difficult aspects of English for non-native speakers to master. Research evidence points to the fact that American children who speak non-standard dialects frequently omit it from their sentences, or if they do use it, the form they use is not likely to agree with the subject of the sentence. Even bright children who speak standard English make mistakes in the use of *be* in their written English until about the fifth grade (Loban, 1966), but interestingly enough, they use *be* more frequently than do less capable children (Loban, 1963). It is no wonder, then, that children with hearing impairments will find the mastery of this verb very difficult. The study of *be* should be continued throughout the deaf child's entire school life.

You will recall that in Lesson 10, we stated that *be* is different from every other verb in English because it has eight forms instead of the usual three, four, or five. The <+ finite> forms include: *are, am, is, was,* and *were;* the <— finite> forms include *be, been,* and *being.* Table 3 relates these forms to the feature, *person,* of pronouns.

Table 3. The Finite Forms of *Be*

Number	*Person*	*Present*	*Past*
singular	first (I)	am	was
	second (you)	are	were
	third (he, she, it)	is	was
plural	first (we)		
	second (you)	are	were
	third (they)		

Linguists explain the appearance of the copula *be* in sentences as resulting from a transformation in which the copula segment is added to a string. In this lesson, we will consider three basic sentence patterns, III, IV, and V, of which the copula is a part. In each pattern, the copula is completed by a different structure. We may add these three new patterns to the two that we have already discussed in Lesson 5. This will complete the number of patterns to be used in this text:

I. $NP + Aux + V_iP$
II. $NP + Aux + V_tP + NP$
III. $NP + be + NP$
IV. $NP + be + Adj$
V. $NP + be + Adv_{p(place)}$

To illustrate patterns III, IV, and V, we will translate them into sentences, and, in the trees, write the terminal strings for only the first of the basic sentences illustrating each pattern.

Pattern III: NP + be + NP

That woman is her companion.

Miss Sullivan was her teacher.

I am her friend.

Sentence Tree 12: That woman is her companion.

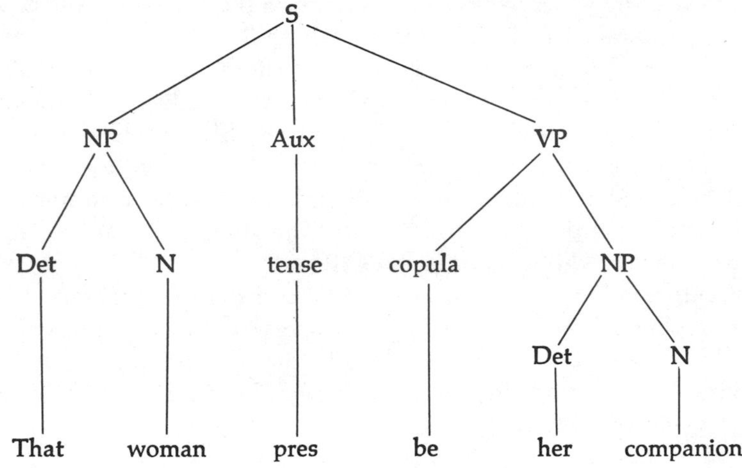

Pattern IV: NP + be + Adj

Helen Keller was indefatigable.

They were inseparable.

She was persistent.

Sentence Tree 13: Helen Keller was indefatigable..

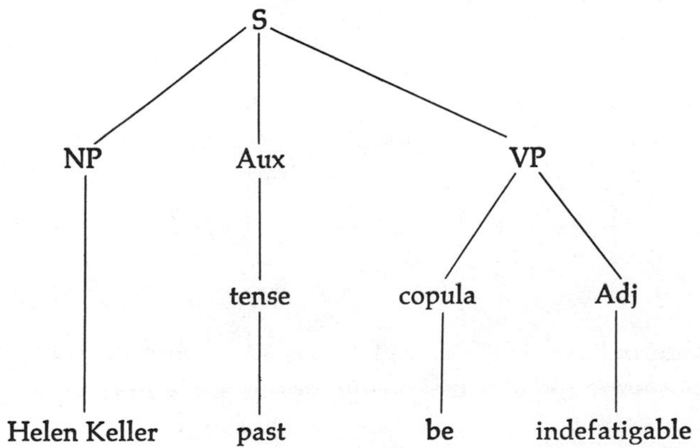

Pattern V: NP + be + Adv_p
Anne Sullivan was in Boston.
Perkins School is there.
We are here.

Sentence Tree 14: Anne Sullivan was in Boston.

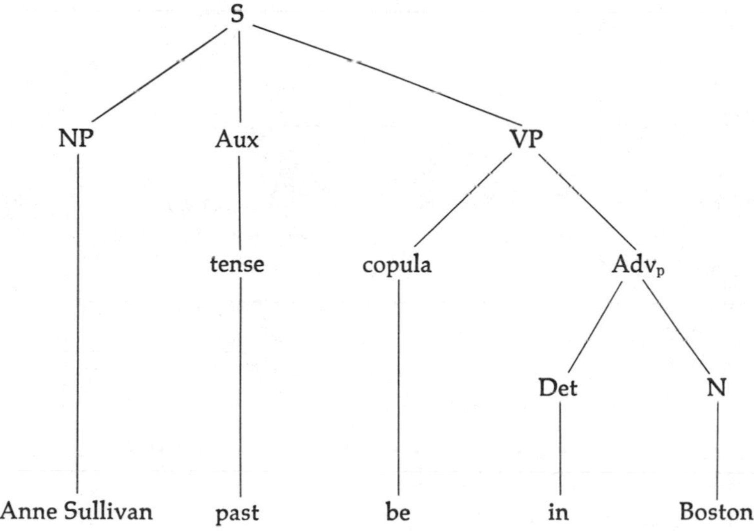

EXERCISE

Write the patterns for these sentences.

Example:

She is clever. NP + be + Adj

1. They are in class. ______
2. They are quiet. ______
3. They are students. ______
4. She is studious. ______
5. The room is there. ______

6. The building is a barracks. ____________________

7. You are welcome. ____________________

8. Miss Sullivan is in the library. ____________________

9. I am her companion. ____________________

Answers:

1. NP + be + Adv_p
2. NP + be + Adj
3. NP + be + NP
4. NP + be + Adj
5. NP + be + Adv_p
6. NP + be + NP
7. NP + be + Adj
8. NP + be + Adv_p
9. NP + be + NP

In passing, we should note that some other verbs known variously as copulative, or linking verbs, pattern in a manner similar to *be*. *Remain* and *become* fit into pattern III, and are followed by NPs. A larger group of verbs including *seem, appear, taste,* and *feel,* plus *remain* and *become,* fit into pattern IV, and are followed by adjectives. However, these are full verbs and do not follow the same transformation rules as the verb *be* does. The rules they follow are those of any other verb in English. These verbs are illustrated for you:

Pattern III:

Helen was a student (at Perkins).

She became a student (at Radcliffe).

She remained a student (all her life).

Pattern IV:

Helen became blind.

Helen appeared blind.

Helen seemed blind.

The doll felt soft.

The plum tasted sour.

She remained calm.

We may thus amplify our basic patterns for the verb *be* by including the verbs of the *become* class and those in the *seem* class in the appropriate patterns:

III. NP + be ($V_{b(become)}$ + NP

IV. NP + be ($V_{s(seem)}$) + Adj

Be is different from other verbs, including those in the above patterns, in respect to some simple transformations. *Be* needs no auxiliary to apply the

T/yes-no transformation. You will recall that in Lesson 6 we learned that the T/yes-no question transposes the auxiliary to the front of the sentence:

Helen could talk. =>
Could Helen talk?

In sentences containing *be,* the verb itself becomes the auxiliary and moves to the front of the sentence:

Miss Sullivan is there. =>
Is Miss Sullivan there?

They are here. =>
Are they here?

Be also differs in how T/neg and T/contr apply to the first person singular (I). There is no contracted form in English which is comparable to: *is not / isn't; are not / aren't; was not / wasn't; were not / weren't; am not / *amn't. *Amn't* is an ungrammatical form. *Ain't* is sometimes substituted for this form, although it is not accepted as standard English. Any contraction of *be* combines the present tense with the pronoun *I,* as in:

I am ready. =>
I'm ready.

I am not ready. =>
I'm not ready.

Negative contractions may take two forms for the second and third persons, as in:

You are not funny. You're not funny. You aren't funny.

You are not twins. You're not twins. You aren't twins.

He is not there. He's not there. He isn't there.

They are not students. They're not students. They aren't students.

EXERCISE

Write the pattern for these sentences in the space to the right.

1. Helen was courageous.____________________
2. She gave a speech.____________________
3. She stood up.____________________
4. She seems indefatigable.____________________

5. She became upset.______________________________

6. She appeared bereaved.______________________________

7. She remained calm.______________________________

8. She became a benefactor.______________________________

9. She traveled widely.______________________________

10. She had a companion.______________________________

Answers:

1. IV	6. IV
2. II	7. IV
3. I	8. III
4. IV	9. I
5. IV	10. II

To compound the difficulties inherent in the use of the copula *be,* we see that it may also be used as an auxiliary in the progressive aspect, as in:

She *is traveling* now.

It retains its eight forms as it combines with the *-ing* form of full verbs. The progressive aspect is discussed in Lesson 14.

A major transformation, the *T/there* transformation, may be performed on the basic pattern, NP + be + Adv_p. The adverb may be a single word like *there,* or a prepositional phrase like *on the table.* We may apply this transformation only if the subject NP contains a non-definite determiner, such as: *a, an, some, many, much, another,* or *no determiner at all* (Ø). We will use the symbol Ø, called a zero determiner, to indicate when a determiner is legitimately omitted from a noun phrase.

If the first NP, or the subject, of the sentence contains any form of a personal pronoun, a proper noun, or a definite determiner, such as *each, every, this,* or *that,* the transformation cannot be applied.

We will now transform some basic sentences based on the above pattern. The *T/there* transformation introduces *there* as the first element in the new sentence, and moves the *be* ahead of the NP:

NP + be + Adv_p => There + be + NP + Adv_p

Old grammar books call this use of *there* an expletive:

Some boys are in the school yard. =>
There are some boys in the school yard.

A red mitten is under the swing. =>
There is a red mitten under the swing.

Many girls are on the merry-go-round. =>
There are many girls on the merry-go-round.

If you say these sentences aloud, you will note that the major stress in the transformed sentences falls on the noun phrases following *there* + *be*. This is one clue to the fact that this is a transformation of the pattern, NP + be + Adv_p.

We cannot apply the *T/there* transformation to the sentence:

Those boys are in the school yard.

It does not meet the criterion for the non-definite determiner in the first NP. Say the following sentence aloud:

There are those boys in the school yard.

(meaning that those boys are there in the school yard) Did you observe that a strong stress falls on *There*? Obviously, *there,* in this sentence is an adverb of place and does not play the same role as the *there* in *T/there sentences.* Hearing people sense the difference between these two uses of *there* because of stress patterns. Children without hearing cannot use this clue unless special auditory training is done with the pattern. Some may never hear the difference, and must rely on other clues in learning how the pattern is used.

EXERCISE

Check the sentences which can be transformed into *T/there* sentences. Write the transformed sentences in the spaces provided.

1. _______ Helen's doll is on her bed. ______________________

____

2. _______ A bug is on the window pane. ______________________

____

3. _______ That bug is a ladybug. ______________________

____

4. _______ Small insects are on the roses. ______________________

____

5. _______ The goldfish are in the bowl. ______________________

____

6. _______ Some glasses are in the cupboard. ______________________

____

Answers:

2. There is a bug on the window pane.
4. There are small insects on the roses.
6. There are some glasses in the cupboard.

Transformed sentences using *T/there* should be used with deaf children in situations that are natural for their use. Children need not be able to perform the transformations you have just completed, but they should be able to discriminate when it is more natural to use a *T/there* sentence than the basic one.

LESSON 14

Some Verb Aspects: Perfect and Progressive

ABSTRACT

- Two aspects of verbs include:
    1. the perfect, which generates verb phrases by combining have and the *-en* form of the verb.
    2. the progressive, or durative, aspect, which generates verb phrases by combining *be* and the *-ing* form of the verb.
- The present perfect aspect expresses a period of time that began before now but continues right up to the present.
- The past perfect aspect is used to express a more remote past time, a past time which occurred before some other past action occurred.
- Adverbs expressing a specific time in the past cannot co-occur with the perfect aspect.
- Adverbs which express frequency and duration, if they also include the present moment, may be used in VPs containing the <+ perfect> aspect.
- The preposition *since*, referring to time, can co-occur with the <+ perfect> aspect.
- Not all verbs carry the <+ progressive> aspect.
- The present progressive aspect conveys different notions involving time, as when, (1) an event is occurring now and is continuing to occur, (2) an event is about to occur in the future, and (3) sporadic or recurring activity is taking place.
- The past progressive is used to express an event or action which was continuing in past time.

We have learned that English has only two tenses, the past and the present. These tenses serve as grammatical signals and do not refer to calendar or clock time. To express what has occurred, what is occurring, what does occur, or what will occur, English employs a complicated system of verb phrases. English also uses verb phrases to express relationships of past events to the present, to the future, or to other past events, and to express degrees of doubt, uncertainty, and willingness. We refer to these varying relationships as *aspects. Aspect* is a feature of verbs.

In this lesson, we shall discuss the perfect <+ perfect> and the progressive <+ progressive> aspects of verbs. The perfect aspect generates verb phrases in combination with *have* and the *-en* form of the verb, while the progressive, or durative, aspect generates phrases in combination with *be,* used as an auxiliary, and the *-ing* form of the verb. Suffice it to say that transformations produce these verb phrases. We shall study only the results of the transformations and note the rules that they have produced. We shall also look rather closely at the semantic connotations of these two aspects.

The perfect aspect is used to indicate a period of time that began before now but continues right up to the present. The action may just have been completed, may still be going on, or even may have been going on or have been completed before some other action occurred. Adverbs expressing a specific time in the past, such as, *yesterday, last month, last week,* cannot co-occur with the perfect aspect. Adverbs which express frequency, as, *often* and *never,* and duration, as, *a long time, all year,* if they also include the present moment, may be used with verb phrases containing the <+ perfect> aspect. The word *since,* when referring to time, and used as a preposition or clause introducer, can also co-occur with the <+ perfect> aspect.

The perfect aspect is contrasted with the simple present and past of full verbs in the following examples. The second sentence of each set contains a perfect aspect:

> All of us *use* the telephone. (Habitual use, present time.)
> All of us *have used* the telephone. (Action started at an undesignated time in the past and continues to the present without designated duration, present perfect.)
>
> The telephone *is* a very sophisticated instrument now. (Present tense generalization.)
> The telephone *has become* a very sophisticated instrument since Bell first invented it. (*Since* requires the use of the perfect aspect, in this case, the present perfect.)
>
> They *listened* to his telelecture yesterday. (Definite time in the past stated.)
> They *have listened* to his lecture regularly every week. (Action taking place at undesignated time in the past, but continuing to the present at stated intervals, present perfect aspect.)
>
> A. G. Bell *experimented* with sound for many years. (Activity recurred regularly in past.)
> A. G. Bell *had experimented* with sound for many years before he invented the telephone. (Action of experimenting started before the inventing did. One action was completed before another was, past perfect.)

I *saw* a movie about A. G. Bell twice last year. (Definite past time stated.)
I've seen the movie about A. G. Bell twice this year. (Action extends from past, but with relevance to the present as indicated by the adverbial *this year*, present perfect.)

The progressive aspect combines present and past tense forms of *be* with the present participles of verbs. Not all verbs can be combined in this manner, for not all verbs carry the <+ progressive> aspect. For instance, we cannot say:

Two and two is equalling four.

A. G. Bell is resembling his father.

I am disliking this book.

When *be* + *-ing* are combined with a verbal form, several meanings may be conveyed, but the meaning first chosen to present to children with hearing impairments refers to an action which is presently occurring, and continues to do so for some time, as in:

Mabel is washing her hands. (Now.)

Miss True is telling the girls a story. (Now.)

The progressive aspect may also convey different notions, such as future time and sporadic recurring activity as illustrated by these sentences:

She is leaving for school soon. (The adverb *soon* connotes future time.)

She is always complaining about her teacher. (Reference is to sporadic or recurring activity.)

These meanings and uses of the progressive aspect must also be included in the language curriculum for deaf children. Note that the auxiliary in these cases is *be*, and that it carries tense. Only the first element of each verb phrase carries tense.

The past form of the progressive aspect is used when a past action continues but does not necessarily terminate in the past, or when two activities are going on simultaneously in the past:

Mabel Hubbard *was reading* to Miss True while her sisters *were studying*. (Two actions were continuing in the past simultaneously.)

Mabel, deafened at four, *was losing* her speech rapidly. (Action continues in past for an undesignated period of time.)

Before long, she *was joining* the others in prayers and songs. (Recurring activity in the past.)

In contrast to the progressive aspect, the past tense is used when an action has been concluded. Note the difference in the use of the simple past and the progressive aspect in the following sentences:

On Saturday, the girls *went* to the woods with their teacher. (Action was terminated.)

They *observed* the animals. (Action was concluded in the past.)

The squirrels *were building* a nest. (Action was not terminated, at least while the girls watched the squirrels.)

The chipmunks *were gathering* food. (Action was not terminated in the presence of the girls.)

A snake *slithered* through the grass. (Action was concluded.)

The introductory word *while* often begins a clause of duration in which the progressive aspect is appropriately used, as in:

Mabel learned to read on her own *while Miss True was teaching her older sisters.* (One action was completed, the other continuing in the past over a period of time.)

Mabel was reading to Miss True *while her sisters were studying.* (Two actions were going on simultaneously in the past.)

EXERCISE

1. Underline the auxiliary *be* in each sentence and indicate its tense in the blanks before the sentences.
2. In the blanks after the sentences, indicate whether the verb phrase represents continuing, sporadic, recurring, or simultaneous activity in present, past or future time.

Example:

present	They are dressing now.	continuing, present
1. ________	The girls are leaving soon.	________________
2. ________	They were planning to spend the day in town.	________________
3. ________	Mabel was looking in the shop windows while Berta was making some purchases inside.	________________
4. ________	Miss True is trying to attract Mabel's attention.	________________
5. ________	She is waving to her.	________________
6. ________	The girls are always playing jokes on each other.	________________

Answers:

1. present, *are,* future
2. past, *were,* continuing, past
3. past, *was,* simultaneous, past
4. present, *is,* continuing, present
5. present, *is,* continuing, present
6. present, *are,* recurring, present

EXERCISE

For each sentence, indicate tense in the first blank and aspect in the second.

1. ________ They have lived here for many years. ________
2. ________ She is redoing the house. ________
3. ________ Mr. Bell had made two trips to Europe the previous year. ________
4. ________ They were awaiting the arrival of their guests. ________
5. ________ They have never heard such tales as yours. ________
6. ________ Elsie's pet turtle is always disappearing. ________

Answers:

1. present, perfect
2. present, progressive
3. past, perfect
4. past, progressive
5. present, perfect
6. present, progressive

LESSON 15

A Phrase Structure Rule for Verbs

ABSTRACT

- Tense is an obligatory element in every verb phrase (VP).
- The modals, as well as *have* and *be*, serve as optional elements in verb phrases.
- Before a terminal string containing the auxiliaries *have* or *be* can become an acceptable English sentence, this transformational rule, Af + V => V + Af, must be applied:
- Af stands for tense, *-ing* and *-en*.
- The phrase structure rule for active verbs in English is: VP → tense (+ modal) (+ have + -en) (+ be + -ing) + V

You already know something about the auxiliary. Here is a brief summary of what you should have learned:

1. Tense is an obligatory element in the auxiliary.
2. Modals (can, may, will, shall, and must) are optional parts of the Aux.
3. The verbs *have* and *be* serve as auxiliaries in the perfect and progressive aspects respectively.

As with all sentence constituents, there are rules of order which apply to the construction of English verb phrases. Happily, we have a relatively simple formula which states the rule for this order. It is:

VP → tense (+ modal) (+ have + *-en*) (+ be + *-ing*) + V

This phrase structure rule may not appear very simple at first glance, but let us analyze it and note its elegance and succinctness. Looking at the Aux in the basic sentence pattern, NP + Aux + NP, we may first view it simply as:

Aux → tense

The terminal strings using the verb *go* appear on the trees that illustrate this rule.

Sentence Tree 15: VP → Tense + go

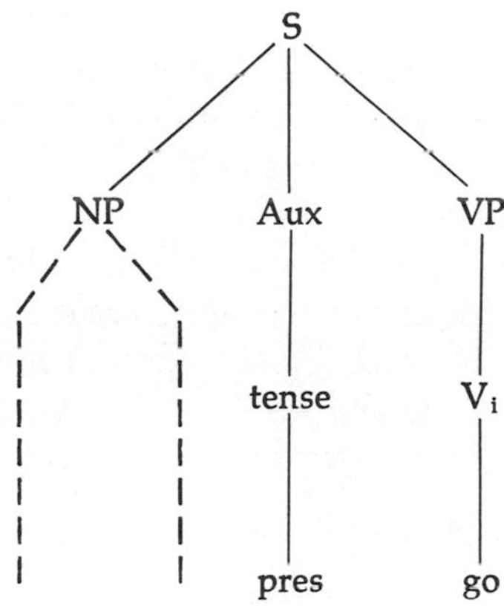

present + go → go, goes
past + go → went

If we wish to construct a simple sentence in which a modal auxiliary is used, we may do so by combining the modal with the stem of the verb. The tense is attached to the modal, the first element in the phrase.

Aux → tense (+ M)

Sentence Tree 16: VP → tense + M + go

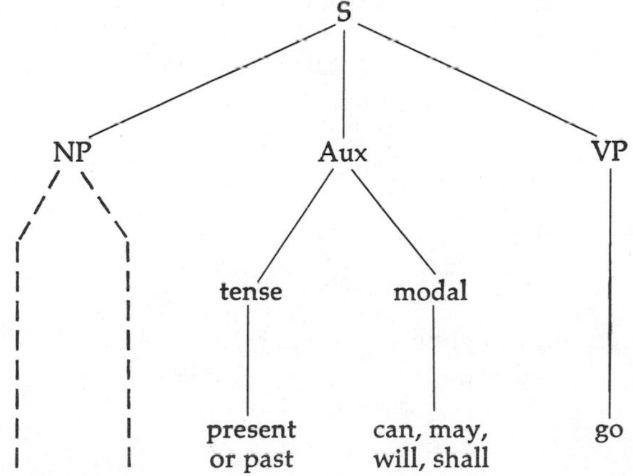

pres + can + go → can go
pres + may + go → may go
pres + shall + go → shall go
pres + will + go → will go
pres + must + go → must go

past + can + go → could go
past + may + go → might go
past + shall + go → should go
past + will + go → would go

In Lesson 14, we observed that the affixes *-en* and *-ing* were involved in the construction of the perfect and progressive aspects. Whenever these affixes are combined with a verb, we must rewrite the rule:

Af + V → V + Af

As an example, the terminal strings illustrated in Trees 17 and 18 must be transformed by adding affixes to the verb *go* in order to make them acceptable in English sentences. *He + has + go* and *he + is + go* are not complete until the affixes *-en* and *-ing*, respectively, are attached to the verb.

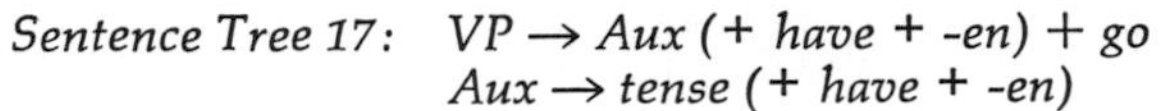

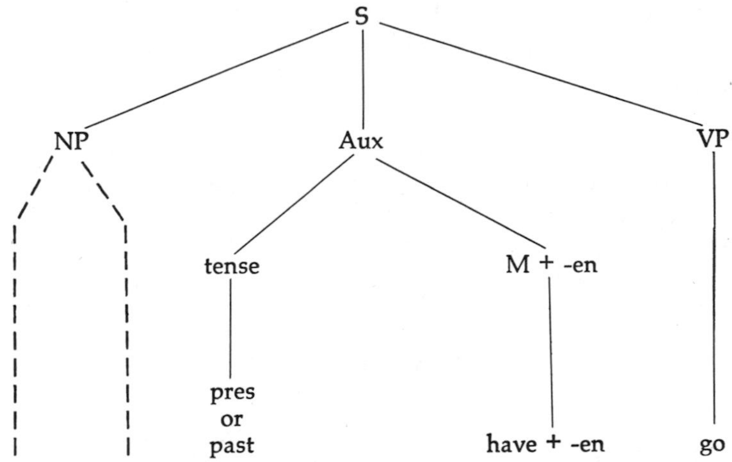

have + -en + go → have gone
had + -en + go → had gone

Sentence Tree 18: *VP → Aux (+ be + -ing) + go*
Aux → tense (+ be + -ing)

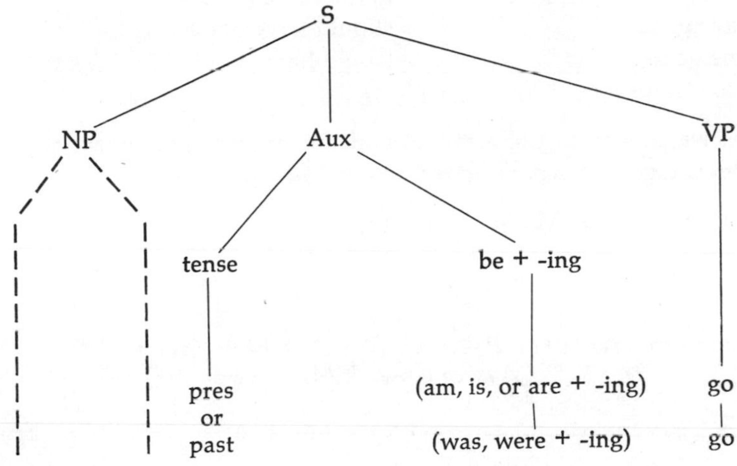

am/is/are + -ing + go → am/is/are/going
was/were + -ing + go → was/were going

If we wish to use a modal with the perfect aspect in a statement, we must write our rule to show that the modal precedes *have + -en*:

Aux → tense (+ M) (+ have + -en) V

Sentence Tree 19: *VP → tense (+ M) (+ have + -en) + go*
Aux → tense (+M) (+ have + -en)

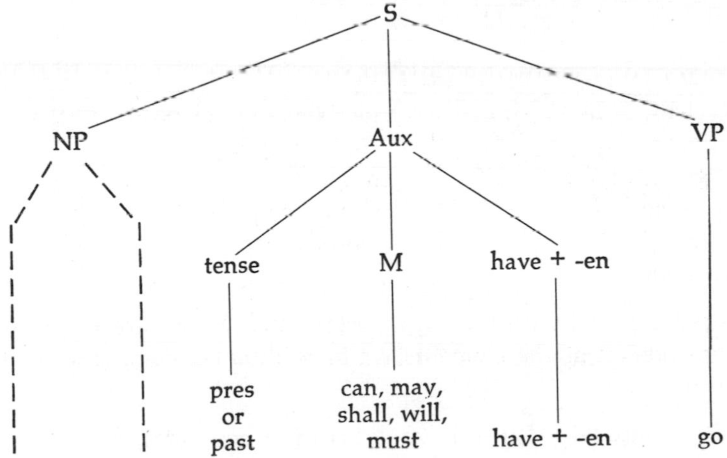

pres (+ M) (+ have + -en) V	past (+ M) (+ have + -en) V
can have gone	could have gone
may have gone	might have gone
shall have gone	should have gone
will have gone	would have gone
must have gone	

Perhaps we choose to use a modal and the progressive aspect (be + -ing) in our sentence. Our rule would be written as follows:

Aux → tense + M (+ be + -ing)

Sentence Tree 20: VP → tense (+ M) (+ be + -ing) + go
Aux → tense (+ M) (+ be + -ing)

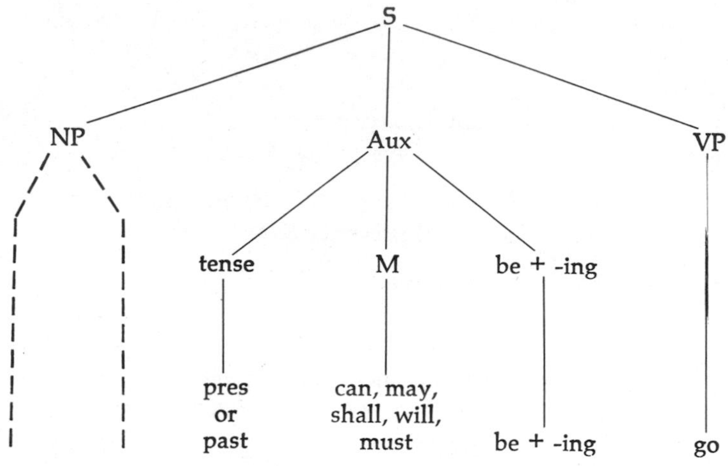

pres (+ M) (+ be + -ing) V	past (+ M) (+ be + -ing) V
can be going	could be going
may be going	might be going
shall be going	should be going
will be going	would be going
must be going	

If we used a modal with both the perfect and the progressive aspects, our rule would include all of the elements we have thus far combined. In fact, it is now complete:

VP → tense (+ M) (+ have + -en) (+ be + -ing) V

Sentence Tree 21: *VP → tense (+ M) (+ have + -en) (+ be + -ing) go*
Aux → tense (+ M) (+ have + -en) (+ be + -ing)

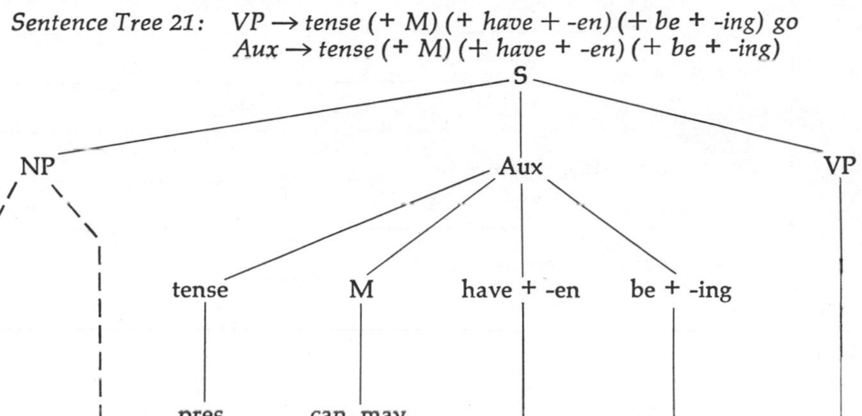

present (+ M) (+ have + -en) (+ be + -ing) go
can have been going
may have been going
shall have been going
will have been going
must have been going

past (+ M) (+ have + -en) (+ be + -ing) go
could have been going
might have been going
should have been going
would have been going

The important generalizations that hearing impaired children must make before they can understand the phrase structure rule for verbs are: (1) only the first constituent in the verb phrase carries tense, and (2) there is a specific order in which the various auxiliaries can be used in verb phrases. If you really understand this very concise and precise rule for active English verbs, you should find no difficulty in helping children construct correct verb phrases. The trick will be to help clarify for children what these phrases mean and when they are used to express certain ideas and relationships.

EXERCISE

Write the verb phrases (VPs) for these strings. Use *he* as the subject.

1. past + have + heard ______
2. pres + have + see ______
3. pres + be + -ing + eat ______
4. pres + can + be + -ing + fake ______
5. pres + be + -ing + tease ______
6. past + shall + have + -en + come ______
7. pres + will + talk ______
8. past + may + ride ______
9. past + will + have + -en + be + -ing + turn ______
10. pres + must + be + -ing + sleep ______

Answers:

1. had heard
2. has seen
3. is eating
4. can be faking
5. is teasing
6. should have come
7. will talk
8. might ride
9. would have been turning
10. must be sleeping

EXERCISE

Write the phrase structure rules for these strings.

1. has been dating ______
2. will have seen ______
3. should have taken ______
4. went ______
5. may have heard ______
6. should be coming ______
7. might have been kidding ______
8. has tried ______
9. had been practicing ______
10. can stay ______

Answers:

1. pres + have + -en + be + -ing + date
2. pres + will + have + -en + see
3. past + shall + have + -en + take
4. past + go
5. pres + may + have + -en + hear
6. past + shall + be + -ing + come
7. past + may + have + -en + be + -ing + kid
8. pres + have + -en + try
9. past + have + -en + be + -ing + practice
10. pres + can + stay

LESSON 16

Future Time and Attracted Sequence

ABSTRACT

- The modals, except for *must*, have only two principal parts, a base and a past tense form.
- The base of a modal serves as an uninflected present tense form.
- The present tense of modals has both a present and future aspect.
- English does not have a future tense, but relies upon varying devices to express futurity or future aspect.
- Some devices used for expressing future aspect involve the modals, the copula *be*, *be* + *going to* + the base form of the verb, and appropriate adverbs.
- In direct discourse a speaker's words are repeated exactly.
- In indirect discourse a speaker rephrases a message.
- If a verb in the main clause is in the present time, each following verb will logically assume its natural aspect.
- In reported speech, a logical or related tense or aspect may not necessarily be used throughout the sequence.
- If a verb in the main clause is in the past tense, it attracts the tense of the following verbs in the sentence to the past.
- If a verb in a main clause expresses future time, a verb in a subordinate clause will use a present tense form.

The modals *can, may, will,* and *shall* have only two principal parts, a present and a past tense form. *Must* has only one form, the present. The *-en* and *-ing* forms are lacking in all modals. In earlier English, the modern present tense was a past tense. Today's present tense of the modals is not inflected in the third person singular as full verbs are. We do not say:

*She cans sew.

*He mays go.

*It wills fly.

The present tense of modals refers not only to present time, but may imply future time, too, depending on the adverb with which it is associated, as in:

I can/may/must go *now*.

I can/may/shall/will/must go *tomorrow*.

This brings us to an interesting observation. How does English express future time? Actually, English does not have a future tense. Instead, it uses many devices to express futurity. Therefore, we shall refer to *future aspect* rather than to *future tense* in this book.

Notice the four different ways in which futurity is expressed in the following sentences:

They *will phone* you tomorrow. (Present tense of the modal is combined with the base form of the verb.)

Tomorrow *is* open house at the Telephone Company. Tomorrow *is* Tuesday, not, Tomorrow *will be* Tuesday. (Present tense of *be*, plus a word designating future time, expresses futurity.)

We *are going to visit* the Telephone Company tomorrow. (Future time is expressed by the phrase *be + going to + base form of the verb (or infinitive)*.

The telephone bill *is coming* tomorrow. (The progressive aspect may connote the future.)

EXERCISE

Express future notional time in this sentence in as many ways as you can:

The girls are practicing basketball at four tomorrow.

1. ______________________________

2. ______________________________

3. ______________________________

4. ______________________________

5. ______________________________

Answers: Answers will vary. Following are five possible answers:

1. The girls will practice basketball at four tomorrow.
2. The girls are to practice basketball at four tomorrow.
3. The girls will be practicing basketball at four tomorrow.
4. The girls are going to practice basketball at four tomorrow.
5. The girls practice basketball at four tomorrow.

In present day English little or no distinction is made in the use of *shall* or *will* to designate future time. *Shall* is used as an obligatory form only in questions with singular and plural subjects with the first person:

Shall I come with you?

Shall we go now?

Contractions of the modals *will* and *shall* in conjunction with personal pronoun subjects are almost universal in ordinary conversation. We say:

I'll come with you, rather than, *I shall* come with you.

He'll wait for you, rather than, *He will* wait for you.

The identity of *shall* and *will* disappears in these contractions, and actually helps simplify oral language for deaf children. These forms should be chosen in preference to the more formal uncontracted phrases for oral speech production.

Many teachers of the deaf introduce their pupils to future time by using the modal *will* in the verb phrase because the form is simple and relatively easy to learn. The form *be* + *going* + *to* + *base of verb* is more difficult since it requires knowledge of all the forms of *be,* but it is a more versatile one. For instance, if we wished to talk about a future action which occurred at a past time, we could say:

I *was going to meet* them at the open house, but I couldn't find them.

We could not substitute a past tense modal for the phrase *was going to meet* in order to express the same idea:

*I would meet them at the open house, but I couldn't find them.

Although alternate ways of expressing the future must be mastered by children with hearing impairments, it is not customary to shift back and forth among the several ways of expressing the same notional time in a series of sentences. For instance, it would be better to use only one form of the future in a paragraph as indicated in the first sequence below rather than mixing them as in the second one:

Tomorrow, our teacher will come to our house right after school. She'll arrive by four-thirty and stay for about two hours. Then she'll leave for Chicago from here.

Tomorrow, our teacher comes to our house right after school, and will arrive by four-thirty. She is going to stay for about two hours and then leaves for Chicago from here.

Hearing impaired children, their teachers, and parents frequently feel the need for checking on what someone else said in order to be sure that they understood the message. This can be done by repeating exactly, or quoting directly, the speaker's words (direct discourse), or by reporting the content of the message in other words (indirect discourse):

Direct: Helen says, "I can ride a bike."
Helen said, "I can ride a bike."

Indirect: Helen says that she can ride a bike.
Helen said that she could ride a bike.

Direct: Mr. K. says, "I will be there."
Mr. K. said, "I will be there."

Indirect: Mr. K. says that he will be there.
Mr. K. said that he would be there.

Note that in direct reporting, when either the present or past tenses are used in the main verb, a natural sequence of tenses follows; but in indirect discourse, a verb in the past tense in the main clause attracts the following verb to the past tense no matter what notional time it indicates. There are some fine nuances in the generalization that a past tense always requires another past tense to follow it in the same sentence, but they will not be mentioned here since correctness will not be violated by having children follow the general rule that past follows past.

If the verb in a main clause indicates future time, the tense of the verb in an adverbial clause modifying the sentence is in the simple present. (See Lesson 36 for more about adverbial clauses.)

The plants *will grow* only if you *water* them. (Main clause: *will grow*, future time; dependent clause; *water*, present time)

I *will meet* you at whatever time you *say*.

When you *are* on your trip, *I'll be thinking* about you.

We're going to invite the principal for lunch when we *see* him.

EXERCISE

Change the direct discourse to indirect discourse.

1. Miss Sullivan says, "Helen must study more."

---

2. Helen said, "Father will bring me a doll."

---

3. Mother said, "I can see an improvement in Helen."

---

4. The doctor says, "Helen should stay in bed."

Answers:

1. Miss Sullivan says that Helen must study more.
2. Helen said that Father would bring her a doll.
3. Mother said that she could see an improvement in Helen.
4. The doctor says that Helen should stay in bed.

EXERCISE

Underline the verbs in the sentences below. Write the phrase structure rule for the verbs in these sentences.

Example: I *will be thinking* about you. *pres + will + be + -ing + think*

1. We may be seeing you. ______
2. They should have been doing their homework. ______
3. The weeks pass too quickly. ______
4. They must have missed the plane. ______
5. We may arrive by ten o'clock. ______
6. They had seen the train go by at high speed. ______
7. They are preparing for their trip. ______

Answers:

1. *may be seeing,* pres + may + be + -ing + see
2. *should have been doing,* past + shall + have + -en + be + -ing + do
3. *pass,* pres + pass
4. *must have missed,* past + have + -en + miss
5. *may arrive,* pres + may + arrive
6. *had seen,* past + have + -en + see
7. *are preparing,* pres + be + -ing + prepare

LESSON 17

How We Use Modals

ABSTRACT

- The past tense of modals is used to express degrees of doubt or possibility.
- Several of the modals have synonyms that can be substituted for them.
- Modals cannot function as finite verbs in sentences, that is, they cannot stand alone in clauses.
- When modals seem to stand alone in a sentence, a deletion transformation has been applied to the verb phrase.
- A question tag involving a modal is negative when the statement preceding it is positive.

Children with language deficits are bound to meet a variety of structures containing the modals in text books and other reading materials. For instance, sentences such as the following might appear in second grade readers:

> "Maybe he *wouldn't* help me," said Ted.
> "Of course, *he'd* help you," replied his mother.
>
> "They *might* not like my pet," said Jim.
> "Why *shouldn't* they?" asked his father.
>
> "Bob *can* go with me, *can't* he?" asked Jerry.
> "He *may,* if you hurry back," said Grandma.
>
> "You *won't* tell, *will* you?" asked Bert.
> "No, I *won't,*" said his mother.
>
> Bert's mother said that she *wouldn't* tell.

Could you define the meanings of the modals in these sentences? This lesson will be devoted to the lexical meanings of modals and to two transformations involving auxiliaries, T/deletion and T/question tag.

We have already noted that the present tense of modals may represent future time as well as present, and that their past tense forms function as regular past tenses in indirect discourse. *Can* becomes *could; may, might; shall, should;* and *will* becomes *would* because of attracted sequence of tenses.

Beyond that, the past tense of modals refers in general to states of obligation, possibility, doubt, necessity, wishes, promises, and conditions contrary to facts. As a result, semantic problems involving subtle shades of meaning may overshadow the syntactical problems for children with hearing impairments. Look up the definitions of all the modals in the dictionary and note that the meanings outlined below encompass only a few possible, but important ones with which children must become familiar:

Can, contrary to what many of us have been taught, now carries the dictionary definition of *have permission to* in addition to *be able to* and *know how to.* Consequently, *can* may alternate with *may* in sentences when reference is to permission:

permission: Mother says I *can* go with you. (or *may* go)
be able to: She *can* sing high C.
know how to: He *can* drive a shift car.

Could expresses a shade of doubt or lesser degree of possibility or permission than *can:*

permission: Perhaps I *could* go if we got home by ten o'clock.
be able to: *Could* you type this letter for me?
know how to: He *could* play the piano before he was five.

May denotes:

permission: You *may* have the funnies now.
possibility or likelihood: It *may* snow.

Might expresses a shade of doubt or lesser degree of possibility than *may*:

It *might* snow.
I *might* have bought that dress if it hadn't cost so much.

Shall is used to express futurity in first person questions and in more formal types of writing:

Shall I help you?
We *shall* expect you for dinner at eight.

Should expresses:

appropriateness: Children *should* be seen but not heard.
expectation: He *should* be here soon.
obligation: He *should* return the book to the library at once.

Will expresses futurity and also carries implications of intention, promise, willingness, and capability:

intention: I promise they *will* meet you at the airport.
willingness: *I'll* treat you to a cup of coffee.
capability: The plane *will* hold 400 passengers.

Would expresses:
conditions contrary to fact: I *would* be pleased if you could come.
habitual action: He *would* boast to all of his friends about his strength.
a softened request: I *would* like some more turkey, please.

Must expresses:
necessity: He *must* pay a fine for the book.
obligation: He *must* return the book to the library at once.
possibility: You *must* be the new librarian.

Several of the modals have synonyms that can be substituted for them. The differences in their meaning as well as their similarities must be brought to the attention of children, for it is important that they become familiar with the alternate ways of expressing the concepts related to the lexical meanings of the modals and with sentence patterns in which they are appropriately used.

When *can* means *be able to*, the latter phrase may be substituted for it, as in:

He *can't* come. He's sick.
He *isn't able to* come because he's sick.

Be to may be substituted for *shall*, *will*, and *must:*

shall: I *shall* go to Europe in May.
be to: I *am to* go to Europe in May.

will: Dr. Brown *will* receive the Nobel Prize.
be to: Dr. Brown *is to* receive the Nobel Prize.

must: They *must* go to the nurse at once.
be to: They *are to* go to the nurse at once.

In like manner, substitutes for *must* have reference to the degree of intensity (or possibility) of the synonym. The idea of *must* is expressed from lesser to greater possibility in the following sentences:

Bob *is to have* an operation.

Bob *ought to have* an operation.

Bob *has to have* an operation.

Bob *must have* an operation.

Table 4 outlines the modals and their equivalents.

Table 4. Modals and Their Equivalents

Can	*May*	*Shall*	*Will*	*Must*
can may be able to	may	shall be to had better	will be to	must be to ought to have to

Modals cannot function as finite verbs in sentences, that is, they cannot stand alone in clauses. Nevertheless, to the uninitiated, it might seem that they do. Please refer to the set of sentences at the very beginning of this lesson. Notice that in some of them no finite verb appears and that the modals are the only stated verbal forms. Actually, the full verbs in these sentences are understood. A T/del (deletion transformation) removes the full verb from the verb phrase when it is expendable and recoverable. A few more examples should suffice to clarify this transformation:

> Mark can go but Beth can't go.
> T/del: Mark can go but Beth can't.
>
> Must I go to bed?
> T/del: Yes, you must.

In short, to avoid repetition, the full verb is often deleted, and, as a result, children have to be taught a new code in which parts of the whole are missing. Incidentally, what we are saying about modals also applies to the auxiliaries *have, be,* and *do*. We have used the modals in prototype sentences that might just as well have contained the other auxiliaries.

EXERCISE

Fill in the sentence with deleted verb phrases.

1. Jerry wondered if his father would let him keep Tiger, but his father wouldn't ________________________.
2. "May I keep him in a box outside?" asked Jerry. "No," said his father, "You can't ________________________.
3. Her mother told Jill she couldn't go outside to play. Jill said, "Please may I go to Mary's house?" "No, you may not ________________.

Answers:

1. let him keep Tiger.
2. keep him in a box outside.
3. go to Mary's house.

EXERCISE

Rewrite these sentences deleting the repetitious items. Note how you rely upon auxiliaries when you delete portions of sentences.

1. My friend, Beth, and I will go on a picnic tomorrow but my brother, Bill, will not go.

2. He has to work, but I don't have to work.

3. I'll take my swimming suit, but Beth will not take her swimming suit.

4. Beth asked her Dad if we could use his car, but he said we couldn't use it.

5. Beth likes to play tennis, but I don't like to play tennis.

6. I went to sleep, but Beth didn't go to sleep.

Answers:

1. . . . but my brother, Bill, won't.
2. . . . but I don't have to.
3. . . . but Beth won't.
4. . . . but he said we couldn't.
5. . . . but I don't.
6. . . . but Beth didn't.

Question tags, which are attached to statements and which involve auxiliaries, may present an additional code-learning task for children:

> Bill can go, /can't he?
> You'll go with me, /won't you?
> You won't tell, /will you, Mama?
> Jan shouldn't run, /should she?
> Fred didn't remember, /did he?
> Betty forgot, /didn't she?

You will note that the question tag is negative if the statement preceding it is positive, and that the tag is positive if the preceding statement is negative. We shall discuss questions at greater length in another lesson, but it is pertinent to point out here how important it is that children have a deep understanding of how auxiliaries function in sentences and questions, and how the two transformations discussed in this lesson require the learning of an additional code.

EXERCISE

In the following dialogue, the speakers are talking about a possible trip to Canada. Complete the dialogue using an appropriate verb or verb phrase as *fly*, *go*, or *drive*.

1. Mr. X: "Do you think they will ____________________?"
2. Mr. Y: "I don't know. They might ____________________."
3. Mr. X: "They would like to ______________, but perhaps they can't ____________________.
4. Mr. Y: "Well, they may sometime later. I hope so, ____________________ ____________________?"

Answers: Since the answers will vary, only a possible answer for Item 1 is given: *fly to Canada?*

Reference: Palmer, F. R.: *A Linguistic Study of the English Verb*. Coral Gables, Florida: University of Miami Press, 1968.

LESSON 18

The Passive Transformation

ABSTRACT

- Verbs that carry the <+ transitive> feature may be transformed to the passive voice.
- Sentences in the active voice are transformed into the passive by bringing the second NP of basic sentence Pattern II, $NP_1 + Aux + V_t + NP_2$, to the beginning of the sentence, by including a form of *be* in the VP, and adding *by* + NP_1 to the end of the pattern.
- $NP_1 + V_t + NP_2$ becomes: NP_2 + be + -en + V_t + by + NP_1.
- When NP_2 is placed in the subject position in the sentence, the auxiliary agrees with the new subject, since the surface subject determines the agreement with the verb.
- The phrase *by* + NP_1 may be deleted when the NP_1 in the active sentence is unknown or unimportant.
- Transitive verbs that take two objects can be transformed to the passive using either object in the NP_1 position.
- Passive sentences may be transformed to yes-no questions by bringing the *be* to the beginning of the sentence.
- A small class of verbs including *have, lack, cost,* and *weigh,* carry a <— passive> feature and cannot be transformed to the passive.

- Verbs used in the T/pass must be chosen with discretion, for the result may be an awkward construction unless semantic elements are considered.
- T/pass → transformation to the passive.

Most verbs that carry the <+ transitive> feature may be transformed to the passive. An active verb is converted to the passive by

1. bringing the second NP of basic sentence pattern II to the beginning of the sentence,
2. combining a form of *be* with the past participle (the -en form of the verb), and
3. adding the phrase *by* + NP_1

Active: The pirates hid the treasure.
Passive: The treasure was hidden by the pirates.

The surface structure of the transformed passive sentence differs from that of the active sentence, but their meanings remain closely related. The surface subjects govern the verb forms used in both active and passive sentences:

The residents *are* evacuating the town.
The town *is* being evacuated by the residents.

Sometimes the phrase *by* + NP_1 may be deleted from the passive, as when the first NP in the active sentence is unknown, implied, or not essential:

Active: Someone will close the pool at 8:00 p.m.
Passive: The pool will be closed at 8:00 p.m. (It is not actually known, nor is it important who will close the pool.)

Active: They drained the pool for repairs.
Passive: The pool was drained for repairs. (By implication the repairmen or the custodians drained the pool.)

Tense and aspect in the passive correspond to those we have studied for active verbs, with the exception that the perfect progressive aspect is not convertible to the passive.

We can say: The water/ is tested.
was tested.
can/may/will/shall/must/be tested.
could/might/would, should/be tested.
has/had/been tested.
is/was/being tested.
can/may/will/shall/must/have been tested.
could/might/would/should/have been tested.

We cannot say: *The water has been being tested.

Table 5 compares sentences with active and passive verb phrases and indicates how various aspects of time or mood can be expressed. Deletable *by* + NP_1 phrases are placed in parentheses.

Table 5. Aspects of Sentences Containing Active and Passive Verb Phrases

Tense	*Aspect*	*Active Voice*	*Passive Voice*
present	recurring expectation	The princess expects her baby momentarily.	Her baby is expected momentarily by the princess.
past	definite past time	The family announced the baby's arrival yesterday.	The baby's arrival was announced yesterday by the family.
present	future time	His mother will name him for his grandfather.	He will be named for his grandfather (by his mother).
present	progressive	The nurse is dressing the baby now.	The baby is being dressed now by the nurse.
present	perfect	The clergyman has just baptized the baby.	The baby has just been baptized (by the clergyman).
past	perfect + possibility	He could have baptized the baby last week.	The baby could have been baptized last week (by him).
past	progressive	The photographer was photographing the happy parents and the child when the baby started to cry.	The happy parents and the child were being photographed (by the photographer) when the baby started to cry.

EXERCISE

Write the verb phrases. You will recall that *-en* is the symbol for the past participle:

Example: pres + be + -en + expect He is expected

1. pres + be + -en + announce It
2. pres + will + be + -en + name She
3. pres + have + -en + be + -en + baptize She
4. past + can + be + -en + arrest They
5. pres + be + be + -ing + -en + feed They
6. past + be + be + -ing + -en + photograph He

7. past + may + have + -en + be + -en + lose It

8. past + shall + have + -en + be + -en + warn They

9. past + be + -en + bomb It

Answers:

1. is announced
2. will be named
3. has been baptized
4. could be arrested
5. are being fed
6. was being photographed
7. might have been lost
8. should have been warned
9. was bombed.

The transitive verbs that take two objects, one a direct object and one an indirect object, can also be transformed to the passive, and either object can be shifted to the beginning of the sentence:

The director sent the graduates invitations. =>

The graduates were sent invitations by the director. =>

Invitations were sent the graduates by the director.

EXERCISE

Change the following sentences to passive. Use whatever formulae are appropriate:

1. $NP_1 + V_t + NP_2 \Rightarrow NP_2 + be + \text{-en} + V_t + by + NP_1$
2. $NP_1 + V_t + NP_2 + NP_3 \Rightarrow NP_2 + be + \text{-en} + V_t + NP_3 + by + NP_1$
3. $NP_1 + V_t + NP_2 + NP_3 \Rightarrow NP_3 + be + \text{-en} + V_t + NP_2 + by + NP_1$

You may delete the $by + NP_1$ phrase, if you consider it unimportant or understood by implication.

1. Dr. Goldstein reported the results of the fund drive at the meeting.

___

2. Next week, the children will present a program in the auditorium.

___

3. The committee gave Dr. Goldstein a check for $1000.00.

___

4. They anticipated a large audience.

---

5. Central Institute for the Deaf recently acquired several more buildings.

---

6. The contractors have just completed the new research center.

---

7. An anonymous donor bought the school an oscilloscope.

---

8. The Board of Directors will dedicate this modern building next week.

Answers:

1. The results of the fund drive were reported at the meeting by Dr. Goldstein.
2. Next week, a program will be presented in the auditorium by the children.
3. Dr. Goldstein was given a check for $1000.00 by the committee. *and* A check for $1000.00 was given Dr. Goldstein by the committee.
4. A large audience was anticipated (by them).
5. Several more buildings were recently acquired by Central Institute for the Deaf.
6. The new research center has just been completed by the contractors.
7. An anonymous donor bought the school an oscilloscope.
   school was bought an oscilloscope by an anonymous donor.
8. This modern building will be dedicated by the Board of Directors next week.

Passive sentences may also be transformed to yes-no questions by shifting *be* to the beginning of the sentence:

> Central Institute for the Deaf was founded by Dr. Goldstein =>
> Was Central Institute for the Deaf founded by Dr. Goldstein?
>
> Central Institute for the Deaf was affiliated with Washington University in the preparation of teachers of the deaf.=>
> Was Central Institute for the Deaf affiliated with Washington University in the preparation of teachers of the deaf?

In informal situations an alternative form for the passive may be used. The verb *got* is substituted for *be* as in:

> The dog *got* run over. The dog *was* run over.
>
> They *got* married. They *were* married.

Nothing *got* accomplished. Nothing *was* accomplished.
The bill finally *got* paid. The bill finally *was* paid.

Hearing-impaired children should be taught this form, for it is important that they understand this idiomatic passive, if they are to read comprehendingly.

EXERCISE

Identify the verbs as being active or passive by placing *A* or *P* in the spaces provided:

_______ 1. The Teacher Training College was organized in 1932.

_______ 2. Dr. Goldstein had raised the funds for the school almost single-handedly.

_______ 3. Dr. Goldstein taught Helen Keller the "two step" in Boston.

_______ 4. A new hearing device was being tested at Central Institute for the Deaf.

_______ 5. Many conferences were held at Central Institute for the Deaf.

_______ 6. Central Institute for the Deaf celebrated its 50th anniversary in 1964.

_______ 7. Hundreds of former students returned to the school at that time.

_______ 8. The school had prepared an elegant smorgasbord for the reunion.

_______ 9. The school's 50th anniversary was being celebrated with a three-day conference.

_______ 10. Three excellent plays were presented by the pupils.

_______ 11. Professional papers were read by graduates of the Teachers College.

Answers: 1. P 2. A 3. A 4. P 5. P 6. A 7. A 8. A 9. P 10. P 11. P

There are two limitations inherent in the passive transformation:

1. A small group of verbs including *cost, have, lack, suit,* and *weigh,* carry a <— passive> feature and cannot be used in passive sentences:

The book costs five dollars.
*Five dollars is cost by the book.

Everyone had a good time.
*A good time was had by all. (This expression may be heard occasionally, but it is not accepted as standard English.)

This story lacks a good plot.
*A good plot is lacked by the story.

The punishment suits the crime.
*The crime is suited by the punishment.

Weigh has both a <+ passive> and a <— passive> feature:

The butcher weighed the fish.
The fish was weighed by the butcher. <+ passive>

The fish weighs five pounds.
*Five pounds is weighed by the fish. <— passive>

2. It is not possible to invert identical noun phrases when the NP_2 is a reflexive pronoun, such as *myself, himself,* or *herself:*

The girl served herself.
*Herself was served by the girl.

The boys taught themselves the tricks.
*Themselves were taught tricks by the boys.
*The boys were taught tricks by themselves.

Besides these two limitations, some attention must be given to the choice of verbs used in passive constructions. Unusual circumstances, in which the actor is unknown, but in which the effect of an action is crucial; events which happen once in a lifetime; and calamities or cataclysms which occur infrequently are often reported in the passive. The semantic aspects must be carefully considered when children with hearing impairments are asked to use the passive. Whatever is to be emphasized is placed first in the sentence. These examples should clarify the selection of the verbs for use in passive sentences:

They were married by a judge.

He was divorced by his fifth wife.

Captain X was buried in Arlington Cemetery.

The windows were shaken by the blast.

Six villages were destroyed by the earthquake.

The bank was robbed of one million dollars.

We generally do not report daily happenings or routine activities in the passive and so avoid sentences such as the following:

My breakfast was eaten by me at 7:00 AM.

Phil's homework was completed by him in one hour.

Mr. John's car was driven to work by him.

If you understand that the passive transformation bears a very close relationship to basic sentence Pattern II, you can help children who are having difficulty learning language to observe and understand the synonymy of active and passive sentences. You can also guide them in becoming conscious of the structure of passive verb phrases, and in identifying and interpreting them in reading materials. You may also want to help children use the passive in their writing when it is appropriate.

LESSON 19

Two-Word Verbs

ABSTRACT

- English transitive and intransitive verbs may be combined with particles or prepositions into linguistic units.
- A particle may be separated from a verb by applying the particle movement transformation (T/prt-movt).
- T/prt-movt is mandatory when the second NP in basic sentence Pattern II is a personal pronoun.
- When the passive transformation is applied to a sentence containing a verb-particle combination, the particle stays with the verb.
- Particles may be confused with prepositions that introduce adverbial phrase complements.
- The preposition in an adverbial phrase may be used to begin a question, but a particle may not be used in this way.
- A prepositional phrase may be separated from a verb by an adverb of manner, but a particle may not.
- The combination of particle or preposition and a verb may change its basic meaning and thus create a multiplicity of meanings, some of which are idiomatic.

Some English transitive and intransitive verbs have a special feature that allows them to be combined into linguistic units with either particles (prt) or prepositions (prep). These combinations are variously called double verbs (Fitzgerald, 1926, 1956), separable verbs (Francis, 1958, p. 265), phrasal verbs (Palmer, 1968, p. 180), and two-word verbs, but the term most frequently encountered in literature on language for deaf children is *double verbs*. Syntactical rules as well as meaning are involved in a study of these verbs.

Listed are some common verbs that may be combined with one or more of the following particles: *away, down, in, off, on, out, over,* and *up:*

beat	come	hand	pass	set	tie
blow	count	hang	pay	shake	turn
break	cut	head	pick	shut	use
bring	dig	help	point	stick	warm
burn	dry	hold	pull	strike	wipe
call	figure	keep	put	string	work
carry	fill	let	roll	take	write
catch	finish	line	rub	talk	
check	get	look	run	tear	
clean	give	make	saw	throw	

Particles look like prepositions or adverbs, but because they function in a particular way when combined with verbs, they have been given a special name that identifies them as being a part of a verb. First we will look at the grammatical rules governing two-word verbs and then at some of the semantic aspects involving them.

In sentences containing transitive verbs, the particle may stay with the verb or may be moved to a position following the second noun in sentence pattern II by the particle movement transformation (T/prt-movt):

$$NP_1 + V_t + prt + NP_2 \Rightarrow NP + V_t + NP_2 + prt$$

In the second of each set of sentences below, T/prt-movt has been applied:

The radio station *gave away* a prize. =>
The radio station *gave* a prize *away.*

The children *took down* the decorations. =>
The children *took* the decorations *down.*

The investigators *looked over* the records. =>
The investigators *looked* the records *over.*

The detectives *brought in* the evidence. =>
The detectives *brought* the evidence *in.*

The particle movement is optional when NP_2 is a noun, but mandatory when it is a personal pronoun:

He missed his exam, so he *made it up.*

Pick up the girls at 7:00 P.M., then *pick us up,* please.

When the passive transformation is applied to a sentence containing a verb-particle combination, the particle stays with the verb:

Prizes *were given away* by the radio station.

The decorations *were taken down* by the children.

The records *were looked over* by the investigators.
The evidence *was brought in* by the detectives.

EXERCISE

Apply T/pass to these sentences:

1. The mayor took over his duties yesterday.

2. The service-men carted the rubbish away.

3. The janitor turned off the lights.

4. The ushers handed the programs out.

5. The reporter wrote the incident up for the paper.

Answers:

1. His duties were taken over by the mayor yesterday.
2. The rubbish was carted away by the service-men.
3. The lights were turned off by the janitor.
4. The programs were handed out by the ushers.
5. The incident was written up by the reporter for the paper.

In sentences containing intransitive verbs, no separation of verb and particle can occur since no NP follows a verb in the pattern: NP + V_i + (Adv). If an adverb of manner, one that answers the question "How. . . ?" completes the sentence, the particle may not be moved to follow the adverb:

She *sat down* quickly.
*She sat quickly down.

The evidence *turned up* unexpectedly.
*The evidence turned unexpectedly up.

The lights *went out* suddenly.
*The lights went suddenly out.

EXERCISE

Young children with hearing disabilities are frequently asked to react to requests such as the following. Underline the two-word verbs in these sentences.

1. Hold out your hand, Beth.
2. Put the toys away, Dan.
3. Pick up the blocks, boys.
4. Pick your feet up, Dale.
5. Hang up your coat, Jill.
6. Pull your socks up, Jane.
7. Get out the blankets.
8. Turn on the lights.
9. Turn them off.
10. Wipe off the table.
11. Clean up your plate.
12. Hurry up! Get down.
13. Wake up. It's time to get up.
14. Fold your blankets up.

Answers:

1. hold out
2. put away
3. pick up
4. pick up
5. hang up
6. pull up
7. get out
8. turn on
9. turn off
10. wipe off
11. clean up
12. hurry up, get down
13. wake up, get up
14. fold up

Identification of the constituents of double verbs is complicated by the fact that words that function as particles can also function as prepositions. In this lesson we will limit the discussion to the differences between particles and their counterpart prepositions, which introduce adverbial phrases, though in a subsequent lesson, prepositions will be discussed in greater detail. Adverbial prepositional phrases are usually referred to as verb complements.

After the T/yes-no and T/do have been applied to a sentence containing an adverbial prepositional phrase, another transformation may place the preposition in the first position in the resulting question:

> The car ran off the road. =>
>
> Did the car run off the road? =>
>
> *Off* what did the car run? (Preposition, *off*, begins the question.)

Particles cannot be brought to the beginning of a question:

> The secretary ran off 100 copies. =>
>
> Did the secretary run off 100 copies? =>
>
> *Off what did the secretary run? (Particle, *off*, cannot begin the question.)

Prepositional phrases may be separated from a verb by an adverb of manner while particles may not:

She looked at the dress longingly. => (preposition)
She looked longingly at the dress.

He worked on his car diligently. => (preposition)
He worked diligently on his car.

The nurse made up the bed quickly. => (particle)
*The nurse made quickly up the bed.

People who hear depend on intonation and pauses in speech to aid them in identifying groups of words that function together as meaningful units, but such help is generally denied hearing-impaired children unless auditory training is emphasized in conjunction with learning language. Notice how similar the following sentences look in their written form, and imagine how difficult it must be for a child who depends largely on vision rather than audition to differentiate between particles, prepositions, and adverbial complements:

They took the Halloween pictures *down* this afternoon. (particle)
They took the injured man *down* the mountain. (preposition)

He turned *in* his expense account. (particle)
He turned *in* his sleep. (preposition)

She took her glasses *off*. (adverbial complement)
She took her glasses *off* the shelf. (preposition)

EXERCISE

In the following sentences identify the italicized words as particles or prepositions. Write *prt* or *prep* in the space provided:

_______ 1. The boys broke *up* the fight quickly.

_______ 2. The boys broke *into* the assembly hall.

_______ 3. She got *in* at 10:00 PM

_______ 4. She got *in* the clothes.

_______ 5. She got *in* the car and drove off.

_______ 6. He was pointing *out* the suspect.

_______ 7. He was pointing *out* the window.

_______ 8. They worked *out* the puzzle together.

_______ 9. They worked *in* the yard together.

_______ 10. He held *onto* the oars.

_______ 11. He held *up* the traffic.

_______ 12. We locked ourselves *out*.

Answers:

1.	prt	5.	prep	9.	prep
2.	prep	6.	prt	10.	prep
3.	prt	7.	prep	11.	prt
4.	prt	8.	prt	12.	prt

Beyond the syntactical intricacies involving two-word verbs there are also complicated semantic aspects with which children must deal. Combining verbs with particles and prepositions allows us to coin hundreds of new meanings without increasing the number of words in our vocabularies. The new meanings may result in more than the sum of the literal meanings of the words in the combination. In short, idioms are created which have to be mastered just as if they were additional words.

Some two-word verbs retain their basic or literal meanings, as in:

I woke up. → I awoke.

Please sit down. → Please sit.

Stand up. → Stand.

But note how the following meanings drastically change the literal meanings of verb, particle, or preposition:

I wouldn't *bank on* that. (depend on)

They *looked after* the sick bird. (cared for)

They *took over* their father's business. (began to manage)

He *gave up* his career. (relinquished)

She *ran across* an old photo. (found)

We *ran into* difficulties. (encountered)

Idioms like those in the above sentences begin to appear in reading materials at about the third grade level. Deaf children should become familiar with many idioms involving double verbs before they encounter them in reading.

EXERCISE

Write out sentences for the following sets of words using the pattern NP + V_t + NP_2. You may use T/prt-movt if you wish:

$$\text{He} + \begin{cases}\text{hold}\\ \text{pass}\\ \text{shake}\end{cases} + \begin{cases}\text{off}\\ \text{out}\\ \text{up}\end{cases} + NP_2$$

Answers: Your answers will be original sentences, but you may have written ones similar to these: He held off the bill collector. He passed off the remark with a shrug. He shook off his ennui.

Now look over your sentences and check those you think contain idioms. If you are in doubt, consult a dictionary of idioms.

In this lesson you have been introduced to only a few of the complexities of double verbs and have learned a few tests that you may apply to identify the constituents of two-word verbs. While tests and rules will be helpful to teachers, they will be of little value to children who must contend with meaning and rules almost simultaneously. Through everyday practice in meaningful situations, children can acquire ability to use double verbs, but it is the responsibility of the teacher to clarify chilren's misconceptions as they arise. Only by understanding the intricacies of double verbs yourself, can you help children understand them.

LESSON 20

The English Determiner System: Regular Determiners

ABSTRACT

- The regular determiners contain three subclasses:
    1. articles (Art)
    2. demonstratives (Dem)
    3. genitives (Gen) (possessive forms of personal pronouns and all nouns)
- There are two types of articles:
    1. definite <+ def> *(the, each, every, neither, either)*
    2. nondefinite <— def> *(a, an, another, some, any, no, enough)*
- Only one regular determiner may be used with a noun at a time. This rule may be used to identify the regular determiners.
- In order to use determiners correctly, it is necessary to have a knowledge of the noun features <+ singular> and <+ count>.
- The T/there transformation can be used only if a *nondefinite* article marks the first NP in the sentence pattern *NP + be +* Adv_p.
- The nonappearing article or zero article in the surface structure of a sentence is represented by Ø.
- The demonstratives carry the <+ def> feature; *this* and *these* carry the feature <+ near> and *that* and *those,* <— near>.
- The genitive forms of the personal pronouns, *my, your, his, her, its, our,* and *their* carry the <+ def> feature.
- There seems to be no rationale for including the definite article *the* before place names.

You will notice that we have rather neglected noun phrases, while we have given a great deal of attention to the verb phrase. The noun phrase in English is as important as the verb phrase, and, in its own way, as complex. In this and succeeding lessons, we will study noun phrases in depth. We will begin by looking at the determiner system. Determiners are structure words that mark nouns.

Lesson 4 has presented these facts about noun phrases:

1. a noun phrase is a constituent of the basic sentence pattern, *NP + Aux + VP*
2. a noun phrase may consist of:
   a. a noun alone: NP → N
   b. a determiner and a noun: NP → Det + N
   c. a determiner, a noun, and a sentence: NP → Det + N + S
   d. a pronoun: NP → Pers Pro
      NP → Indef Pro

Native speakers of English are generally not aware that there is a complex determiner system since they use it easily and correctly. It would be safe to say that second only to verb errors in the writing of hearing-impaired youngsters and adults are those errors related to the use of determiners.

Determiners are a large enough class of words to require subcategorization. The regular determiners contain three subclasses:

1. articles: Det → Art
2. demonstratives: Det → Dem
3. genitives: the possessive forms of personal pronouns and nouns: Det → Gen

Only one at a time of these subclasses may be used to mark a noun.

There are two types of articles, nondefinite and definite. Some linguists (Jacobs and Rosenbaum, 1968) consider that articles are represented as features of nouns in deep structures rather than as constituents of NPs. Nouns are said to carry the feature <+ Def> and <— Def>. Our purposes are better served by considering the phrase structure rules governing the use of articles than by trying to incorporate the feature <+ Def> or <— Def> into the noun lexicon. It is necessary, however, that children be familiar with the noun features <+ count> and <— count>, <+ singular> and <— singular> in order to use articles correctly. It is also very important that they understand clearly the phrase structure rules governing the use of determiners.

The first rule for articles states:

Art → Nondefinite

Art → Definite

Nondef → a, an, some

Def → the

The articles *a, an,* and *some* are the most common nondefinite articles. We will look at them in considerable detail, for they are the prototypes of the other nondefinite articles. They appear before nouns when it is the intention of the speaker or writer to name one of a possible number of like things as:

1. a notebook (one of several notebooks, one of all notebooks, or a class of items identified as *notebooks*)
2. some erasers (an indefinite number of a group of things entitled *erasers*)
3. some ink (part of a mass entitled *ink*)

The nondefiniteness of the article does not imply that the noun marked by the article does not convey a specific meaning in the context of its setting. It merely means that the noun is an unspecified one of many of its kind. After all, a noun is only a symbol that stands for a large class of objects. In order to name a chair, a child must have generalized the concept that things with four legs that are used to sit on are *chairs*. A *chair* could be a big chair, a little chair, a wooden chair, an arm chair, or any chair in sight or out of sight. Reference is to any of its class when a nondefinite article is used.

A is used before count nouns beginning with consonants. The vowel, *u*, as in *ųnion*, is a diphthong which begins with the glide [j], thus requiring that it be preceded by the article *a*, as in a *u*nion, *a u*niform, *a u*tility. *An* is used before count nouns beginning with the vowels, *a*, *e*, *i*, *o*, and *u* (pronounced [ə], as in *umbrella*), and before words beginning with silent *h* as in *heir*. Since the use of articles is somewhat dependent on a knowledge of speech, those hearing-impaired children who have not been brought up in the oral tradition may find these rules somewhat difficult to understand.

When a modifier intervenes between a nondefinite article and a count noun, the choice of *a* or *an* depends on the first sound in the modifier rather than on the noun as in:

an egg, *an* inedible egg, *a* boiled egg

a size, *a* big size, *an* average size

a community, *an* organized community, *a* united community

Three other nondefinite articles that mark singular nouns are *any*, *another*, and *no*. *No* also marks plural nouns. Their meaning as well as their use must be clarified for the children with hearing impairments. If you are not sure of their meaning, or of that of any other determiners, refer to your dictionary. Since determiners are involved in idiomatic language and are not always used according to the rules we are studying here, you might also find a dictionary of idioms very useful.

Examples of the use of *another*, *any*, and *no* are:

Another piece is in the box on the table.

Any piece will be O.K.

No piece is large enough.

In Lesson 13 we learned that the T/there transformation can be applied only if a nondefinite article marks the NP in the sentence pattern, $NP + be + Adv_p$. We can apply the T/there transformation to sentences containing *no, another,* and *any,* as well as *a, an,* and *some* in the NP.

Any is substituted for *some* and *no* in statements in which the verb has undergone a negative transformation. Since *some* is a nondefinite article, its substitute, *any,* can also be used in this transformation:

Some milk is in the refrigerator. =>
T/there: There is *some* milk in the refrigerator.
T/neg: There isn't *any* milk in the refrigerator.

No pencils are here (in this box). =>
T/there: There are *no* pencils here. =>
T/neg: There aren't *any* pencils here.

Another piece is in the box. =>
T/there: There is *another* piece in the box. =>
T/neg: There isn't *another* piece in the box. or
There isn't *any other* piece in the box.

Some is used with mass nouns <— count> as in *some bread, some money, some knowledge,* and with plural forms <— sing> of count nouns as in *some grapes, some ideas* and *some mistakes.*

He has *some knowledge* of the subject.

They have *some money,* but they aren't really rich.

Some mistakes are costly.

Get *some grapes* and *some apples* out of the refrigerator.

Proper nouns and plural nouns frequently are not preceded by an article in the surface structure of a sentence, but are interpreted as having a nondefinite article in their deep structure. This nonappearing, or zero, article is written Ø to indicate its presence in the deep structure even though it is deleted in the surface structure. The use of the zero article is as difficult for hearing-impaired children to learn as is the use of those articles that do appear before nouns:

A child is *a* blessing.

Ø Childen are *a* precious cargo.

Ø Children will be Ø children.

A kiwi is *a* bird.

Ø Kiwis are Ø birds.

The nondefinite article may be omitted before noncount nouns when the reference is to a generality, but it is included when a portion of the mass is referred to:

Ø Bread is nourishing.

Put *some* bread on the table.

Ø Inflation seems to be a way of life in the United States.

Some inflation can be expected.

There are quite a few nouns that can be used both as count and noncount nouns. Hearing-impaired children must become aware of them if they are to master the correct use of the articles. Teachers must be sure to point out the dual nature of these nouns. Here is a very short list of such nouns:

fire(s) <+ count>	I am going to light a fire under him. The fires started spontaneously.
fire <— count>	Fire swept through the valley.
food(s) <+ count>	Oatmeal is a breakfast food. Some foods are fattening.
food <— count>	I like good food.
grain(s) <+ count>	Wheat is a grain. Barley and oats are grains.
grain <— count>	Grain is raised in the midwest.
hair(s) <+ count>	There is a hair on your collar.
hair <— count>	Your hair is pretty.
time(s) <+ count>	We had a good time. He tried many times, but failed.
time <— count>	I'll have time later.
currency(s) <+ count>	The German mark is a strong currency now.
currency <— count>	We accept only currency here.
rock(s) <+ count>	He threw a rock at me. They threw rocks at us.
rock <— count>	The underlying stratum is rock.
precaution(s) <+ count>	A strong lock is a good precaution against theft.
precaution <— count>	He threw precaution to the wind.

The is the most important of the definite articles. It singles out a specific thing from its group or class. Its pronounciation varies depending on the sound following it. When it precedes a vowel, it is pronounced *thi*, as in th*i* air, rather than the usual *the* before consonants, as in th*e* sky.

Ordinarily, we use a nondefinite article when we first mention a thing in order to give the reader or listener an opportunity to locate it in its class. Thereafter, when we refer to it, we use the definite article *the* since it becomes a specific item in reference to both speaker and listener:

I caught *some* fish.

We cooked *the* fish.

However, if there is only one thing of a kind in the world, in the home, in the room, or in the environment, we use the definite article the first time we mention it, since the thing has been identified by its uniqueness:

The moon is full tonight. (only one moon)

The tide is coming in. (only one tide in the environment)

Pull down *the* shades. (only one group of things called shades in the house)

Let's move *the* stuff over here. (only one group of things referred to as *stuff* in the room)

We washed *the* car today. (only one car in the family)

Even though there is more than one light or one floor in a house or building, we use *the* idiomatically in such expressions as:

Turn on *the* light.

Sweep *the* floor.

The use of *the* can be puzzling to hearing-impaired children. For instance, there seems to be no rationale for including or omitting it in sentences employing the verb *went*:

We went to/ *the* store/ *the* movies/ *the* opera/ *the* circus/ *the* office/ *the* library/ *the* museum/ *the* bank/ *the* lake/ *the* mountains/ *the* country/ *the* city.

We went to/ Ø church/ Ø school/ Ø bed/ Ø dinner/ Ø work/ Ø class/ Ø Disneyland.

We went to/ *a* play/ *a* show/ *a* dance/ *a* party/ *a* wedding.

The is used when referring to the parts of a noun already identified, as in:

Please help yourself to *an* orange. Put *the* peel and *the* seeds in this bag.

Mr. Smith took his car to the garage, because *the* brakes wouldn't hold and *the* distributor was not operating efficiently.

The is used before names of musical instruments, as in:

He plays/ *the* violin/ *the* piano/ *the* tuba/ *the* bass drum.

We omit *the* before the names of games:

They play/ Ø tennis/ Ø golf/ Ø hockey/ Ø football/ Ø baseball/ Ø tag/ Ø checkers/ Ø bridge.

The is an integral part of the names of many newspapers, magazines, buildings, and businesses, but in others, it is omitted. For instance, we say:

He reads *The Wall Street Journal* and *The Saturday Review.*

He reads *Newsweek/Life/Time.*

His office is in *the Empire State Building.*

He lives at *The Towers.*

He ate lunch at *The Top Steak House.*

He ate breakfast at *Pancake Heaven.*

If a genitive form of a noun is used in a title or name, no other regular determiner is allowed, since use of the genitive excludes the use of another regular determiner:

I shop at Walgreen's/Woolworth's/Penny's/Macy's.

*I shop at *the* Field's.

The use of *the* before place names is an example of the kind of knowledge which the hearing-impaired must acquire. Table 6 outlines how determiners are used with place names.

Table 6. Examples of Use of the Ø Article and the Definite Article, *the*, before Place Names

Category	*Ø*	*The*
Continents	North/South America, Australia, Antarctica, Asia, Africa	
Countries	France, Egypt, Vietnam, Tanzania, India, Canada, Great Britain, Argentina, Scandinavia	The United States, The USSR (The United Soviet Socialist Republics), The Argentine, The Netherlands, The Balkans
States	Arizona, Wisconsin	The Commonwealth of Virginia
Cities	San Francisco, Miami	The Hague (exception)
Streets	Main Street, Lake Drive, Michigan Boulevard, Broadway	The Avenue of the Americas, The Street of Sorrows
Oceans, seas, straits		The Atlantic Ocean, The Mediterranean Sea, The Straits of Gibraltar
Bays, sounds, gulfs	Green Bay, Manilla Bay, Long Island Sound	The Bay of Pigs, The Bay of Biscay, The Gulf of Mexico
Islands	Manhattan, Treasure Island, Bali	The Philippine Islands, The Virgin Islands
Mountain ranges		The Rocky Mountains, The Alps, The Laurentians
Mountain peaks	Mount Washington, Mount Rainier, Mount Vesuvius	
Rivers		The Amazon, The Mississippi, The Rhine, The Euphrates
Lakes and groups of lakes	Lake Michigan, Lake Placid, Fox Lake	The Great Lakes

When names of rivers, mountain ranges, or musical instruments are used as modifiers of plural or mass nouns, the article is omitted, as in:

> I like violin music better than piano music.
>
> Rocky Mountain roads are treacherous in stormy weather.
>
> Mississippi River traffic is heavy all summer.
>
> United States citizens enjoy many privileges.

Children with hearing impairments find it very difficult to understand and use idioms, so they will need constant guidance and practice in gaining control over them as well as over the regular phrase structure rules governing determiners.

There are several other definite articles with which children must become acquainted. These are *each, every, either,* and *neither:*

> *Each* day offers us a new challenge.
>
> *Every* dollar saved is a dollar earned.
>
> *Either* road is fine.
>
> *Neither* road is good.

These definite articles, like all definite determiners, cannot be used in the T/there transformation:

> *Each* girl is in her place.
> *There is *each* girl in her place.
>
> *Every* boy is here now.
> *There is *every* boy here now.
>
> *Neither* dish is in the cupboard.
> *There is *neither* dish in the cupboard.

The demonstratives, *this, these, that,* and *those* also carry the <+ Def> feature. *This* and *these* refer to a noun near the speaker, while *that* and *those* refer to nouns more distant from the speaker. *This* pencil may become *that* pencil merely by shifting its position nearer to or farther away from the speaker. What may be *this* pencil to one speaker may be *that* pencil to another, depending on his proximity to it. *This* and *these* carry the feature <+ near>, while *that* and *those* have the feature <— near>. They cannot be used in the T/there transformation.

The and the demonstratives differ somewhat in their patterning. We may use demonstratives, but not *the* with *one,* where it is used as a noun:

> *This/that* one is mine/yours/theirs.
>
> **The* one is mine.
>
> *These/those* ones are mine/yours/theirs.
>
> **The* ones are mine.

When an adjective modifier accompanies *one*, it is possible to use the definite determiner in the NP:

> *The* white one is mine.
>
> *The* one on the table is his.
>
> *The* blue ones are hers.
>
> *The* ones with the fringes are theirs.

Ones is usually omitted in the plural, so sentences like the following would be more commonly encountered:

> *These/those* are mine.
>
> *Those* with the fringes are theirs.

The subclass of genitive forms of the personal pronoun, *my, your, his, her, its, our,* and *their* completes the three categories of regular definite determiners. They carry the <+ def> feature. The T/there transformation cannot be applied when a genitive is used with the first noun in the pattern $NP + be + Adv_p$. An important thing to remember is that only one regular determiner can be used with a noun at a time. This mutual exclusiveness makes it impossible to say:

> *that each desk
>
> *a this pen
>
> *those his papers

EXERCISE

1. Underline the determiners in these sentences.
2. In Column I, list the regular determiners.
3. In Column II, identify them as being (Art), (Dem), or (Gen).
4. In Column III, identify the determiner as carry the <+ def> or <— def> feature.

	Column I	*Column II*	*Column III*	*Sentence*
1.	________	________	________	1. That woman takes her baby for a walk in the park every day.
	________	________	________	
	________	________	________	
	________	________	________	

2. ________ ________ ________

________ ________ ________

________ ________ ________

________ ________ ________

________ ________ ________

2. Each time I look at the picture, I think of our picnic at that lake in Maine.

3. ________ ________ ________

________ ________ ________

________ ________ ________

________ ________ ________

3. Children believe that visiting the zoo is a lark for grownups, too.

Answers:

1. *Column I:* that, her, a, the, every; *Column II:* dem, gen, art, art, art; *Column III:* < + def>, < + def>, < — def>, < + def>, < + def>.
2. *Column I:* each, the, our, that, Ø; *Column II:* art, art, Gen, Dem, art; *Column III:* <+ def>, <+ def>, <+ def>, <+ def>, <— def>.
3. *Column I:* Ø, the, a, Ø; *Column II:* art, art, art, art; *Column III:* < — def>, <+ def>, <— def>, <— def>.

EXERCISE

Mark with an *X* which of these determiners may be used in the T/there transformational.

1. ______his
2. ______the
3. ______an
4. ______any
5. ______these
6. ______this
7. ______neither
8. ______each
9. ______some
10. ______their
11. ______every
12. ______that
13. ______a
14. ______those
15. ______my
16. ______no
17. ______either

Answers: *X* in blanks 3, 4, 9, 13, 16.

EXERCISE

Write sentences illustrating the T/there transformation using the nouns *book/books* and *egg/eggs* and the adverb phrases *in the library* and *on the table.*

1. There is ______________________________
2. There are ______________________________
3. There was ______________________________
4. There were ______________________________
5. There isn't ______________________________
6. There aren't ______________________________
7. There wasn't ______________________________
8. There weren't ______________________________
9. There will be ______________________________
10. There won't be ______________________________

Answers: Sentences will vary, but these are possibilities:

1. There is an egg on the table.
2. There are some eggs on the table.
3. There was no egg on the table.
4. There were many books in the library.
5. There isn't a book on the table.
6. There aren't any books on the table.
7. There wasn't an egg on the table.
8. There weren't any eggs on the table.
9. There will be some books on the table.
10. There won't be any eggs on the table.

LESSON 21

The English Determiner System: Prearticles, Postdeterminers, and Predeterminers

ABSTRACT

- Prearticles, *all, both, just, only,* and *even,* may appear optionally before the regular determiners and serve as restricters of the nouns they precede.
- Not all prearticles can be used with each of the regular determiners.
- Like regular determiners, prearticles appear before adjectives that modify a noun.
- The postdeterminers, *ordinals, cardinals,* and *comparatives,* also precede prenominal adjectives but follow the regular determiners.
- The post determiners can co-occur with one another, but in a fixed order: 1. ordinals, 2. cardinals, 3. comparatives.
- Ordinals indicate the order of rank in a series.
- Cardinals indicate the number of items in a set.
- Comparatives express a difference in degree from the positive.
- To understand the correct use of postdeterminers, a knowledge of the noun features $<\pm$ singular$>$ and $<\pm$ count$>$ is necessary.
- *Much* alternates with *a lot of/lots of* in T/neg, just as *any* does with *some* in negative statements.
- Predeterminers are formed by combining prearticles, regular determiners, post determiners, or nouns of quantity with the morpheme *of.*
- The rule for predeterminers is:

$$\text{Predet} \rightarrow \begin{Bmatrix} \text{Preart} \\ \text{N}_{\text{quantity}} \end{Bmatrix} \begin{Bmatrix} \text{Art} \\ \text{Dem} \\ \text{Gen} \end{Bmatrix} \ (\text{Postdet}) + \text{of}$$

- When a noun of quantity appears in the first NP of a sentence, it governs the form of the verb following it.
- The noun following a predeterminer usually governs the verb form. Children must learn which word in the NP governs the verb.
- The rule for determiners in English can be written:

$$\text{Det} \rightarrow \ (\text{Predet}) \ \ (\text{Preart}) \begin{Bmatrix} \text{Art} \\ \text{Dem} \\ \text{Gen} \end{Bmatrix} \ (\text{Postdet})$$

In Lesson 20 we learned that the regular determiners, the articles, the demonstratives, and the genitive forms of personal pronouns were mutually exclusive as markers of nouns, thus allowing only one at a time of these three subclasses to be used before a noun. We have also noted that determiners may be deleted in the surface structure before some proper nouns, plural count nouns, and mass nouns as in:

I like Ø John. (proper noun)

I like Ø onions. (plural count noun)

I like Ø coffee. (noncount noun)

The rule thus far for determiners is:

Det + N

$$\text{Det} \rightarrow \left\{ \begin{array}{l} \text{Art} \\ \text{Dem} \\ \text{Gen} \end{array} \right\}$$

$$\text{Art} \rightarrow \left\{ \begin{array}{l} \text{Nondef} \\ \text{Def} \end{array} \right\}$$

Nondef → *a(n), another, some, any, no, enough*

Def → *the, each, every, either, neither, this, that, these, those,* and the genitive forms of nouns, *my your, his, her, its.*

There is a small group of words—*all, both, just, only,* and *even*—that may precede an article. They are called *prearticles* because they may appear optionally before articles, genitives, and demonstratives. As prearticles, *just* and *only* have approximately the same meaning. However, *just* is used idiomatically in quite a few expressions and its meaning is controlled by the context in which it is used, as in *just the same.*

Prearticles serve as restricters of the meaning of the nouns that they precede. Not all prearticles can be used with all of the regular determiners. For instance, *both* and *all* must be used with plural nouns marked by definite determiners. We cannot say:

*both no boys

*all some boys

We can say:

Both the boys entered the contest.

Both my boys enjoyed the game.

Both those boys were invited.

All his actions were funny.

All these animals are strange ones.

All the children enjoyed the circus.

The following sentences show that many combinations of prearticles and articles are possible:

It's *just an* idea of mine.

They're *just some* children I know.

I'd like *just another* chance.

I've had *just no* luck at all.

It's *only his* idea, not mine.

He had *only some* small change in his pocket.

Even that boy could do better.

All of the prearticles and articles may appear before any adjective that precedes a noun, as in:

They bought *only the* biggest apples.

They want *just those* large pumpkins.

So far, the rule for determiners reads:

$$\text{Det} \rightarrow \quad (\text{Preart}) \begin{Bmatrix} \text{Art} \\ \text{Dem} \\ \text{Gen} \end{Bmatrix}$$

There is another set of words that follow the regular determiners but precede the adjectives before nouns. They are the *postdeterminers*. The three groups of postdeterminers are: *ordinals, cardinals,* and *comparatives*. Ordinals indicate the order of rank in a series as: *first, second, third*. Cardinals indicate the number of items in a set as: *one, two, three*. Comparatives express a difference in degree from the positive as: *fewer, fewest; less, least; more, most*.

These words, unlike the regular determiners, may occur with one another, but only in a fixed order: 1. ordinals, 2. cardinals, 3. comparatives.

Now the rule reads:

$$\text{Det} \rightarrow \quad (\text{Preart}) \begin{Bmatrix} \text{Dem} \\ \text{Gen} \\ \text{Art} \end{Bmatrix} \quad (\text{Postdet})$$

Postdet → (ordinals) (cardinals) (comparatives)

Ordinals (Ord) → *first, second, third . . . , final, last, next, same, other*

Cardinals (Card) → *one, two, three . . . , few, several, many, much*

Comparatives (Comp) → *fewer, fewest, less, least, more, most*

While it is possible that all three subclasses of postdeterminers can be used together, it is unlikely that they will be found in a single phrase. Native users of English sense the rightness of combinations while non-native speakers and children with hearing defects will require considerable clarification as to which postdeterminers pattern with which articles and nouns. Children must be very familiar with the noun features <± singular> and <± count> in order to understand the use of the postdeterminers.

Here are a few possible combinations that children might encounter:

the *final* game

the *first several* times

some *more* milk (used with <— count> noun)

some *more* kittens (used with plural <+ count> noun

these *last five* years

John's *other two* sisters

much less noise (used with <— count> noun)

the *next most* important task

EXERCISE

Add appropriate prearticles to these phrases:

Example: just/only/even __________ the first several times

1. ______________________________ the same few boys
2. ______________________________ some more milk
3. ______________________________ those last three candidates
4. ______________________________ John's other two brothers
5. ______________________________ their final five years
6. ______________________________ much less noise
7. ______________________________ the many accusations
8. ______________________________ the next most popular item

Answers: Answers will vary, but these are possibilities:

1. just, only, even
2. just, only, even
3. all, just, only, even
4. just, only, even
5. all, just, only, even
6. just, only, even
7. all, just, only, even
8. just, only, even

Much alternates with *a lot of* in negative sentences just as *any* does with *some,* though with *much,* the alternative is often optional:

We took *some* charcoal to the picnic.
*We didn't take *some* charcoal to the picnic. =>
We didn't take *any* charcoal to the picnic.

The boys had *a lot of fun* at the picnic.
The boys didn't have *a lot of fun* at the picnic. =>
The boys didn't have very *much* fun at the picnic.

Sentences containing *lots of* and *a lot of* in the first NP in the pattern, NP + be + Adv_{L}, may be used in the T/there transformation:

Lots of girls were at the dance. =>
T/there: There were *lots of* girls at the dance.

A *lot of* paper is in the drawer. =>
T/there: There is *a lot of* paper in the drawer. =>
T/neg: There isn't *a lot of* paper in the drawer.
There isn't *much* paper in the drawer.

EXERCISE

Write the phrase structure rules for these noun phrases:

Example: the first two passengers def art + ord + card + N

1. only the first two passengers ______
2. just the third time ______
3. all the many changes ______
4. both these boys ______
5. my first few thoughts ______
6. the next fewest stops ______
7. a final try ______
8. all those last few days ______
9. just his fourth offense ______

Answers:

1. preart + def art + ord + card + N
2. preart + def art + ord + N
3. preart + def art + card + N
4. preart + dem + N
5. gen + ord + card + N
6. def art + ord + comp + N
7. nondef art + ord + N
8. preart + dem + ord + card + N
9. preart + gen + ord + N

EXERCISE

Apply T/neg to the following statements and questions:

1. There are some paper sacks in the drawer.

____

2. We have a lot of time to do our homework.

____

3. Do you have some hand lotion I could use?

____

4. They ate a lot of popcorn at the party.

____

5. Bill thought up some good games for the party.

____

Answers:.

1. There aren't any paper sacks in the drawer.
2. We don't have a lot of (much) time to do our homework.
3. Don't you have any hand lotion I could use?
4. They didn't eat a lot of (much) popcorn at the party.
5. Bill didn't think up any good games for the party.

The rule for determiners can be expanded once more to include another set in the English determiner system, the *predeterminers.* Predeterminers always contain the morpheme *of,* which terminates a string composed of one or several of the determiners we have already studied. Besides the articles, nouns of quantity (N_Q) are used to form predeterminers. Following are examples of predeterminers based on the subcategories of determiners:

1. prearticles: *all of, both of*
2. regular determiners: *some of, none of ,either of, neither of, enough of, any of*
3. postdeterminers: *the first of, the last of, one of, twenty of, few of, a few of, several of, much of, many of, the fewest of, the least of, most of*
4. nouns of quantity: *a barrel of, a quart of, a bottle of, a lot of, lots of, half of*

A predeterminer may be used before a regular determiner and is separated from it by the word *of.* A predeterminer may include several subcategories of determiners according to the following rule:

$$\text{Predet} \rightarrow \left\{ \begin{array}{c} \text{Preart} \\ \text{N}_{\text{Quantity}} \end{array} \right\} \left\{ \begin{array}{c} \text{Art} \\ \text{Dem} \\ \text{Gen} \end{array} \right\} \text{(Postdet)} + \text{of}$$

Examples are:

neither of the books

just enough of your foolishness

only a few of my friends

even the last four of those cupcakes

Nouns may be marked by rather long strings of determiners, though in general practice we use only one or two per noun. For instance, it would be correct but unusual to write a sentence such as:

He played in *only the first two quarters of the last few* games.

Many predeterminers that contain nouns of quantity, as in *a quart of* and *a bushel of,* may be used either with plural <+ count> or with <—count> nouns:

a quart of cherries <+ count>

a quart of molasses <— count>

a bushel of potatoes <+count>

a bushel of grain <— count>

The noun of quantity, not the plural count noun following it, governs the form of the verb when the noun of quantity occupies the subject position in the sentence:

A quart of cherries costs 49 cents.

A bushel of potatoes weighs 50 pounds.

However, in sentences containing predeterminers such as *all of, some of, lots of,* and *most of,* which may also be used with plural <+ count> and with <— count> nouns, the noun following the predeterminer governs the verb form:

All of his *energies were* dissipated.
All of his *energy was* devoted to the task.

Some of these *girls expect* to help you.
Some of their *fun has been spoiled.*

Lots of *vegetables are* in storage.
Lots of their *trouble stems* from their improvidence.

Most of the *apples were* bruised.
Most of my *time was* wasted.

It is very difficult for non-native speakers and hearing-impaired children to learn to use the English determiner system. They must become aware of complex phrase rules that prescribe the order of determiners and also the rules for verb agreement in noun phrases involving predeterminers. Knowing this rule for the determiner system:

$$\text{Det} \rightarrow \text{(Predet)} \quad \text{(Preart)} \quad \left\{ \begin{array}{c} \text{Art} \\ \text{Dem} \\ \text{Gen} \end{array} \right\} \quad \text{(Postdet)}$$

will help you analyze children's problems in their struggles with the system, but only practice in using determiners will help them master it.

EXERCISE

Write sentences using the following phrases as subjects (NPs) with a form of *be* in the verb phrase (VP):

1. Several of my friends ______________________.
2. All of his cousins ______________________.
3. All of his work ______________________.
4. Six of their puppies ______________________.
5. Each of his last three classes ______________________.
6. Most of the four last days ______________________.
7. A lot of the berries ______________________.
8. Lots of water ______________________.
9. A pound of walnuts ______________________.
10. Only the first three bottles of juice ______________________.

Answers:

1. were 2. were 3. was 4. were 5. was 6. were 7. were 8. was 9. was 10. were

EXERCISE

Underline the prearticles, the regular determiners, and the postdeterminers in each of these sentences, and write the phrase structure rules for them. Be sure to note the Ø article before some of the nouns.

Example:

The house that __ John Alden built still stands.

the — def art + N, Ø + N (John Alden)

---

1. Our forefathers built their homes near waterways.

---

2. I would like to see that problem solved.

---

3. The first ten applicants will be accepted.

---

4. Some of the children rode the final two miles.

---

5. Henry was one of the boys who walked the ten miles.

---

6. The last two guests finally arrived.

Answers:

1. our = gen + N, their = gen + N, Ø + N (waterways)
2. Ø + Pro (I), that = dem + N
3. the first ten = def art + ord + card + N
4. some of the = predet + def art + N, the final two = def art + card + ord + N
5. Ø + N (Henry), one of the = predet + def art + N, the ten = def art + card + N
6. the last two = def art + ord + card + N

LESSON 22

Pronouns: Personal and Reflexive

ABSTRACT

- Pronouns are diverse enough to contain subclassifications: personal pronouns, reflexive pronouns, relative pronouns, indefinite pronouns, and interrogative pronouns.
- A pronoun may replace a noun in a sentence when the noun is repeated in that sentence or in the following sentence. The second noun carries the <+Pro> feature.
- All personal pronouns carry the <+def> feature and so cannot participate in the T/there transformation.
- Personal pronouns also have these features: person, number, gender, and case.
- There is a close concordance between the nominative case of personal pronouns and the forms of the copula *be*.
- The neuter pronoun, *it*, has uses beyond those of the other personal pronouns. Sometimes it acts only as a place holder in a sentence.
- The second genitive form is used in the pattern $NP + be + NP_1$, when the first NP contains a definite article and the second NP a genitive form.
- The nominative form is used in the subject position, the accusative in object position, and the genitive is used as a determiner.
- Understanding and using indirect discourse requires a knowledge of the referents of pronouns.

- By a transformation (T/reflexive) the reflexive pronouns, such as *myself* and *yourself*, are required replacements for a noun or pronoun when the second NP in the same sentence is identical to the first or has the same referent.
- Reflexive forms of pronouns may be used as intensifiers.

A dictionary lists the derivation of the English word *pronoun* from the Latin *pronomen* (*pro* = for, and *nomen* = noun or name), but modern linguists prefer not to define a pronoun as "A word that can stand for a noun or that can be substituted for it," since the various subclasses of pronouns have their own characteristics differentiating them from other pronoun subclasses as well as from nouns. They are not at all a homogeneous group with similar characteristics. The various subclasses of pronouns include personal pronouns, reflexive pronouns, relative pronouns, interrogative pronouns, and indefinite pronouns.

Personal pronouns originate as noun segments in the deep structure of sentences in which the noun carries the feature <+ Pro>. A pronoun may replace a noun in a sentence when the noun is repeated in that sentece or in the following sentence. The second noun carries the <+ Pro> feature as in:

> Dr. Goldstein was an otologist, but more than that *he* was a humanitarian.

Personal pronouns all carry the <+ def> feature and so cannot participate in the T/there transformation, if the subject noun contains any form of a personal pronoun:

His hat is in the closet.
T/there: *There is his hat in the closet.

They are on a march to the stadium.
T/there: *There are they on a march to the stadium.

Besides the feature <+def>, personal pronouns have these important features:

person: <I, (first person)> <II, (second person)> <III, (third person)>

number: <+ singular> <— singular>

gender: <+ masculine> <+ feminine)> (neuter) <— masculine> <— feminine>

case: <+ nom (inative)> <+ acc(usative)> <+ gen(itive)>

Table 7 indicates the various forms of the personal pronouns and classifies them according to these features. Notice that *you* and *it* serve both as nominative and accusative forms, and that only the third person singular pronouns have gender. The genitive of all personal pronouns has two forms.

Table 7. Forms of Personal Pronouns

	NOMINATIVE		ACCUSATIVE		GENITIVE	
PERSON	<+ Sing>	<— Sing>	<+ Sing>	<— Sing>	<+ Sing>	<— Sing>
I	I	we	me	us	my/mine	our/ours
II	you	you	you	you	your/ yours	your/ yours
III	he <+ masc> she <+ fem> it (neuter) <— fem> <— masc>	they	him <+ masc> her <+ fem> it (neuter) <— fem> <— masc>	them	his/his <+ masc> her/hers <+ fem> its (neuter) <— fem> <— masc>	their/ theirs

By referring to Table 3 in Lesson 13 you will recognize that there is a close concordance between the forms of the copula *be* and the nominative forms of personal pronouns. They seem to be made for each other, and, consequently, should be learned in conjunction with each other by children who have difficulty learning language.

A speaker uses the first person pronoun when he is referring to himself. When he is including himself in a group of one, two, or more persons, he uses the plural form of the first person. The second person pronoun is used when a speaker addresses one or more persons directly.

You is sometimes indefinite, as in: "You can't be sure of anything today."

Third person pronouns are employed when reference is made to someone or something other than the speaker or those spoken to.

The plural first person pronouns, *we* and *us*, do not mean two or more I's, but rather the person speaking *and someone else*. We may use *we* without an antecedent, as it is used to introduce this sentence, if it is understood who *we* are. *We* takes on a general and indefinite quality in this case. *They* refers to groups or sets consisting of two or more persons or objects as *an apple and an orange; ten boys;* or *a boy, his kite, and his dog.*

Personal pronouns that carry the noun feature <+ N> put the same restrictions on verbs as do nouns. A neuter pronoun cannot be used with verbs carrying the <+ human> feature .We cannot say (except, I suppose, if the *it* in the next sentence refers to a computer):

It recalled its mistake.

but we can say:

He recalled his mistake.

It is interesting to note that when people name their dolls, pets, or cars, they confer animation and sometimes even sex upon them. In children's stories, ordinarily inanimate fire engines, trains, airplanes, and even steam shovels come to life and are legitimately referred to as *he* or *she* instead of *it*. The concept of aliveness, real or imaginary, along with the <+ human> feature is one that children with hearing impairments must learn at an early age in order to understand referents to pronouns.

The neuter pronoun *it* has uses beyond those of the other personal pronouns. In some instances *it* bears a resemblence to *zero* in the number system, for it acts as a place holder in sentences. As a place holder in the subject position, *it* governs the form of the verb following it:

> *It* is raining.
>
> *It* is ten o'clock.
>
> *It* seems cozy in here.

It refers to nothing in the previous sentences, but since every English sentence seems more comfortable with a subject, *it* serves this purpose:

> *It's* me. (with heavy emphasis on *me*)
>
> *It* was George who did it. (emphasis on *George*)
>
> *It* was my fault. (emphasis on *my fault*)

In the above sentences *it*, again, has no specific referents. We might have stated the same idea in this manner:

> I am here.
>
> George did it.
>
> The fault was mine.

For purposes of emphasis in the spoken language, we begin the sentence with the innocuous *it* and then emphasize that part of the sentence which seems most relevant to the speaker. This is a semantic problem rather than one of syntax.

In Lesson 20 you learned that the genitive forms of personal pronouns were classified as determiners, but two nominatives, *we* and *you*, also carry this feature:

> You boys will have to wait.
>
> We teachers should state our case clearly.

These forms may precede adjectives in noun phrases just as articles may:

> You big boys ought to know that.
>
> We new teachers have every right to be heard.

Under certain conditions the second form of the genitive, *mine, yours, his, hers, its, ours,* and *theirs,* is required in sentences. For instance, in those based on Pattern III, *NP + be + NP,* where the second NP contains a regular genitive pronoun determiner or in yes-no questions based on this pattern, a deletion transformation removes the second noun and replaces it with the second genitive forms:

The dishes are her dishes. =>
The dishes are hers.

Is this scarf your scarf? =>
Is this scarf yours?

Notice that the determiner used to mark the first noun is a definite determiner. Only then is the second genitive applicable. When the determiner is nondefinite or Ø, we cannot use the second genitive after the copula:

*Some dishes are mine.

*Ø Dishes are mine.

In the subject position of a sentence the nominative forms are used, and in the object position the accusative forms are used. The accusative is also used when the pronoun is in indirect object or the object of a preposition:

They gave *him* the books for *her.*

Between *you* and *me, I* wonder if *he* will deliver *them.*

Some hearing people have difficulty using the diverse forms of pronouns correctly. Modern spoken English tolerates *It's me,* when *me* is in object territory, but not as yet **between you and I,* where it is in object territory. Children with hearing defects and language learning difficulties usually do not make these kinds of errors. Their errors consist mainly of faulty reference, that is, of not matching the correct form for person with the correct inflected form of present tense verbs or with the many forms of the copula *be* as in:

**He like* candy.

*It *grow* in South America.

*Julie and David *was* here.

*They *is* happy.

Children often omit *be* from their sentences.

In reading, children with hearing defects have great difficulty identifying antecedents of pronouns and need guidance in relating them to the proper antecedents.

Direct and indirect discourse is a case in point. To understand and use direct and indirect discourse, children must have firm control over the referents of pronouns. Pronouns shift in person from <+ I> to <+ III> or from <+ II> to <+I> or <+ III>, or to any other combinations depending on who is speaking, spoken to, or spoken about, and who is reporting what was said. In an oral conversation with hearing-impaired children, parents or teachers often find it necessary to restate, or have the children restate, what they have heard or seen on the lips to check their understanding of the message. Such restatement could be a repetition of the direct quotation or transformation to a statement about the statement. Indirect discourse requires changing not only verb tenses but replacing pronouns so that the referent and the pronoun agree in person and in number.

When we report a person's exact words in written form, we enclose them in quotation marks. Indirect discourse, except when it is a part of a direct quotation, is not identified by any special punctuation marks.

Assume that a mother is speaking to her children about a trip she has to take. She has arranged for a baby sitter, Linda, to stay with the children while she is gone. Mother says to her children:

> "I feel better about going away when I know Linda is here looking after you. There is enough chili in the refrigerator for your supper, and I'll open a can of pears for you. Linda can bake some cookies and you can help her."

Later when Linda arrives, Mother, in speaking to her, first uses indirect discourse to report what she had told the children and then addresses Linda directly. Notice how the pronouns differ from those above, not only in the indirect discourse but also in the direct discourse.

> "I told the children that I felt better about going away when I knew you were looking after them."

(Indirect discourse now changes to direct.)

> "There is enough chili in the refrigerator for your supper, and I'll open a can of pears for you. You can bake some cookies and they can help you," said Mother to Linda.

Mother then telephones to Grandma and reports what she had told both Linda and the children. The content of her message is a report of her direct conversation with the children and Linda.

> "I told the children that I felt better about going away when I knew Linda was looking after them. I said that there was enough chili in the refrigerator for their supper and that I'd open a can of pears for them. I told them, too, that Linda could bake some cookies and that they could help her," Mother said to Grandma.

Notice how verb tenses change in the indirect discourse and how the pronouns change to conform to the proper referents according to the deliverer and receiver of the message.

This brief introduction to direct and indirect discourse points out that personal pronouns present sufficient difficulties to warrant careful planning on the part of teachers in helping children use them correctly.

The reflexive pronouns, *myself, yourself, himself, herself, itself, ourselves, yourselves,* and *themselves* are required replacements for a noun or pronoun when the second noun or pronoun in the same sentence is identical with the first, or has the same referent, as the first noun or pronoun in the sentence:

> *The cat found *the cat* on a hot tin roof.
>
> The cat found *itself* on a hot tin roof.

T/reflexive is used to avoid ambiguity:

John got *him* a new suit.

John got *himself* a new suit.

In these sentences *him* refers to someone other than John; *himself* refers to John, the subject of the sentence.

When a pronoun is the subject of a sentence the same rule applies:

She hurt herself. — not:

*She hurt her. (if *she* and *her* have identical referents)

In the following example we are actually dealing with two sentences. The boundaries of the second sentence are marked by double crosses, (# S # → sentence boundaries):

We told ourselves # We ought not be late. #

The second *we* is the subject of the second sentence, and thus does not come under the T/reflexive rule as does the reflexive *ourselves*.

Occasionally, you may hear a sentence like this:

Mr. Jones and *myself* did this without their consent.

This use of *myself* does not follow the rule we have just learned.

In the following sentences, the reflexive pronouns are used as intensifiers. If the pronoun serves to intensify the whole sentence, it may be moved to the end of the structure by a pronoun movement (T/pro movt):

I, I heard it. =>
T/intens: I myself heard it. =>
T/pro movt: I heard it myself.

We, we don't know # who's coming # =>
T/intens: We ourselves don't know # who's coming # =>
T/pro movt: We don't know ourselves who's coming.

EXERCISE

1. Underline the *personal* pronouns.
2. Identify the personal pronouns as to number, person and case.
3. Indicate whether or not the personal pronoun is employed as a determiner.

	SENTENCE	*Singular* <+> *or* <−>	*Person*	*Case*	*Determiner* <+> *or* <−> *or place holder*
Example:	We freshmen students have formed a club.	<—>	I	Nom	<+ Det>
1.	You students are not understanding me.				
2.	Charles, will you pick up the book, please?				
3.	His house burned down yesterday.				
4.	The book is mine.				
5.	It is my book.				
6.	It is hot in here.				
7.	That girl is her daughter.				
8.	You gave it to me.				

Answers:

1.	You	<— S>	II	N	<+ Det>; me, <+ S>, I, A, <— Det>
2.	you	<+ S>	II	N	<— Det>
3.	His	<+ S>	III	G	<+ Det>
4.	mine	<+ S>	I	G	<+ Det>
5.	it	<+ S>	III	N	<— Det>; my, <+ S>, I, G, <+ Det>
6.	it	<+ S>	III	N	place holder
7.	her	<+ S>	III	G	<+ Det>
8.	you	<+ S>	II	N	<— Det>; it, <+ S>, III, A, <— Det>
	me	<+ S>	I	A	<— Det>

EXERCISE

1. Apply the T/reflexive or T/intensifier transformation to the appropriate noun or pronoun in the sentences below. Write out each sentence.
2. Underline those reflexive form(s) that are used as intensifiers:

1. We, we, wondered about that.

____

____

2. I taught me how to type.

____

3. John, help John to the dessert.

____

4. The robber gave the robber up to the police.

____

5. The idea in the idea is useful.

____

6. We found us in a quandry.

____

7. They drove they mad trying to solve the problem.

____

8. Help you to happiness.

____

Answers:

1. We ourselves wondered about that.
2. I taught myself how to type.
3. John, help yourself to the dessert.
4. The robber gave himself up to the police.
5. The idea in itself is useful.
6. We found ourselves in a quandry.
7. They drove themselves mad trying to solve the problem.
8. Help yourself to happiness. (first pronoun understood)

LESSON 23

Joining Sentences: The Use of Coordinating Conjunctions

ABSTRACT

- Two or more sentences can be joined together with coordinating conjunctions, if the sentences have similar structures and some semantic relationship.
- Two or more nouns, pronouns, verbs, and other classes of words may be joined with coordinating conjunctions.
- Diverse word classes may not be joined with coordinating conjunctions
- The most common connectors are *and, but,* and *or.*
- Two related positive or two related negative statements or questions may be combined by *and.*
- The connector *but* is used when the second sentence contains an idea contrary to what was stated in the first sentence.
- *Or* is used when there are two or more alternatives.
- A deletion transformation (T/del) may be applied to conjoined sentences, thus altering their surface structures but not destroying their original meaning.
- In sentences combining NPs used as subjects, the new subject dominates the verb phrase.
- A form of *do* with *so* may replace a verb phrase when the verb phrase in the second sentence is almost identical to that in the first sentence.

The transformations we have studied thus far can generally be described as the rearrangement of the constituents of sentences based on Patterns I through V. We have transformed such sentences into:

1. yes-no questions
2. negative statements
3. sentences using the passive
4. sentences beginning with *There is/are/was/were . . .*

We have also directed our attention to phrase structure rules for verbs, determiners, and personal pronouns as they apply in sentences and their transformations.

Now we are ready to explore the ways in which sentences may be combined. In your earlier school writing experiences, your teachers have undoubtedly called your attention to "run-on" sentences connected by *and*, which seem to go on and on and on. We all tend to violate the syntactic rule stating that only similar constituents can be joined. We can join two nouns, two pronouns, two adjectives, two adverbs, or two verbs with *and*. We cannot join a pronoun and a verb or a noun and an adverb, or any dissimilar constituents:

*I and ran.

*a girl and quickly

If the sentences have similar structures, we can also join them with connectors (coordinating conjunctions), the most common of which are *and*, *but*, and *or*. Besides, the sentences must bear some semantic relationship to each other. It would be folly to teach hearing-impaired children to say:

The cat is asleep, and John is funny.

Teachers of hearing-impaired children must bear in mind that lexical meanings and thought relationships are closely tied to the teaching of all syntax. Only logical semantic relationships should be used when demonstrating syntactical rules.

Children with hearing impairments and/or language learning disabilities will have to learn the differences in the use of the various connectors when compounding sentences. For instance, two related positive or two related negative statements may be combined by *and:*

The girls went to homemaking class.
The boys went to woodworking class. =>
The girls went to homemaking class *and* the boys went to woodworking class.

The girls don't mind the snow.
They don't object to walking to class in the cold. =>
The girls don't mind the snow *and* they don't object to walking to class in the cold.

The structure of these conjoined sentences has not changed. Only the punctuation changes. In the following sentences, the second sentence, enclosed by double crossed bars only for purposes of clarification, contains an idea contrary to what was expected, thus requiring the use of *but* as the conjunction. You may recall that the boundary of a sentence is written # S #:

The girls *went* to homemaking, # *but* the boys *didn't go* to woodworking today. #

The suit *was* the right size, # *but* I didn't like the color. #

I didn't want to see the movie, # *but* I went to please them. #

Linda *fell*, # *but* she didn't cry. #

Or is used when there are one or more alternatives, expressed in two or more sentences:

He can stay.
He can leave. =>
He can stay *or* he can leave.

We must finish now.
We'll be late for gym. =>
We must finish now *or* we'll be late for gym.

I must leave.
I'll start to laugh. =>
I must leave *or* I'll start to laugh.

The relationship of the ideas in sentences containing *or* is less obvious than those containing *and* and *but,* so it becomes especially necessary to clarify for hearing-impaired children the conditions under which *or* may be used.

EXERCISE

Combine the two sentences with the appropriate connector: *and, but, or.*

1. The sun was shining.
The snow wasn't melting. =>

---

2. It was cold.
The wind was blowing. =>

---

3. It was cold.
The wind wasn't blowing. =>

---

4. Shall I get up?
Shall I go back to bed? =>

---

5. The filling station was closed.
Jack was out of gas. =>

---

6. He wouldn't go to bed.
He wouldn't do his homework. =>

Answers: 1. but 2. and 3. but 4. or 5. and 6. and/or (depending on meaning)

Sometimes we can shorten sentences combined by coordinating conjunctions through deletion yet not destroy their original meaning. As an example, we can combine:

John ran.
John fell. =>
John ran and John fell. =>

The second *John* may be deleted since it is recoverable. Our sentence now reads:
John ran and fell.

In the next two sentences, we join two coordinate nouns that serve as the subject of the sentence by deleting the recoverable verb *ran:*

Billy ran.
Mary ran. =>
Billy ran and Mary ran. =>
Billy and Mary ran.

In the following sentences, we combine two coordinate nouns that serve as objects of the sentence:

Bill ate his meat.
Bill ate his potatoes. =>

Bill ate his meat and Bill ate his potatoes. =>
Bill ate his meat and potatoes.

In sentences combining NPs used as subjects with the copula *be* or with verbs in the third person singular of the present tense, the new subject dominates the verb:

The ball *is* here.
The bat *is* here. =>
The ball *is* here and the bat *is* here. =>
The ball and bat *are* here.

John walk*s* to school.
Mary walk*s* to school. =>
John walk*s* to school and Mary walk*s* to school. =>
John and Mary *walk* to school.

When a verb phrase in the second sentence is almost identical to the one in the first sentence, it cannot always be deleted but may be replaced by a form of *do + so:*

The astronauts practiced their routines.
Later, the astronauts practiced their routines again. =>

We can combine these sentences with *and* because they have similar structures and because they are related in meaning:

> The astronauts practiced their routines and later the astronauts practiced their routines again. =>

We are able to deleate the NP, astronauts, from the second sentence wtih T/del:

> The astronauts *practiced their routines* and later *practiced their routines* again.

We still have two identical verb phrases in this sentence except for the adverbial modifier *again,* but we cannot remove the second verb phrase:

> *The astronauts practiced their routines and later again.

In sentences such as these, we have a replacement device which employs a form of *do* + *so* for the verb phrase:

> The astronauts practiced their routines and later *did so* again.

In the following sets of sentences notice that when the subject of the second sentence is not the same as that of first sentence, the subject is transposed to follow *so do:*

> John plays football. =>
> I play football.
> *John plays football and I do so.
> John plays football and so do I.
>
> Anita wears size 9 shoes. =>
> Alice wears size 9 shoes.
> Anita wears size 9 shoes and so does Alice.

When the copula is the verb in a sentence coordinated by *and,* a deletion of the second verb requires that an appropriate form of the copula be used with *so,* as in *so am, so was,* and *so were:*

> Alice was tired. =>
> Anna Belle was tired.
> Alice was tired and so was Anna Belle.

Such replacements are very commonly encountered in reading materials and should be called to the attention of and clarified for children with hearing impairments.

EXERCISE

Combine these sentences using T/coord conj, T/del, and T/do-so, and replace nouns with pronouns where appropriate.

1. The girls put on their new dresses.
   The girls modeled their new dresses for their mothers. =>

2. The girls made tea.
   The girls forgot the sugar for the tea. =>

3. We can go now.
   We can wait for Dad a little longer. =>

4. Betty can babysit for me.
   Betty can do my shopping for me.

5. We ought to go.
   We should wait for Dad. =>

6. After school, the boys played baseball.
   The boys played baseball again after supper. =>

7. Where is the ball?
   Where is the bat? =>

Answers: (Order may vary slightly.)

1. The girls put on their new dresses and modeled them for their mothers.
2. The girls made tea, but forgot the sugar for it.
3. We can go now or wait for Dad a little longer.
4. Betty can babysit for me or do my shopping.
5. We ought to go, but we should wait for Dad.
6. The boys played baseball after school, and did so again after supper.
7. Where are the ball and bat?

The rules for combining sentences with coordinating conjunctions, *and, but,* and *or,* are relatively simple for language-impaired children to understand. However, some difficulty may arise from a lack of understanding of the semantic relationships required for conjoining sentences. The children must be given many opportunities to make choices concerning the connectors to use and the kinds of sentences that may logically and meaningfully be put together.

LESSON 24

Sentence Embedding: Relative Clauses

ABSTRACT

- Every NP, no matter where it appears in a sentence, can support an embedded sentence.
- A transformation that allows a sentence to be embedded after an NP in another sentence is called the relative clause transformation (T/rel).
- In the T/rel transformation, a noun is relativized by replacing it with a relative pronoun (rel pro).
- The relative pronouns are *who, whom, whose, which,* and *that. That* is the most versatile of the relative pronouns.
- *S/rel* indicates the presence of an embedded relative clause, or of a sentence that is to be transformed to a relative clause.
- # S # → sentence boundary.
- Some relative clauses restrict or limit the meaning of the NP they follow and are called *restrictive* clauses.
- Some relative clauses provide additional information about the NP they follow and are called *nonrestrictive* clauses.
- Rules involved in the T/rel transformation:

    1. The nouns in S/rel and in the matrix sentence, the sentence in which another is embedded, must be identical.

2. The grammatically correct relative pronoun must be chosen as a replacement of the noun.
3. *That* may alternate with *which, who,* and *whom,* but not with *whose.*
4. When the relative pronoun is not in the subject position in S/rel, the relative pronoun movement (T/rel pro movt) is necessary to bring the pronoun to the beginning of S/rel.
5. Relative pronouns may be deleted when they are not subjects of S/rel.
6. When the relative pronoun is the object of a preposition, the preposition may remain at the end of the sentence or the entire prepositional phrase may engage in the relative pronoun movement (T/prep + rel pro movt).
7. *That* may not replace a relative that stays with the preposition.

The lengthening of sentences is not at all limited to the conjoining of two sentences with coordinating conjunctions. English has a device that allows a new sentence to be embedded directly into a noun phrase. Every NP, no matter where it appears in a sentence, can support such a sentence. The transformation that allows this operation to take place is called the *relative clause transformation* (T/rel). It is a very important transformation because a whole family of transformations is derived from it. In Lesson 25, we will investigate them.

The relative clause transformation may be applied as many times as there are NPs in the original sentence or in the embedded sentences. For instance, here is a sentence containing no less than six relative clauses:

> The Wisconsin legislature/*which met in 1912*/selected the Normal School/*which was located in Milwaukee,*/*which had a well-established day school for the deaf,*/to begin a program/*that would train teachers of the deaf*/*whose education had previously been exclusively the prerogative of residential schools for the deaf*/*which were large enough to engage in in-service training of teachers.*

Just as run-on sentences are uninteresting and boring, so are sentences containing too many relative clauses. Moreover, one has to search too hard for meaning to tolerate the lengthening of sentences inordinately by the embedding of relative clauses. Sentence organization is a matter of style as well as grammar. While T/rel quite commonly is used in oral English, its impact and importance are felt mainly in written English. Consequently, if hearing-impaired children are to grow in competence in their written language, they must become conversant with this very important transformation.

In the T/rel transformation, the NP in the insert or embedded sentence is relativized by replacing Det + N with a relative pronoun. Sentence Tree 22 illustrates the embedding of the sentence: *Students must work* in the NP of the sentence: *Students should carry fewer credits.*

Sentence Tree 22: Students who must work should carry fewer credits.

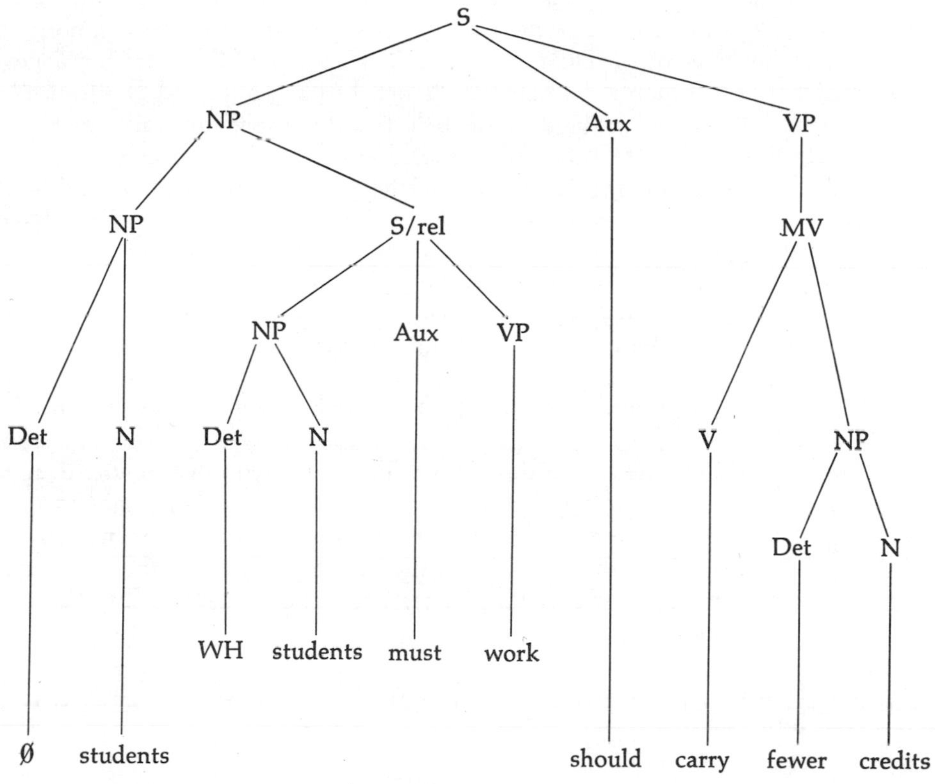

In the tree, *WH* stands for the feature that allows for the replacement of the noun by a relative pronoun. In the following sentences we see how the NP, *Students*, is replaced by the relative, *who*, in the sentence that becomes the relative clause (S/rel):

> Students # S/rel # should carry fewer credits.
> Students # Students must work # should carry fewer credits. =>
> Students who must work should carry fewer credits.

A relative clause like the one above restricts or limits the meaning of the NP it follows. Notice that it is not set off by commas. Suppose you were asked to identify the two sentences which make up the following example:

> All children who are five years old by September 1 may enter kindergarten at the beginning of the fall term.

This would not be difficult, for it is evident that the two sentences are:

> All children may enter kindergarten at the beginning of the fall term.
>
> All children are five years old by September 1.

These sentences are grammatically correct but neither is "true" in the sense that all children may enter kindergarten, or that all children are five years old by September 1. But when the second of these sentences is used to qualify and restrict the meaning of *all children* in the first sentence, the total message becomes factually acceptable. Sometimes we ask hearing-impaired children to put two sentences together for the sake of drill, but this procedure falls far short of helping children understand the process of relativization. If it becomes necessary to explain how one sentence may be inserted into another sentence, it is very important that only sentences that make up total meaningful wholes be employed in the demonstration. Otherwise, children may be satisfied in their own productions to write sentences with irrelevant clauses such as:

My father who is a man is working for the Electric Company.

With this caution in mind, we may proceed to look at some details of the T/rel transformation.

The first rule to note is that the noun to be relativized must be identical with the noun in the sentence into which the relative clause (S/rel) is embedded. The sentence that receives the clause is referred to as the matrix sentence. In your earlier school grammar you may have called such a sentence the independent clause. The determiners in the noun phrases need not be identical but the nouns must be the same:

Matrix: Some registration procedures will be changed next term
S/rel: Some of the procedures are now outdated. } ==>
Some registration procedures *which* are now outdated will be changed next term.

The second rule states that when the relative pronoun *who* replaces a noun and its determiner, it is necessary to choose one of its three forms: *who, whose,* or *whom.* The choice will depend not only on the function of the NP that the relative pronoun is to replace but also on the features of the noun in that NP. Table 8 indicates the features of the relative pronouns which govern their selection for use in relative clauses.

Table 8. Selection of Correct Relative Pronoun to Replace NP

Noun Feature	*<+ Nominative>*	*<+ Genitive>*	*<+ Accusative>*
<+ human>	who	whose	whom
<− human> <± animate>	which		which
<+ human> <± animate>	that		that

When the subject of S/rel is <+ human> and is identical to the NP in the matrix sentence, then *who* (nominative case) is chosen. Later in this lesson we will amplify this rule to include the relative, *that*, as a replacement for *who*. The following examples illustrate how relative pronouns are incorporated into sentences:

> Matrix: Mrs. Truex advises some students.
> S/rel: The students major in the education of the deaf. =>
> Mrs. Truex advises some students *who* major in the education of the deaf.

Which is chosen in the next sentence because the NP carries the feature <— animate>.

> Matrix: Dr. Strawn has directed the program.
> S/rel: The program prepares teachers of the deaf. =>
> Dr. Strawn has directed the program *which* prepares teachers of the deaf.

The relative pronoun *that* may be alternated with either *who, whom,* or *which.* Such flexibility is desirable when it is natural, expedient, or necessary to add variety to expression. We may say:

> Mrs. Truex advises students *that* major in the education of the deaf.
>
> This afternoon Mrs. Truex will see the students *that* she advises.
>
> Dr. Strawn directs the program *that* prepares teachers of the deaf.

When the relative pronoun, *whose,* is used in S/rel, it replaces a <+ human> genitive determiner. The determiner must have as its referent the noun in the matrix sentence:

> Matrix: That's the girl.
> S/rel: I forgot her name. —>
> That's the girl whose name I forgot.

This set of sentences also illustrates the third rule for the use of relative pronouns. When the relative pronoun is not in the first position in S/rel, the relative pronoun movement (T/rel pro movt) brings the pronoun to the beginning of the relative clause. If the relative pronoun replaces a genitive form, the noun in S/rel moves with the relative pronoun. The steps taken to achieve the correct embedding in the above set of sentences are as follows:

> That's the girl. # I forgot her name. # =>
> T/rel pro: *That's the girl # I forgot *whose* name. # =>
> T/rel pro movt: That's the girl whose name I forgot.

Here are two more illustrations of this rule; the relative pronouns *whom* and *which* are used:

Matrix: She is a student.
S/rel: I know the student very well. =>
T/rel pro: *She is a student # I know whom very well. # =>
T/rel pro movt: She is a student whom I know very well.
Matrix: Here is a composition.
S/rel: She wrote the composition. =>
T/rel pro: *Here is a composition # she wrote which. # =>
T/rel pro movt: Here is a composition which she wrote.

That may replace *whom* and *which* in these sentences:

She is a student that I know very well.

Here is a composition that she wrote.

Another rule tells us that relative pronouns that are not subjects of S/rel may be optionally deleted since their removal does not disturb the meaning of sentences. In applying T/rel pro del to the above two sentences, we still maintain grammatically and semantically correct sentences:

She is a student I know very well.

Here is a composition she wrote.

T/rel pro del does not apply to sentences in which the relative pronoun is a subject:

Mrs. Truex advises some students *who* major in the education of the deaf.

*Mrs. Truex advises some students major in the education of the deaf.

The next rule states that when the NP is the object of a preposition, the preposition may remain at the end of the sentence or the entire prepositional phrase may engage in the relative pronoun movement (T/prep + rel pro movt). *Whom* or *which* cannot be replaced by *that* when the preposition moves with the relative pronoun.

Matrix: He is someone.
S/rel: I owe allegiance to someone. =>
*He is someone # I owe allegiance to someone. # =>
T/rel pro: *He is someone # I owe allegiance *to whom*. # =>
T/rel pro movt: He is someone *whom* I owe allegiance *to*. =>
T/prep + rel pro movt: He is someone *to whom* I owe allegiance.

We can also say:

He is someone *that* I owe allegiance *to*.

but not:

*He is someone to that I owe allegiance.

Another example follows:

Matrix: The motion was adopted. =>
S/rel: We made a few additions to the motion.
*The motion was adopted # we made a few additions to the motion. # =>
T/rel pro: *The motion # we made a few additions *to which* # was adopted. =>
T/rel pro movt: The motion *which* we made a few adidtions *to* was adopted. =>
T/prep + rel pro movt: The motion *to which* we made a few additions was adopted.

We can also say:

*The motion *that* we made a few additions *to* was adopted.

but not:

The motion *to that* we made a few additions was adopted.

EXERCISE

1. Without further transforming the sentences below, underline the relative pronouns for which *that* may alternate.
2. In those instances where *that* may *not* alternate, write the rule that does not allow the substitution.

Examples:

A. I like the dress which you made.
I like the dress that you made.

B. He wrote a poem for which he was paid.
That may not be substituted for *which* when the preposition moves with the relative pronoun.

1. He read the letter which he got this morning.

2. He never answered the letter to which he should have replied at once.

3. The baby whose shoe fell off couldn't walk without falling.

---

4. Everyone who heard the lecture thought it was great.

---

5. The cookies which I made this morning disappeared like magic.

---

6. I couldn't find any of the bargains which I went downtown for.

Answers:

Underlined: 1. which 4. who 5. which 6. which
Rules: 2. *That* may not substitute for which when the preposition moves with the relative pronoun. 3. *That* can substitute for *who, whom,* or *which,* but not for *whose.*

It is important to remember that in all the illustrations thus far the relative clause restricts or limits the meaning of the NPs. No special punctuation is required for restrictive clauses.

EXERCISE

Relativize the italicized noun phrases in these sentences. Indicate which of these transformations you used in the process:

1. T/rel pro	3. T/rel pro deletion
2. T/rel pro movement	4. T/prep + rel pro movement

Examples:

I ordered *the book.*

I ordered which ___1___

which I ordered ___2___

I ordered ___3___

1. *The motor* races.

_______________ ____

_______________ ____

_______________ ____

_______________ ____

2. *The girls* acted coy.

3. *The students* will graduate.

4. He gave *the book* to his father.

5. I don't know *those people.*

6. He was loyal *to the coach.*

7. He paid $50.00 for *the coat.*

8. I don't remember *the author's name.*

______________________________ ______

______________________________ ______

______________________________ ______

______________________________ ______

Answers:

1. which races, 1
2. who acted coy, 1
3. who will graduate, 1
4. he gave which to his father, 1
   which he gave to his father, 2
   he gave to his father, 3
5. I don't know whom, 1
   whom I don't know, 2
   I don't know, 3
6. he was loyal to whom, 1
   whom he was loyal to, 2
   he was loyal to, 3
   to whom he was loyal, 4
7. he paid $50.00 for which, 1
   which he paid $50.00 for, 2
   he paid $50.00 for, 3
8. I don't remember whose name, 1
   whose name I don't remember, 2

Sometimes relative clauses are used not to limit or restrict the meaning of an NP but rather to add more information about the NP. This kind of relative clause is called a nonrestrictive clause and is set off by commas.

> The University of Wisconsin-Milwaukee, which has prepared teachers of the deaf for more than fifty years, has sent its graduates to every state in the Union.

In this sentence the relative clause could be omitted without disturbing the meaning of the matrix sentence. The matrix is an adequate factual statement with or without an embedded sentence:

> The University of Wisconsin-Milwaukee has sent its graduates to every state in the Union.

Here are two more sentences containing nonrestrictive relative clauses:

> The Department of Education for Exceptional Children, which was established in 1929 at the University of Wisconsin-Milwaukee, now prepares teachers of the deaf, the mentally retarded, the emotionally disturbed, and teachers of children with language learning disorders.
>
> He belongs to the Council for Exceptional Children, which is a professional organization for teachers of the handicapped.

The relative pronoun *that* cannot be substituted for *who* or *which* is nonrestrictive clauses:

> *He belongs to the Council for Exceptional Children that is a professional organization for teachers of the handicapped.

EXERCISE

Punctuate these sentences and tell which are restrictive (Res) and which are nonrestrictive (Nonres) relative clauses.

1. The book to which I referred has disappeared from the library. ________
2. Our library which has 150,000 volumes is open twenty-four hours a day. ________
3. Phil who looks exactly like his twin brother likes to play tricks on people. ________
4. The author whose name I don't recall made some good points. ________
5. Where is the woman who cleans this part of the building? ________
6. I wish I could meet President Flexnor whom I greatly admire. ________
7. Elevated Train #53 which stops here is a local. ________

Answers:

1. Res
2. Nonres; commas after *library* and *volumes*
3. Nonres; commas after *Phil* and *brother*
4. Res
5. Res
6. Nonres; comma after *Flexnor*
7. Nonres; commas after *#53* and *here*

LESSON 25

Relative Clause Reduction: Noun Modifiers

ABSTRACT

- The relative clause results from the embedding of a sentence in a noun phrase, which, in turn, creates the possibility of a great many other transformations.
- These transformations all involve *be* and result in a variety of noun modifiers.
- Relative clause reductions include the following transformations:

    1. T/rel pron del: deletion of the relative pronoun
    2. T/rel pron + *be* del: deletion of the relative pronoun and the form of *be* following it
    3. T/Adj shift: shift of adjective in *NP + be + Adj* to a prenominal position (MN) in matrix sentence
    4. T/participle shift: shift of participle to a prenominal position in matrix sentence

- When the VP in S/rel contains a form of *be,* or is based on either the progressive aspect or passive transformation, the S/rel sentence may partake in the relative clause reduction process.
- The appearance of prenominal modifiers can occur by embedding S/rel based on:

    1. *NP + be + Adj*
    2. when *NP + be + ing + V* is not followed by an adverbial modifier
    3. when nothing follows the verb in T/pass, *NP + be + en + V*

- The appearance of postnominal modifiers can occur by embedding S/rels based on:

    $NP + be + Adv_p$
    $NP + be + ing + V_t + NP_1 + (Adv)$
    $NP_2 + be + en + V_t + by + NP_1 + (Adv)$
    $NP + be + NP$

- A single word, a coordinated group, or a series of words usually precedes a noun. Only coordinated groups follow nouns.
- A phrase or clause follows a noun.

The relative clause that results from the embedding of a sentence in a noun phrase is the parent of a great many transformations. This family of transformations, all involving *be,* creates a variety of noun modifiers in the NP. Let us look at these transformations one by one.

We will start by embedding sentences based on pattern III, *NP* + *be* + *Adj:*

Matrix: He signed up for the course. (+ S rel)
S/rel: The course is easy. =>
*He signed up for the course # the course is easy. # =>
T/rel pro: He signed up for the course, which is easy.

The relative clause may be reduced by deleting the relative pronoun, *which,* and *is* which follows it (T/rel pro + *be* del):

T/rel pro + *be* del: *He signed up for the course easy.

This resulting sentence is incorrect until we shift the adjective to the prenominal position, that is, to a position before the noun (MN) by using the adjectival shift transformation (T/Adj shift) thus making the sentence syntactically correct:

T/Adj shift: He signed up for the easy course.

In like manner, S/rel sentences containing forms of *be (is, are, was, were)* in the VP, may partake in the relative clause reduction process. This occurs when the verb phrase in S/rel is based on either the progressive aspect or the passive transformation, and is *not* followed by any other constituent:

Matrix: The students (+S rel) were warned not to create a disturbance.
S/rel: The students were congregating. =>
*The students # the students were congregating # were warned not to create a disturbance. =>
T/rel pron: The students who were congregating were warned not to create a disturbance.
T/rel pron + *be* del: The students congregating were warned not to create a disturbance. =>
T/Adj shift: The congregating students were warned not to create a disturbance.

In the last sentence the present participle became a prenominal modifier, that is, a modifier preceding a noun (MN).

In the next set of sentences, the passive transformation has already been applied to S/rel:

Matrix: The road (+ S rel) ran through the center of the campus. =>

T/pass + S/rel: The road was blocked.

*The road # the road was blocked # ran through the center of the campus. =>

T/rel: The road which was blocked ran through the center of the campus. =>

T/rel pron + *be* del: *The road blocked ran through the center of the campus.

The shift of the past participle *blocked* to the prenominal position makes the sentence grammatical. The past participle may become a prenominal modifier just as the present participle may become a noun modifier:

T/part shift: The blocked road ran through the center of the campus.

Prenominal modifiers, along with determiners, may appear in a series before nouns:

The student's broken-down, battered old car finally had to be junked.

Will that milling, shouting crowd converge on the stadium?

If a two-word intransitive verb is composed of a verb and an adverb, the adverb stays with the verb in the reduction process. T/rel pro + be del is applied to the embedded sentence below:

Matrix: The players (+ S/rel) were second string men. =>

S/rel: The players were warming up.

*The players # the players were warming up # were second string men. =>

T/rel pro: The players who were warming up were second string men. =>

T/del pro + be del: The players warming up were second string men.

Since the two words *warming up* make a phrase, they remain in the postnominal position.

Two-word verbs may also become prenominal modifiers as in these sentences. They are usually past participles and are hyphenated in this position:

The warmed-over food was not very tasty.

The ripped-out seams began to fray.

These wrapped-up packages should be mailed.

When two or more S/rels are coordinated and embedded in a matrix to which a deletion transformation is then applied, the resulting modifier may remain in the postnominal position. Notice that the coordinated postnominal modifiers are set off by commas in the next sentence. In speech they are distinguished by stress.

Matrix: The car (+ S/rel and S/rel 2) drove away on its own power.
S/Rel 1: The car was ancient.
S/Rel 2: The car was battered up.
*The car # the car was ancient and the car was battered up # drove away on its own power.
T/rel pro: The car which was ancient and which was battered up drove away on its own power.
T/rel pro + be del: The car, ancient and battered up, drove away on its own power.
T/Adj shift: The ancient and battered-up car drove away on its own power.

We may apply still another deletion to remove the coordinator, *and*. The result is a series of words before the noun:

The ancient, battered-up car drove away on its own power.

Postnominal adjective modifiers are used in coordinated patterns. A single adjective, on the other hand, does not follow a noun, but single adjectives, coordinated adjectives, and adjectives in a series are all found in prenominal positions.

EXERCISE

Write out the sentences from which these transformed sentences were derived:

Example:

The attractive coeds were selling kisses.

The coeds were attractive.

The coeds were selling kisses.

1. The charred remnants called up sad memories.

____

____

2. That attentive young man bores her.

3. Here are the missing keys.

4. The exhausted players called for time out.

5. That was a thrilling nerve-wracking game.

6. The dean suggested intensive and sincere participation in the project.

7. These are recent, unsettling developments.

Answers:

1. The remnants were charred. The memories were sad. The remnants called up memories.
2. That man is young. That man bores her. That man is attentive.
3. Here are the keys. The keys are missing.
4. The players called for time out. The players were exhausted.
5. That was a game. The game was thrilling. The game was nerve-wracking.
6. The dean suggested participation in the project. The participation is intensive. The participation is sincere. The participation is intensive and sincere.
7. These are developments. The developments are recent. The developments are unsettling.

Some prenominally placed present participial modifiers do not seem to be generated from the phrase structure *NP* + *be* + *ing* + *V* but rather from another base, as in:

> There is room *for standing only.* => standing room only
>
> Those fixtures are *for lighting.* => lighting fixtures
>
> The room is *for waiting.* => waiting room

Postnominal modifiers result from embedding sentences based on *NP* + *be* + Adv_p, when Adv_p → prepositional phrase, on *NP* + *VP* + *NP*, when VP → *be* + *ing*, and on passive sentences which all contain a form of *be:*

> Matrix: Please bring me the book. (+ S/rel) =>
> S/rel: The book is on your desk.
> T/rel pro: Please bring me the book that is on your desk. =>
> T/rel pro + be del: Please bring me the book on your desk.
>
> Matrix: The class (+ S/rel) has only a few living members. =>
> S/rel: The class is planning a reunion.
> T/rel pro: The class which is planning a reunion has only a few living members. =>
> T/rel pro + be del: The class, planning a reunion, has only a few living members.
>
> Matrix: The meeting (+ S rel) finally proceeded. =>
> S/rel: The meeting was interrupted by a series of questions.
> T/rel pro: The meeting which was interrupted by a series of questions finally proceeded. =>
> T/rel pro + be del: The meeting, interrupted by a series of questions, finally proceeded.

EXERCISE

Apply the necessary deletions to arrive at the greatest possible reduction of each relative clause. Write the transformed sentences on the lines provided and be sure to punctuate them correctly. In the space to the right indicate the transformations you have used. Cross out the words you expect to delete.

1. T/rel pro del
2. T/rel pro + be del
3. T/Adj shift or participle shift.

Example:

The trails ~~which were~~ blazed by the pioneers hardly resemble the highways we travel today. ____2____

The trails blazed by the pioneers hardly resemble the highways

we travel today.

1. The parade which was scheduled for the day before Homecoming was rained out.

2. Mary urged the scouts who were working for merit badges to finish them.

3. The game which was exciting ended in a tie that disappointed everyone.

4. He made a final effort which was gratifying.

5. The two dozen roses which he sent her were drooping when they arrived.

6. The convocation which was interesting and which was well planned celebrated the school's anniversary.

7. The four officers who were recently elected will take over at the next meeting.

Answers:

1. The parade ~~which was~~ scheduled for the day before Homecoming was rained out. The parade scheduled for the day before Homecoming was rained out. (2)
2. Mary urged the scouts ~~who were~~ working for merit badges to finish them. Mary urged the scouts working for merit badges to finish them. (2)
3. The game ~~which was~~ exciting ended in a tie which disappointed everyone. The exciting game ended in a tie which disappointed everyone. (2, 3)

4. He made a final effort ~~which was~~ gratifying. He made a final gratifying effort. (2, 3)
5. The two dozen roses ~~which~~ he sent her were drooping when they arrived. The two dozen roses he sent her were drooping when they arrived. (1)
6. The convocation ~~which was~~ interesting and ~~which was~~ well planned celebrated the school's anniverstary. The interesting and well-planned convocation celebrated the school's anniversary. (2, 3)
7. The four officers ~~who were~~ recently elected will take over at the next meeting. The four recently elected officers will take over at the next meeting. (2, 3)

The embedding of S/rel based on Pattern III (NP + be + NP) results in another kind of noun modifier, the appositive. The same transformations we have been discussing also apply to this series of sentences:

> The coach (+ S/rel) received an award. =>
> The coach was a great fellow.
> *The coach # the coach was a great fellow # received an award. =>
> The coach, who was a great fellow, received an award.
> The coach, a great fellow, received an award. (appositive → a great fellow.)

We may make sentence modifiers of appositives preceding the NP by shifting the appositive to the beginning of the sentence as in:

> The Pennsylvania Limited, a fast train, made its final run last night. =>
> A fast train, the Pennsylvania Limited, made its final run last night.

In the same way, we may shift participial phrases to the beginning of sentences:

> The team, waiting for the gun to go off, was poised for play. =>
> Waiting for the gun to go off, the team was poised for play.

We have learned how dispensable *be* is in transformations involving noun modifiers. This information should help you, the teacher, to understand the origin of the various kinds of noun modifiers. Language-impaired children, in their first language-learning experiences cannot be expected to understand these transformations. They will rather learn and practice the patterns involving noun modifiers which *you* know have resulted from the transformations. If they understand (1) that a single word, series of words, or coordinated groups of words may precede a noun and (2) that a phrase or clause follows a noun, they will have learned a great deal to help them use noun modifiers correctly. If they then learn that there are permissive shifts of these modifiers, their ability to understand what they read will be enhanced.

LESSON 26

Features of Adjectives and a Phrase Structure Rule for Prenominal Modifiers

ABSTRACT

- A modifier that precedes a noun → MN.
- Prenominal modifiers may be adjectives, verbal forms, or nouns.
- Adjectives have some of the same features as verbs; some cannot be used in request sentences or in the progressive aspect.
- *Complements* are functional linguistic units which may follow nouns, verbs, and adjectives.
- Some adjectives may be followed by complements.
- Adjectives may be preceded by qualifiers, or limiting words, such as, *extremely, somewhat, quite, pretty, very,* and others.
- Adjectival quality may be tested by placing the word to be tested in the open slots in the following sentence frame:

  The very __________*(noun)* is very __________.

- Nouns may legitimately serve as prenominal modifiers. They are called *noun adjuncts.*
- A phrase structure rule for prenominal modifiers is:

  MN → descriptive adjective + color + noun adjunct + N

- Many adjectives are derived from nouns and verbs.
- It is important that children with language problems learn how words of one form-class may be changed to another form-class by the addition of suffixes.

In Lessons 24 and 25, we discovered how adjectives and verbal forms originated as modifiers of nouns. We have also learned that determiners precede these modifiers in noun phrases. To refresh your memory, do the following exercise.

EXERCISE

In the spaces provided under each phrase write:

I. The words included in the determiner system.
II. The words that are prenominal modifiers. Indicate whether the modifier of the noun (MN) is an adjective (A) or a verbal form (V).
III. The noun.

Example:

their amusing antics

I. their ____ II. amusing (V) ____ III. antics ____

1. some of the milling crowd

I. ____ II. ____ III. ____

2. the first two valid points

I. ____ II. ____ III. ____

3. most of their early attempts

I. ____ II. ____ III. ____

4. only one of the regular players

I. ____ II. ____ III. ____

5. some of the most unruly spectators

I. ____ II. ____ III. ____

6. the unyielding umpire

I. ____ II. ____ III. ____

7. that cheering throng

I. ____ II. ____ III. ____

8. the three side-lined players

I. ____ II. ____ III. ____

9. a screeching halt

I. ____ II. ____ III. ____

10. screaming fans

I. ____ II. ____ III. ____

Answers:

I		II		III	
1.	some of the	1.	milling (V)	1.	crowds
2.	the first two	2.	valid (A)	2.	points
3.	most of their	3.	early (A)	3.	attempts
4.	only one of the	4.	regular (A)	4.	players
5.	some of the most	5.	unruly (A)	5.	spectators
6.	the	6.	unyielding (V)	6.	umpire
7.	that	7.	cheering (V)	7.	throng
8.	the three	8.	side-lined (V)	8.	players
9.	a	9.	screeching (V)	9.	halt
10.	Ø	10.	screaming (V)	10.	fans

We have spoken about adjectives from time to time throughout this book without trying to define them in any traditional sense. In this lesson we will point out some of their features and present a phrase structure rule for the order of modifiers appearing before nouns. We will also discuss the derivation of adjectives from other form-class words.

Some linguists think that adjectives are more like verbs than like any other form-class words. For instance, there are some adjectives, just as there are some verbs, that cannot be used in request sentences or in the progressive aspect. We cannot request that someone:

> *Be tired/thirsty/lonesome/afraid. (adjective)
>
> *Own this dog/Belong to Belinda. (verb)

nor can we say:

> *He is being cold/hungry/crazy/unhappy. (adjective)
>
> *It is containing a powerful drug./She is resembling her mother. (verb)

But we can say:

> Be quiet/honest/patient/liberal/good. (adjective)
>
> Get on with it./Try this recipe./Open the door. (verb)
>
> He is being quiet/patient/obnoxious/lazy. (adjective)
>
> He is ordering a new car./He is waiting for it. (verb)

Besides, some adjectives, like some verbs, may be followed by an additional linguistic unit called a complement, a term used to designate the function of a constituent rather than its structure. Complements will be discussed more fully in Lesson 30. The following sentences contain complements following the adjective and the verb and are included here merely to point out similarities in the appearance of their surface patterns:

The dean is *eager to see you.*
The dean *wants to see you.*

He is *happy that you have returned safely.*
He *knows that you have returned safely.*

Adjectives have a feature that allows them to be preceded by words like *extremely, exceedingly,* and *enormously.* These words qualify or limit the meanings of adjectives following them:

extremely interesting movies

exceedingly capable teachers

enormously succesful books

There are a few more qualifying words with which we should become acquainted. They have the role of indicating the degree of meaning applicable to the adjective. These same words may also pattern with adverbs:

a bit	mighty	so
a little	quite	somewhat
enough	pretty	very
indeed	rather	

All of the above words precede the adjective, except for *enough,* which follows it; *indeed* may precede or follow an adjective.

a bit disturbed	rather stupid
a little inconsistent	so happy
indeed horrified	somewhat deficient
mighty funny	too big
pretty cool	very boring

foolish enough
horrified indeed

Several of the qualifiers may be combined in patterns as in:

a bit too expensive	quite a bit better
quite satisfied indeed	very happy indeed
indeed quite satisfied	rather too old
not so very steady	

A test for adjectival quality consists of placing a word to be tested in the open slots in the following test frame based on pattern IV, *NP + be + Adj,* in which the qualifier *very* has been introduced before the word to be tested:

The very ___________ *(noun)* is very ___________.

The very *big* bird is very *big.*

The very *perishable* produce is very *perishable.*

The very *tired* baby is very *tired.*

The very *charming* woman is very *charming.*

Any word that fits into this frame may be considered an adjective.

Let us analyze the words *text, organ,* and *paper* for adjectival quality by using the test frame:

> *The very *text* book is very *text.*
>
> *The very *organ* recital is very *organ.*
>
> *The very *paper* dress is very *paper.*

Ungrammatical sentences result when we insert the words *text, organ,* and *paper* in the open slots. We cannot use other qualifiers in these phrases either:

> *an extremely organ recital
>
> *an enormously text book
>
> *an exceedingly paper dress

The words *organ, text,* and *paper* are obviously not adjectives. They are nouns which legitimately act as modifiers of other nouns. It is perfectly grammatical to say:

> a text book/two text books
>
> an organ recital/Ø organ recitals
>
> a paper dress/some paper dresses

The words *text, organ,* and *paper* have the feature <± singular> and so must be nouns. They cannot be classified as adjectives, even though they may appear as modifiers of nouns. In a series of prenominal modifiers, the words identifiable as adjectives precede any noun modifier in a sequence. The noun as modifier, or *noun adjunct,* as it is called, is the last in the series and is always contiguous to the noun it modifies, as in:

> an attractive *table* cloth

This order may be stated in rule form:

> MN → descriptive adjective + noun adjunct + noun

For want of a better term, we shall designate words used to describe feelings, sizes, shapes, sounds, textures, physical and mental qualities, and other categories too numerous to mention, as descriptive adjectives, if they fit into the test frame we have been using:

> Descriptive adjectives → sad, happy, wild, interested, daring, applicable . . .

These phrases further illustrate the rule:

> controversial church services
>
> unexpected audience reaction
>
> winning football teams
>
> handsome totem poles

The rule may be expanded to include words naming colors:

MN → descriptive adjective + color + noun adjunct + noun

long red nylon underwear

large orange paper chrysanthemums

Violation of this order creates an ungrammatical phrase:

*a blue, two-door new convertible

When these prenominal modifiers are combined with determiners and qualifiers in noun phrases, the results may be quite unwieldy:

She sold *only three of the many rather large bedraggled orange paper chrysanthemums.*

It would be safe to say that in normal spoken English we place limits on the number of prenominal elements in noun phrases. Ordinarily we use just a determiner and perhaps one other form-class word, such as an adjective cr a noun, or a determiner and a postnominal phrase modifier. In written language we may increase the number of noun modifiers especially when we are trying to write vivid descriptions. Since the production of long strings of words before nouns requires a sophisticated grasp of a very complex organizational task, it seems wise to suggest that hearing-impaired children not be held to a mastery of the kinds of phrases that even native users of English seldom use.

EXERCISE

Write the following groups of words in their correct order. Then indicate in the form of a rule the category to which each word belongs.

Example:

sable gorgeous a (jacket)

a gorgeous sable jacket

article + descriptive adjective + noun adjunct + N

1. best three girl of my (friends)

______

______

2. cradle old that miserable (snatcher)

______

______

3. my party velvet blue new (dress)

4. red snappy new a (convertible)

5. exam final that (question)

Answers:

1. three of my best girl friends; predet + gen + descr adj + noun adjunct + N
2. that miserable old cradle snatcher; dem + descr adjs + noun adjunct + N
3. my new blue velvet party dress; gen + descr adj + color + noun adjunct + noun adjunct + N
4. a snappy new red convertible; art + descr adjs + color + N
5. that final exam question; dem + descr adj + noun adjunct + N

Many adjectives are derived from nouns and verbs. The most common derivational suffixes used to create adjectives are illustrated in Table 9.

Table 9. Adjective Derivational Suffixes

Suffix	*Example*	*Derived from: N (Noun) V (Verb)*
-able, -ible	bear + -able → bearable	V
	digest + -ible → digestible	V
-al, -ial	derivation + -al → derivational	N
	benefi (t) + -ial → beneficial	N — V
-ant, -ent	continu(e) + -ant → continuant	V
	depend + -ent → dependent	V
-ar	pol(e) + -ar → polar	N
-ary, -ory	illusion + -ary → illusionary	N
	promis(e) + -ory → promissory	V
-en	wax + -en → waxen	N — V
-ful	hope + -ful → hopeful	N — V
	wake + -ful → wakeful	V
-ic	acrobat + -ic → acrobatic	N
-ish	girl + -ish → girlish	N
-ive	attract + -ive → attractive	V
-less	brain + -less → brainless	N
-like	bride + -like → bridelike	N
-ly	coward + -ly → cowardly	N
-ous, ious	nerv(e) + -ous → nervous	N
	spac(e) + -ious → spacious	N
-ual	contract + -ual → contractual	N — V
-y	air + -y → airy	N

A very important aspect of vocabulary study for children with language impairments is learning how words of one form-class may be changed to another form-class by addition of suffixes. This table can serve as a reference when you plan a program including the study of derivational suffixes for adjectives.

LESSON 27

Comparison of Adjectives

ABSTRACT

- A feature of adjectives is that of comparison.
- In general, adjectives of one and two syllables have three forms:

    1. the base form
    2. the comparative, formed by the addition of the suffix *-er*
    3. the superlative, formed by the addition of the suffix *-est*

- Most adjectives of three or more syllables have no comparative or superlative forms and are used with the function words *more* and *most* in structures of comparison.
- The comparative form is used when two NPs are involved in the comparison.
- The use of the comparative form of regular one-syllable adjectives requires the deletion of the function word *more* in the formula, *more + adj + than*, and the addition of *-er* to the stem of the adjective.
- Noun features <+ concrete>, <+ animate>, and <+ human> must be observed when making comparisons.
- Sentence patterns involving the comparative aspects of adjectives vary considerably.
- The superlative form is used when three or more items are involved in the comparison.
- Sentences in which the superlative of adjectives is used often require additional restrictive clauses to clarify the comparison.

A feature of adjectives is that of comparison. In general, adjectives of one and two syllables have three forms: the base form, the comparative form, and the superlative. The inflectional suffix *-er* is added to the base form to make the comparative, and *-est* to make the superlative as in:

rich, richer, richest

However, some two-syllable adjectives like *rugged* require the use of the function words *more* and *most* when they are used in the comparative and superlative degrees:

rugged, more rugged, most rugged

Most adjectives with three or more syllables have no comparative or superlative forms and are used with the function words *more* and *most* in structures of comparison. A few two- or three-syllable adjectives, such as *handsome,* and especially those compounded with the prefix *un-*, as in *uneasy* and *unlikely,* may be used both with the function words or by adding the suffixes *-er* or *-est,* but they are exceptions to the rule.

Table 10 gives examples of one syllable adjectives that are regularly and irregularly compared. Spelling rules must be taught when an inflectional suffix is added to an adjective. The first four adjectives in the table are prototypes of the spelling variations that will be encountered.

Table 10. Comparative and Superlative Forms of Common Adjectives

	Base Form	*Comparative Form* + *-er*	*Superlative Form* + *-est*
	fine	finer	finest
Regular	tall	taller	tallest
Comparison	hot	hotter	hottest
	tricky	trickier	trickiest
	ill — bad	worse	worst
	well — good	better	best
Irregular	less	lesser	least
Comparison	little	less	littlest
			least
	far	farther	farthest
		further	furthest
		inner	innermost
	eastern		
	northern	more northern	northernmost
	southern		
	western		
Not Usually	singular		
Compared	round		

Sentence structures employing the comparative forms of adjectives have their origin in two sentences. The sentence:

The Rockies are more rugged than the Sierras.

is derived from:

The Rockies are rugged.

The Sierras are rugged.

First, we delete the second identical VP, in this case *are,* and then add the comparative signals *more* and *than.* The sentence formula reads:

NP + be + more + adj + than + NP

When we use the comparative form of a one-syllable adjective, we still follow the formula:

more + adj + than

but replace *more + adjective* with *adjective + -er,* so the rule now reads:
adj + -er + than

For example:

The Pan-American Building is tall.
The Empire State Building is tall. =>

*The Empire State Building is more tall than the Pan-American Building. =>
The Empire State Building is tall*er than* the Pan-American Building.

The noun features <+ concrete>, <+ animate>, and <+ human) must be observed in making comparisons, and must apply to both sentences to be used in the transformation. It would be quite incorrect to say:

*My house <— animate> is more beautiful than your kitten <+ animate>.

*Truth <— concrete> is more desirable than oatmeal <+ concrete>.

It is unwise to ask hearing-impaired children to compare items such as ants with elephants, toy trucks with dolls, or birds with fish since these comparisons are not conceptually compatible. We can begin by comparing familiar objects such as one piece of fruit with another in terms of size, sweetness, or ripeness; one cookie with another in terms of size, freshness, or cost; or two pads of paper with each other in terms of thickness or size. We must choose our examples wisely if language-impaired children are to discover what is comparable and what is not.

Children may have some difficulty in understanding that *bigger than* does not always mean *big,* or *smaller than* does not necessarily mean *small.* We may say that a small piece of candy is *bigger than* another small piece, or that one very long string is *shorter than* another long one. The teacher's job is to clarify the semantic relationship of the items being compared and match the vocabulary to be used with the concept presented in the comparison.

The sentence pattern, *NP + be + more + adj + than + NP,* is the one most frequently used when introducing the comparative transformation to hearing-impaired children. However, constructions in which the comparative forms of adjectives may be found vary considerably. The children should be able to identify items being compared in any sentence type. Deletions of parts of verb phrases and replacement of nouns with pronouns in the following sentences may obscure the meanings of the comparisons. Children should be given the opportunity mentally to fill in these deletions or replace the nouns so that they really understand which items are being compared:

> The losers appeared *more dejected* than I had anticipated (they would appear).
>
> He looked *weaker* than he had (looked) for some time.
>
> Mother had never prepared a *more delicious* dinner (than today's).
>
> I expected a *more interesting* lecture (than the one he gave).
>
> The new rifle proved itself a *more potent weapon* (than the old one).

When the superlative degree of an adjective is used, it may appear before a noun in sequential order with determiners just as any other adjective does:

> That is her prettiest dress.
>
> The shortest way home is the sweetest way.
>
> They took their youngest daughter with them.

In these sentences the implication is that there are more than two dresses, two ways, or two daughters involved in the comparisons.

Sometimes it is necessary to add an additional restrictive relative clause after the noun to make the comparison clear. The usual deletions, *T/rel pron + be del,* may be applied where suitable. We sometimes hear sentences like this:

> Phil is the cleverest person!

but normally, it is ncessary to set limits in order to indicate clearly the desired comparisons:

> Phil is the cleverest person (that) I know.
>
> Phil is the cleverest person (who is) alive.
>
> Phil is the most talented young man (who is) among my friends.
>
> The Mississippi is the longest river (which is) in the United States.

EXERCISE

Use the comparative or superlative forms of as many of the following adjectives as possible to complete the sentences:

intolerable	good	cheerful	fast
happy	disorderly	great	

1. That was the ____
____ meeting I ever attended.
2. Five is ____ three.
3. Which do you like ______________________________ pears or peaches?
4. She is the ____
____ person I have ever met.
5. They decided that the ______________________________ way to finish the job was to call in a mason.

Answers:

1. most disorderly, most cheerful, cheerfullest, best, greatest
2. greater than
3. better
4. most intolerable, happiest, most disorderly, best, most cheerful, greatest
5. best, fastest

LESSON 28

Sentence Embedding: Relative Adverbs

ABSTRACT

- The relative adverbs, *when* and *where,* act very much like relative pronouns in the expansion of noun phrases.
- *When* replaces nouns carrying the feature <+ time>.
- *Where* replaces the adverbs *here* and *there* and nouns with the feature <+ place>.
- There is a synonomy between sentences employing the relative adverb, *where,* and the relative pronoun, *which,* as the object of the prepositions, *at, in,* and *on,* in transformations that embed sentences.

We have devoted several lessons to the expansion of the NP and still we have not completed all there is to say about this subject. We have seen how one, two, three, and even half a dozen determiners, predeterminers, and post-determiners may precede a noun and how the relative clause and its family of transformations add both prenominal and postnominal modifiers to the NP.

Besides the relative pronouns, *who, which,* and *that,* the relative adverbs *when* and *where* function to introduce relative clauses. *When* and *where* are also interrogative pronouns, which may introduce embedded questions into sentences, and they are also introductory words for adverbial clauses, but in this lesson we will deal only with their function as relatives.

When replaces nouns carrying the feature <+ time>, as *time, minute, hour, day, week, month,* and *year*. For example.

> He told me about the *time when* he almost died.
>
> This is the *month when* our taxes are due.

In the following set of sentences, the same steps are taken to embed a sentence headed by a relative adverb as those taken to embed any relative clause. The relative adverb, *when,* like the relatives, *whom, which,* and *that,* may also be deleted from the embedded sentence:

Matrix: I remember the day (+ S/rel).
S/rel: We visited Lexington School one day. =>
*I remember the day # we visited Lexington School one day. # =>
T/adv-time-shift: *I remember the day # one day we visited Lexington School. # =>
T/rel adv: I remember the day *when* we visited Lexington School. # =>
T/rel adv del: I remember the day we visited Lexington School.

Where replaces the adverbs *here* and *there* and nouns with the feature <+ place>:

I like it here where I can go snowmobiling.
She went there where the climate is drier than it is here.
This is a school where all the children have excellent speech.

In embedding sentences introduced by the relative adverb, *where,* the noun replaced by the relative may be part of a prepositional phrase beginning with *at, in,* or *on.* The transformation removes the preposition from the sentence structure:

Matrix: This is the building. (+ S/rel)
S/rel: The Child Development Center is housed in the building. =>
*This is the building # the Child Development Center is housed in the building. # =>
T/adv prep phrase shift: This is the building # in the building the Child Development Center is housed. # =>
T/rel adv: This is the building *where* the Child Development Center is housed.

The presence of the preposition, *in,* is required when the regular relative pronoun, *which,* is used as an alternative to the relative adverb, *when:*

This is the building *in which* the Child Development Center is housed.

In Lesson 24 you learned that there is a choice of moving the preposition with the relative pronoun or leaving it at the end of the sentence. Since *where* takes the place of *in which,* it cannot be deleted in this sentence:

*This is the building the Child Center is housed.

It is useful for children to understand that there are these two ways of expressing time and place relationships when embedding sentences:

He'll never forget the day *when* he learned to swim.
He'll never forget the day *on which* he learned to swim.

This is the corner *where* I'll meet you.
This is the corner *on which* I'll meet you.

In these sentences the relative pronoun transformation sounds more formal than the relative adverb transformation does. Children who are advanced enough to use relative clauses should be encouraged to use the relative adverb construction in their speech.

In the following sentences deletions of another sort have taken place:

> Let's move somewhere where we can see better.
> Let's move where we can see better.
> Let's go to someplace where we can see better.
> Let's go to where we can see better.

The general terms *somewhere* and *someplace* can be considered as being in the same category as PRO forms. They are not indispensable in these sentences and can be deleted.

EXERCISE

Rewrite the two sentences using the T/rel pron or T/rel adv transformations, or both, if appropriate. In the space before the sentence indicate the number(s) of the transformation(s) used.

1. T/rel adv_t 2. T/rel adv_p 3. T/rel pron

Example:

The 1940's was a time (+ S rel).
Hearing aids were greatly improved at the time. =>

2. The 1940's was a time when hearing aids were improved.

3. The 1940's was a time in which hearing aids were improved.

1. New York is a city (+ S rel).
   You can find excitement there. =>

2. Do you remember the day?
   The King of England renounced his throne that day. =>

3. New York is a city (+ S rel).
   There are several schools for the deaf. =>

4. I took a bus to Queens (+ S rel). =>
Lexington School is located in Queens.

____

____

5. The month passed all too quickly (+ S rel). =>
I stayed in New York that month.

____

____

6. That was a year (+ S rel).
Many important events occurred in that year.

____

____

Answers:

1. New York is a city where you can find excitement. (2)
New York is a city in which you can find excitement. (3)
2. Do you remember the day when the King of England renounced his throne? (1)
Do you remember the day on which the King of England renounced his throne? (3)
3. New York is a city where there are several schools for the deaf. (2)
New York is a city in which there are several schools for the deaf. (3)
4. I took a bus to Queens where Lexington School is located. (2)
5. The month when I stayed in New York passed all too quickly. (1)
The month in which I stayed in New York passed all too quickly. (3)
6. That was a year when many important events occurred. (1)
That was a year in which many important events occurred. (3)

LESSON 29

Nominalization: Nouns Derived from Other Form-Classes and Their Function as Noun Phrases in Sentences

ABSTRACT

- Nouns can be created from other form-class words.
- Several derivational suffixes may be added to words, but after an inflectional suffix is added, no more derivational suffixes may be attached to that word.
- The present participle of some verbs may function as nouns in sentences. They are referred to as *action nominals* when they occupy noun positions in sentences.
- Noun phrases may function as subjects, objects, or complements in sentences.
- Noun phrases may be generated from an entire sentence by transforming the verb to a noun through the addition of a derivational suffix or through the use of its present participle, and substituting the possessive form for the nominative form of the subject noun.
- An alternative form for the possessive of nouns is *of* + *NP*.

This lesson will deal with nominalization in English, that characteristic allowing for the creation of nouns from other form classes, and the positioning of words not normally considered nouns in places occupied by nouns in sentences.

Just as adjectives may be derived from other form-class words, so nouns may be formed from adjectives and verbs, and even from other nouns. The most common endings that identify nouns are: *-age, -al, -ee, -er(-or), -cy, -ist, -ity, —(+c)ion, -ism, -ment, -ness, -ship,* and *-ure.* Table 11 gives examples of derived nouns.

Table 11. Nouns Derived from Verbs, Adjectives, and Other Nouns

Derivational Suffix	*From Verb to Noun*		*From Adjective to Noun*		*From Noun to Noun*	
	Verb	*Noun*	*Adjective*	*Noun*	*Noun*	*Noun*
-al	dispose	disposal				
-ee	draft	draftee				
-er	teach	teacher				
-or	act	actor				
-ion	act	action				
-ment	curtail	curtailment				
-ure	proceed	procedure				
-ism			active	activism		
-ity/-ty			real	reality		
			loyal	loyalty		
-ness			foolish	foolishness		
-age					mile	mileage
-cy					diploma	diplomacy
-ist					botan(y)	botanist
-ship					friend	friendship

The ending *-al* as in *cathedral* and in *loyal* identifies both nouns and adjectives. Confusion as to the form-class to which these words belong is eliminated if all new vocabulary is presented in the context of a sentence, and if children are given sufficient practice in using the items correctly.

Nouns appear in certain positions in basic sentences and function as *subjects, objects,* or *noun phrase complements.* These terms refer to their roles in surface structures of sentences. Subjects usually appear before a verb and prescribe the form of the verb if the present tense or the copula is used, while objects, direct and indirect, ordinarily follow the verb. The objects of prepositions follow the preposition to create linguistic units which carry structural as well as semantic meaning. Noun phrase complements are transformed sentences that are embedded in NPs. They will be discussed in some detail in the next lesson. Transformations can rearrange these constituents. You have already studied some of them, and you will be introduced to others as we go along.

The following simple sentence illustrates the functional elements, subject, indirect object, direct object, and object of a preposition, in the pattern, $NP + VP + NP + NP + Adv_t$:

> The teacher gave his students an exam on Monday.
> Subject: the teacher
> Indirect object: his students
> Direct object: an exam
> Object of preposition: Monday

The present participles of some verbs function as nouns in sentences. They are referred to as *action nominals* and have the features of nouns. Most of them call up an image of movement or at least suspended action. They can appear in noun positions and serve as subjects and objects:

Subject: *Spelling* is next on the program.
Dancing is her profession.

Direct Object: The dentist put two *fillings* in my teeth.
I hated the *drilling*.

Object of Preposition: It's time for *reading*.
Thank you for *waiting*.

Entire sentences containing either intransitive or transitive verbs may be nominalized by a series of transformations. We will not go into great detail concerning these transformations but only observe the results of their application.

In order to transform the next sentence into an NP, the verb is first nominalized by adding a noun derivational suffix and then substituting the possessive for the nominative form of the subject noun:

the teachers decided =>
decided => decision
the teachers => the teachers'

The resulting phrase:

the teachers' decision

may be used in various noun positions, and may function as a subject or object in sentences:

Subject: The teachers' decision created an uproar among the students.

Indirect object: They gave the teachers' decision serious thought.

Direct object: The principal approved the teachers' decision.

Object of preposition: The students objected to the teachers' decision.

When the subject noun has the feature <+ human>, the alternative form of the possessive, *of* + *NP*, may be used in transforming the sentence into a noun phrase, but when the subject noun has the <— human> feature, the alternative form of the possessive is usually, though not necessarily, chosen:

<+ human> subject:

the speaker arrives => the speakers' arrival =>
the arrival of the speaker
the children recover => the children's recovery =>
the recovery of the children

<— human> subject:

the story continues => the continuation of the story

the lease expires => the expiration of the lease

An action nominal can be used in this same transformation:

the dogs bark => the dogs' barking =>
the barking of the dogs

the door slams => the door's slamming =>
the slamming of the door

the airplane lands => the airplane's landing =>
the landing of the airplane

These noun phrases also appear in noun positions in sentences:

Subject: The dogs' barking annoyed the neighbors.

Object: The hunter heard the barking of the dogs in the distance.

Object of preposition: She was awakened by the barking of the dogs.

When a sentence to be nominalized contains two nouns, the second of which is a direct object, as in $NP + V_t + NP$, an additional transformation inserts *of* before the second *NP*. The regular possessive form is chosen to transform the subject noun whether it has the <+ human> or <— human> feature:

The doctor curtailed John's activities. =>
The doctor's curtailment *of* John's activities

John won the Cutest Baby Contest. =>
John's winning *of* the Cutest Baby Contest

The poll rated the candidate's popularity. =>
The poll's rating *of* the candidate's popularity

The storm destroyed their property. =>
The storm's destruction *of* their property

When hearing-impaired children are first learning the use of the possessive case, it may be of help if they understand that the possessive form of nouns is related to the basic meaning of the verb, *have*, which, according to most dictionaries, is: "To hold in possession." For instance, these sentences may be paraphrased as follows:

Don has two sisters =>
Don's two sisters

The dog has a bone =>
The dog's bone

EXERCISE

Write the sentences form which these noun phrases were derived.

1. the residents' survival

____

2. the town's recovery

____

3. the decision of the chairman

4. the children's acting out

5. her letter writing

6. John's appreciation of the award

7. their sending of the mission

8. the behavior of the crowd

9. the president's resigning

10. his practicing of the sonata

Answers:

1. The residents survived.
2. The town recovered.
3. The chairman decided.
4. The children acted out.
5. She wrote letters.
6. John appreciated the award.
7. They sent the mission.
8. The crowd behaved.
9. The president resigned.
10. He practiced the sonata.

EXERCISE

How do the italicized groups of words function in the sentence? Write the name of the function — S (subject), IO (indirect object), DO (direct object), OP (object of preposition) — in the space provided.

Example:

DO I hung up *the washing.*

______ 1. They very much enjoyed *his telling of the story.*

______ 2. *The tailings* from the mine were piled mountain high.

______ 3. The audience was impressed by *the participation of the nominees.*

______ 4. The president's secretary held *a press briefing.*

______ 5. *The ringing of the doorbell* woke the family.

______ 6. The council gave *the alderman's proposal of a curfew* absolutely no consideration.

______ 7. *The boys' discovery of the treasure* made headlines.

______ 8. They received the *president's greetings* by telephone.

______ 9. Her family wondered about *her departing so suddenly.*

______ 10. The submarine made *soundings* in the deepest part of the ocean.

Answers: 1. DO 2. S 3. OP 4. DO 5. S 6. IO 7. S 8. DO 9. OP 10. DO

Children with hearing defects will be greatly aided in their reading if they understand the synonomy of noun phrases derived from simple sentences.

LESSON 30

Sentence Embedding: Noun Phrase Complements

ABSTRACT

- A sentence that is embedded in a noun phrase following certain nouns such as *fact, idea,* or *news,* is known as a *factive clause.*
- A factive clause functions as a *noun phrase complement.*
- A complementizer introduces a transformation that embeds one sentence in another.
- A factive clause is introduced by the complementizer, *that.*
- *Which* cannot be substituted for *that* in a factive clause as it can in a relative clause.
- The passive transformation may be applied to sentences containing a noun phrase complement if all conditions for T/pass are met.
- An intermediate sentence is one that is not a basic sentence nor a completely transformed one, but a sentence to which other transformations may still be applied.
- The shifting of a noun phrase complement to the end of the sentence, away from the noun to which it was attached, is called the extraposition transformation (T/extrap).
- The passive transformation may be used as a test to substantiate any kind of noun phrase complement.
- The cleft-sentence transformation (T/cleft-sent) also identifies noun phrase complements.
- The cleft-sentence test is based on sentence Pattern III, but the first NP is transformed to a clause beginning with *what.* The pattern for this test is: *What clause + be + NP.*

- If a single noun or pronoun is to be tested with T/cleft sent, it must have the feature <— human>.

In this lesson we will continue the study of noun phrase constituents. Let us review briefly the rules we have learned thus far about NPs:

$$NP \rightarrow \begin{Bmatrix} N \\ Pro \end{Bmatrix}$$

$$NP \rightarrow (Det)\ N$$

$$NP \rightarrow (Det)\ N\ (S)$$

Lesson 24 dealt with the relative clause, a clause derived from a sentence embedded in a noun phrase. The tree diagram below illustrates how this embedding is accomplished. It shows that the nouns in both the matrix sentence and in the relative clause are identical.

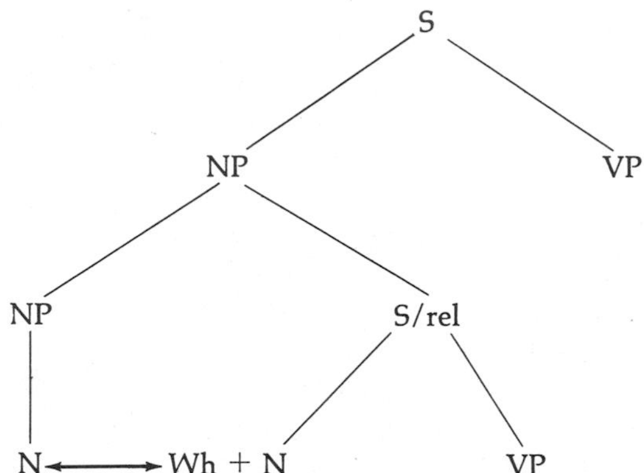

There is yet another way of embedding a sentence in a noun phrase. A sentence introduced by *that* may follow such nouns as *fact, claim, conclusion, decision, feeling, idea, news, opinion, statement, supposition,* and *theory.* The resulting clause is called a *factive clause* by many grammarians. The introductory word *that* is not a relative pronoun in this case, but a *complementizer,* and the sentence it introduces is a *noun phrase complement.*

The next sentence contains a factive clause which functions as a noun phrase complement:

The fact *that Congress passed the law* makes sense.

The noun in the embedded sentence is not identical to the noun it follows, nor is it possible to substitute a relative pronoun for *that* in this clause. You recall that in relative clauses an appropriate relative pronoun is interchangeable with *that.*

Compare this tree which embeds a factive clause with the tree for a relative clause above:

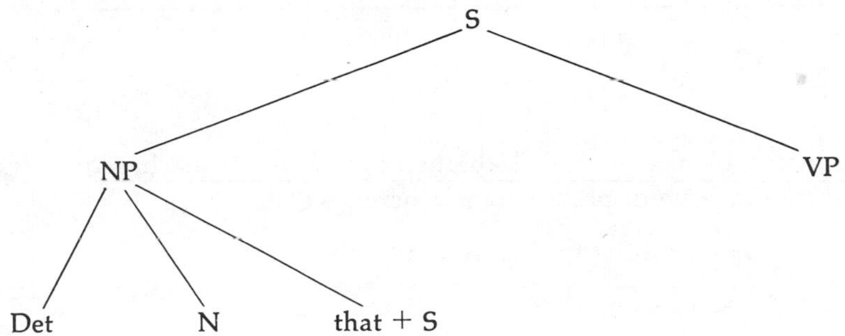

The next tree illustrates the embedding that produced this transformed sentence:

The news that the law had passed pleased everyone.

The Aux is purposely omitted from the tree, since its presence is not critical to the discussion at hand.

Sentence Tree 23: The news that the law had passed pleased everyone.

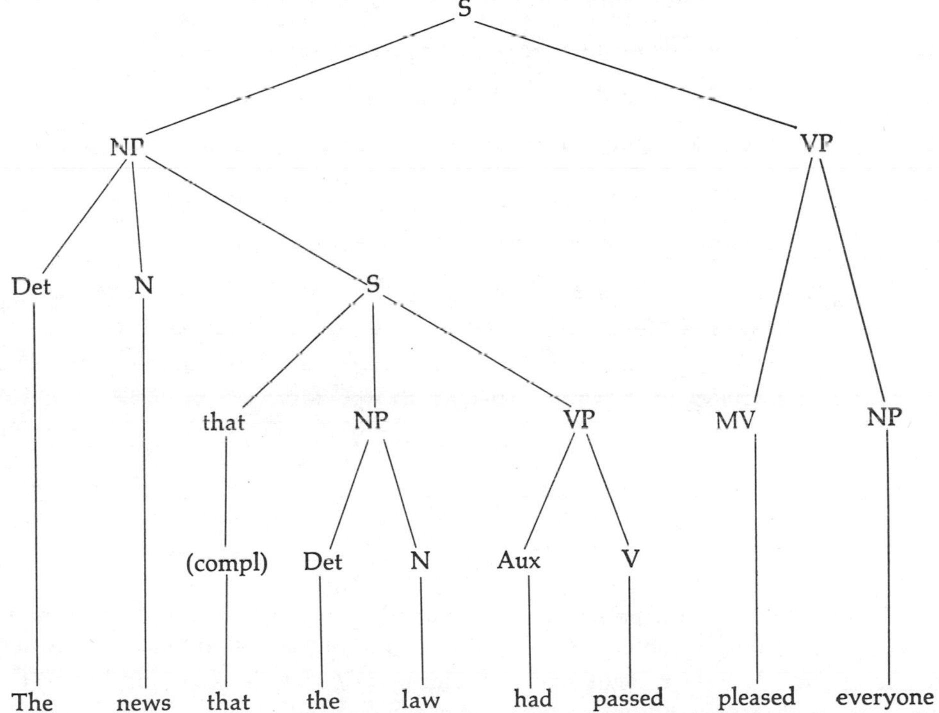

At first it may be difficult to distinguish between relative clauses introduced by the relative pronoun *that*, and factive clauses introduced by the complementizer *that*. The next exercise should help you improve your skill in discriminating between these two kinds of clauses.

EXERCISE

Indicate in the blanks provided whether the clause in each sentence is a relative clause (R) or a noun phrase complement (NPC).

1. _______ I have a feeling that he will soon be here.
2. _______ I have a feeling that depresses me.
3. _______ The opinion that he expressed was ill-founded.
4. _______ The opinion that the world will soon come to an end is held by some people.
5. _______ We came to the conclusion that the discussion should terminate.
6. _______ The conclusion that we came to is known to everyone.
7. _______ The supposition that the moon is made of green cheese is ridiculous.
8. _______ It was his supposition that confused all of us.
9. _______ He holds to the theory that Einstein propounded.
10. _______ He holds to the theory that matter is destructible.
11. _______ The fact that you are here pleases me.
12. _______ The fact that you just disclosed astounds me.
13. _______ The idea that you have is an excellent one.
14. _______ The idea that someone can make a million dollars overnight is preposterous.

Answers: 1. NPC 2. R 3. R 4. NPC 5. NPC 6. R 7. NPC 8. R 9. R 10. NPC 11. NPC 12. R 13. R 14. NPC

The passive transformation may be applied to a sentence containing a noun phrase complement in the subject position. You may recall that this transformation is applicable only to sentences containing a V_t. In the example below the entire noun phrase including the complement becomes the object of the preposition *by* in the phrase *by + NP:*

The news that the law had passed pleased everyone.
T/pass: Everyone was pleased *by the news that the law had passed.*

EXERCISE

Apply T/passive to these sentences where it is applicable.

1. The report that Lexington School had raised five million dollars surprised no one.

2. The fact that everyone worked hard on the fund drive pleased the Committee.

3. Knowledge that the vaccine for rubella was effective cheered the medical community.

4. The theory that deafness can be genetic has been proved.

5. News that the vaccine was impotent disappointed his fellow workers.

Answers:

1. No one was surprised by the report that Lexington School had raised five million dollars.
2. The Committee was pleased by the fact that everyone worked hard on the fund drive.
3. The medical community was cheered by the knowledge that the vaccine for rubella was effective.
4. Not applicable.
5. His fellow workers were disappointed by the news that the vaccine was impotent.

T/passive serves as a good test for noun phrases and noun phrase complements. If you are in doubt about a constituent that you think might be a noun phrase, use the passive test.

Another transformation may be applied to the sentences in the above exercise whose verbs are in the active voice. This transformation deletes the noun preceding the *that* clause. For instance, if the nouns *report, fact, knowledge, theory,* and *news* are deleted, the sentences remain quite correct and are still synonymous with the original ones:

1. That Lexington School had raised five million dollars, surprised no one.
2. That everyone worked hard on the fund drive, pleased the Committee.
3. That the vaccine for rubella was effective cheered the medical community.
4. That deafness can be genetic has been proved.
5. That the vaccine was impotent disappointed his fellow workers.

The result of the deletion is an intermediate kind of structure, one to which other transformations can still be applied. An intermediate sentence is not a basic sentence nor a completely transformed one. If we wished to include a noun head in the above intermediate type of sentence but did not know what it was, we could substitute the pronoun *it* for the unknown noun. The sentences would then read:

*1. It, that Lexington School had raised five million dollars, surprised no one.

*2. It, that everyone worked hard on the fund drive, pleased the Committee.

These sentences are ungrammatical, but a shifting of the noun phrase complement to the end of the sentence by a transformation called the *extraposition transformation (T/extrap)* makes them syntactically acceptable:

1. It surprised no one that Lexington School had raised five million dollars.
2. It pleased the Committee that everyone had worked hard on the fund drive.

EXERCISE

Transform the sentences below using the extraposition transformation. Begin the sentences with *It*.

1. That the vaccine for rubella was effective cheered the medical community.

____

____

2. That deafness can be genetic has been proved.

3. That the vaccine was impotent disappointed his fellow workers.

4. That the child would recover was his opinion.

5. That deafness will disappear is our hope.

6. That the virus is isolated is a fact.

7. That her mother worried is understandable.

8. That the deaf learn language at all is miraculous.

9. That he left is O.K. with me.

10. That she disappeared suddenly is very strange.

Answers:

1. It cheered the medical community that the vaccine for rubella was effective.
2. It has been proved that deafness can be genetic.
3. It disappointed his fellow workers that the vaccine was impotent.
4. It was his opinion that the child would recover.
5. It is our hope that deafness will disappear.
6. It is a fact that the virus is isolated.

7. It is understandable that her mother worried.
8. It is miraculous that the deaf learn language at all.
9. It is O.K. with me that he left.
10. It is very strange that she disappeared suddenly.

When a noun phrase complement appears with the object of a sentence, we may also apply T/extraposition if first we apply T/passive, which brings the noun phrase complement into the subject position:

The Board made the decision *that the school would remain an oral school.* =>

T/pass: The decision *that the school would remain an oral school* was made by the Board. =>

T/extrap: The decision was made by the Board *that the school would remain an oral school.*

These three sentences have essentially the same meaning. The reading ability of hearing-impaired children will be improved considerably if they are able to recognize such synonomy. Teachers who prepare original materials for use with hearing-impaired children should be aware of this feature and should incorporate sentences containing these synonymous sets into the language program at an appropriate time.

EXERCISE

Apply T/passive and T/extraposition to these sentences where they are applicable. Remember that relative clauses do not engage in the T/extraposition transformation as do noun phrase complements.

1. The president reported the news that the school had received a large grant.

T/pass: ______________________________

____

T/extrap: ______________________________

____

2. The children discovered the fact that water is expandable.

T/pass: ______________________________

____

T/extrap: ______________________________

____

3. The children discovered the dog that had been hiding in the yard.

T/pass: ______________________________

____

T/extrap: ______________________________

____

4. A famous scientist stated the theory that there is life on Mars.

T/pass: ______________________________

____

T/extrap: ______________________________

____

5. The police officer held the opinion that all drivers were law violators.

T/pass: ______________________________

____

T/extrap: ______________________________

____

6. The girls presented an idea that was very novel.

T/pass: ______________________________

____

T/extrap: ______________________________

____

Answers:

1. T/pass: The news that the school had received a large grant was reported by the president.
   T/extrap: It was reported by the president that the school had received a a large grant.
2. T/pass: The fact that water is expandable was discovered by the children.
   T/extrap: The fact was discovered by the children that water is expandable.

3. T/pass: The dogs that had been hiding in the yard was discovered by the children.
   T/extrap: Not applicable in sentences with relative clauses.
4. T/pass: The theory that there is life on Mars was stated by a famous scientist.
   T/extrap: The theory was stated by a famous scientist that there is life on Mars.
5. T/pass: The opinion that all drivers were law violators was held by the police officer.
   T/extrap: The opinion was held by the police officer that all drivers were law violators.
6. T/pass: An idea that was very novel was presented by the girls.
   T/extrap: Not applicable in sentences with relative clauses.

The passive transformation is a good test for noun phrases, but since not all sentences can be converted to the passive we look to another test to aid us in identifying NPs, especially those that are somewhat complex. This test, called the *cleft-sentence test* is based on sentence Pattern III, *NP + be + NP,* but requires considerable transformation of the first NP. The test sentence begins with the word *What,* introducing a clause formed by the words in the sentence to be tested. The constituent to be tested is placed in the second NP position after an appropriate form of *be*. Whatever follows *be* may be considered a *noun phrase complement.*

The pattern for the cleft-sentence test is:

What clause + be + NP

In order to check on whether the words *lightning* and *schoolhouse* are NPs in the sentence:

Lightning struck the schoolhouse.

we will use the cleft-sentence test:

T/cleft-sent: What struck the schoolhouse was lightning.

T/cleft-sent: What lightning struck was the schoolhouse.

Your prior knowledge that *lightning* and *schoolhouse* were NPs was substantiated because the resulting two synonymous sentences were grammatical.

If single nouns or pronouns are to be tested, they must have the feature <— human> since the word *What* in the test sentence refers to the PRO form *Something* rather than *Someone*. This test, like the passive, has its limitations. For example, the test applied to the next sentence does not result in grammatical statements:

Edward Nitchie taught many hard of hearing people.

T/cleft-sent: *What Edward Nitchie taught was many hard of hearing people.

T/cleft-sent: *What taught many hard of hearing people was Edward Nitchie.

It is relatively simple to recognize NPs containing single nouns, but as phrases and sentences grow more complex the task becomes more difficult. The cleft-sentence transformation helps in identifying more complicated constituents as NPs. Here are some examples of more complex NPs that we can test:

Their retreating from their positions left everyone in utter confusion.

T/cleft-sent: What left everyone in utter confusion was *their retreating from their positions.*

She noticed *that Edward was an excellent lipreader.*

T/cleft-sent: What she noticed was *that Edward was an excellent lipreader.*

In this sentence we might first substitute the PRO form, *Something,* for the clause, as in, *She noticed Something,* and then apply the test because we know the clause carries the <— human> feature.

That people were vitally interested in joining the League for the Hard of Hearing soon became evident.

T/cleft-sent: What soon became evident was that people were vitally interested in joining the League for the Hard of Hearing.

It came to me that she was his cousin.

T/cleft-sent: What came to me was that she was his cousin.

In sentences beginning with *It,* which substitutes for a noun deleted from a factive clause, *what* may be substituted for *it.* In the above sentence the deleted noun might have been *the thought* in the sentence:

The thought that she was his cousin came to me.

When a sentence, to which the cleft-sentence test is applied, does not yield a grammatical structure, it is entirely possible that the constituent in question is not a noun phrase complement. For instance, apply the test to the sentence:

It was George that paid the bill.

T/cleft-sent: *What was George was that paid the bill.

We get an ungrammatical result (1) because *it* has no real referent but is merely a place holder in the sentence, (2) because George has a <+ human> feature, and (3) because *that paid the bill* is a relative clause.

The cleft-sentence test, like other tests we have studied, is a device that native users of English can apply in order to clarify for themselves the functions of constituents. It is not a test to be taught to hearing-impaired children who at best are uncertain about what constitutes correct usage. Their job is to learn to speak (and/or spell manually) and write English automatically. Learning tests and rules will not help them do this.

EXERCISE

Practice your ability to use the cleft-sentence transformation. First underline the constituent you wish to test, then write out the transformed sentence. If the cleft-sentence test does not apply, write *Not applicable.*

1. The children's being late upset the schedule.

   ____

2. They didn't know that they were to return promptly.

   ____

3. The fact that no one had a watch explained the delay.

   ____

4. They raced each other back to the classroom building.

   ____

5. The principal took all the children to the office.

   ____

6. Their evident astonishment at being scolded proved their innocence.

   ____

7. It was true that they were innocent.

   ____

Answers:

1. What upset the schedule was *the children's being late.*
2. What they didn't know was *that they were to return promptly.*
3. What explained the delay was *the fact that no one had a watch.*
4. Not applicable.
5. Not applicable.
6. What proved their innocence was *their evident astonishment at being scolded.*
7. What was true was *that they were innocent.*

LESSON 31

Introduction to Infinitives

ABSTRACT

- Infinitives may occupy noun positions in sentences.
- Infinitives can be embedded in NPs as noun phrase complements.
- The complementizer that embeds noun phrase complements is:

  for . . . to

- The pattern for embedding an infinitive sentence in a noun phrase is:

  for + subject NP + to + base form of verb

- The pronoun subject of an insert infinitive sentence is in the accusative case.
- The subject of an infinitive sentence must be deleted when it is identical to a noun in the matrix sentence. The word *for* is also deleted in this transformation (T/for + subj N del).
- An embedded infinitive may be moved to the end of a sentence by the extraposition transformation.
- The complementizer *for . . . to* also introduces infinitive sentences into verb phrases.
- The infinitive of purpose answers the question *Why . . . ?* and functions as a verb phrase complement.

Infinitives are widely used both in spoken and written forms of English and are very important sentence components with which language-impaired children must become familiar. Infinitives are versatile constituents because they can be used in noun positions and because they can also function as complements of verbs.

In Lession 10 you learned that the infinitive is the base form of the verb and that it can appear in structures with or without its sign *to*. This sentence contains six infinitives:

> Just for us *to get* Phil *to say* yes was enough *to make* us *forget to ask* him not *to change* his mind.

The excessive use of infinitives in a single sentence is certainly not recommended since overuse of any one type of constituent tends to becloud meaning.

Simple infinitives (those without their sign) and those with the sign *to*, may occupy noun positions in surface structures:

> Subject: *To cheat* is considered a necessity by some students.
>
> Object: The boys really wanted *to confess.*
>
> Object to preposition: They could think of nothing but *to apologize.*
> She did nothing all day long but *mope.*

The *-ing* form of a verb, the action nominal, is often preferred to the infinitive as a subject:

> *Cheating* is considered a necessity by some students.
> (vs. *To cheat* is considered a necessity by some students.)
>
> *Walking* is very good exercise.
> (vs. *To walk* is very good exercise.)

The infinitive in the object position, however, is one which children must learn to use early in their acquisition of language.

We can transform any English sentence into an infinitive sentence and embed it in a noun phrase with much the same result as we achieved when we embedded factive clauses in noun phrases.

The complementizer that introduces an infinitive sentence is *for . . . to.* The pattern for embedding the infinitive sentence in a noun phrase is:

> *for + subject NP + to + base form of verb*

Here are three examples of the infinitive transformation T/for . . . to:

Gallaudet left for Europe. =>
T/for. . . to: for Gallaudet to leave for Europe

Dr. Goldstein devoted his full efforts to the education of deaf children. =>
T/for. . . to: for Dr. Goldstein to devote his full efforts to the education of deaf children

Nitchie founded the New York League for the Hard of Hearing. =>
T/for. . . to: for Nitchie to found the New York League for the Hard of Hearing

The transformed infinitive sentences can be embedded in noun phrases as noun phrase complements.

In these sentences the infinitive follows the subject nouns, *time, inspiration* and *opportunity:*

> The time *for Gallaudet to leave for Europe* drew near.
>
> The inspiration *for Dr. Goldstein to devote his full effort to the education of deaf children* came from his deep interest in their welfare.
>
> The opportunity *for Nitchie to establish the New York League for the Hard of Hearing* came soon after World War I.

The function of the embedded infintive sentences as noun phrase complements can be tested by applying the cleft-sentence transformation. What follows *be* is a noun phrase complement.

> What drew near was *the time for Gallaudet to leave for Europe.*
>
> What came from his deep interest was *the inspiration for Dr. Goldstein to devote his efforts to the education of deaf children.*
>
> What came after World War I was *the opportunity for Nitchie to establish the New York League for the Hard of Hearing.*

When the subject of the insert infinitive sentence is a personal pronoun, a further transformation is necessary to change the pronoun from the nominative to the accusative case:

> Matrix: The time arrived all too soon.
> Insert: He went.
> *The time # he went # arrived all too soon.
> T/for . . . to: *for he to go=>
> T/acc pron: for him to go=>
> The time for him to go arrived all too soon.

The complementizer, *for,* and the subject NP of an infinitive insert sentence (*for + subj NP*) may be deleted provided their removal does not interfere with the meaning of the sentence. The clue for the deletion of *for + subj NP* in the next sentence is the fact that the subject of the insert sentence was not known:

> The opportunity (for Someone) to interview the candidates was granted. =>
> T/del: The opportunity to interview the candidates was granted.

When the subject of the infinitive sentence is the same as the noun after which it is embedded, it *must* be deleted. In fact, all recoverable items are deleted according to the rules we have studied in previous lessons. The next two sets of sentences illustrate these deletions:

> Matrix: The woman bought a dress.
> Insert: She will wear the dress at the reception. =>
> T/for . . . to; + T/acc pron: for her to wear the dress at the reception
> *The woman bought a dress *for her* to wear the dress at the reception. =>

T/for + subj NP del: *The woman bought a dress to wear the dress at the reception. =>

T/ident obj NP del: The woman bought a dress to wear at the reception.

Matrix: The woman made a dress.
Insert: Her daughter will wear it at the reception. =>
T/for . . . to: for her daughter to wear it at the reception.
*The woman made a dress for her daughter to wear *it* at the reception. =>
T/ident obj NP del: The woman made a dress for her daughter to wear at the reception.

The subject of the infinitive is retained because it is not identical with the subject in the matrix, but the pronoun *it* is deleted because it becomes a repeated item in the same sentence.

An embedded infinitive may be moved to the end of a sentence by the extraposition transformation just as embedded factive clauses may be moved. This is especially true when the verb in the matrix is the copula *be*. Rather than start sentences with infinitives we begin them with *it:*

For him to take his vacation now is out of the question. =>
T/extrap: It is out of the question for him to take his vacation now.

For teachers of the deaf to improve their skills in teaching language to deaf children is very important. =>
T/extrap: It is very important for teachers of the deaf to improve their skills in teaching language to deaf children.

EXERCISE

Combine these sentences so that they contain infinitives. Indicate in the space provided the transformations you used to achieve your results:

1. T/for . . . to
2. T/acc pron
3. T/for + N deletion
4. T/identical obj N deletion

Example:

Matrix: The opportunity came unexpectedly.
Infinitive insert sentence: He went to college. =>
1, 2 The opportunity for him to go to college came unexpectedly.

1. Matrix: The agency found a baby.
   Insert: The Smiths adopt the baby. =>

_____ ______________________________

_____ ______________________________

2. Matrix: The doctor established a regimen. =>
   Insert: She will follow the regimen.

   ______ ______________________________

   ______ ______________________________

3. Matrix: The fisherman brought in the fish. =>
   Insert: The processing plant canned them.

   ______ ______________________________

   ______ ______________________________

4. Matrix: That was a high price. =>
   Insert: He paid it.

   ______ ______________________________

   ______ ______________________________

5. Matrix: John's attempt created a roar of approval. =>
   Insert: John climbs the greased pole.

   ______ ______________________________

   ______ ______________________________

6. Matrix: The worst attitude was one of indifference. =>
   Insert: He adopts it.

   ______ ______________________________

   ______ ______________________________

7. Matrix: It took a long time. =>
   Insert: The ink dried.

   ______ ______________________________

   ______ ______________________________

Answers:

1. The agency found a baby for the Smiths to adopt. (1) (4)
2. The doctor established a regimen for her to follow. (1) (2) (4)
3. The fisherman brought in the fish for the processing plant to can. (1) (4)
4. That was a high price for him to pay. (1) (2) (4)
5. John's attempt to climb the greased pole created a roar of approval. (3)
6. The worst attitude for him to adopt was one of indifference. (1) (2) (4)
7. It took a long time for the ink to dry. (1)

We have learned about the infinitive as a noun phrase complement, but before we observe how the same complementizer, *for . . . to,* produces verb phrase complements, we will briefly review what constitutes a verb phrase. By inspecting the following tree diagrams of basic sentence patterns it is evident that what follows the verb becomes part of the verb phrase. Pattern III is not applicable because what follows the copula in this pattern is a noun phrase complement. Pattern I is based on intransitive verbs while pattern II is based on transitive verbs. The constituents following the copula in patterns IV and V are considered verbal complements.

Pattern I: Glen swims well.

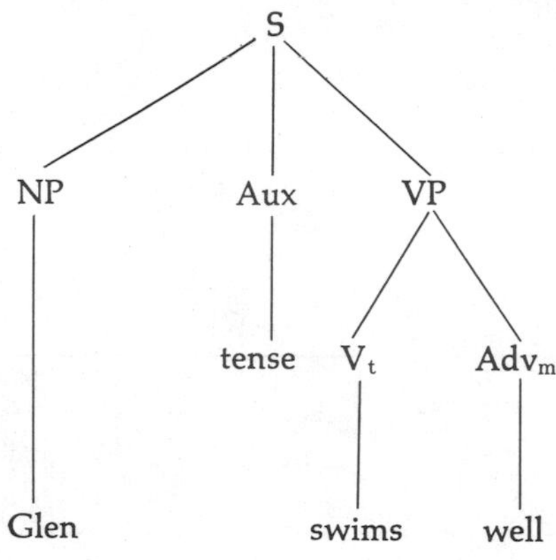

Pattern II: He can tread water easily.

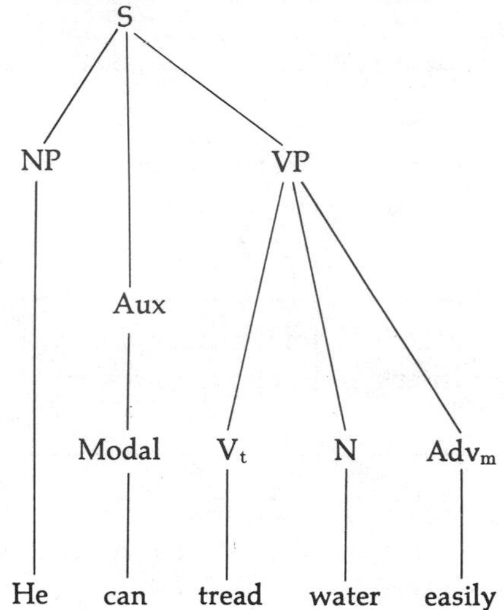

Pattern IV: He was victorious.

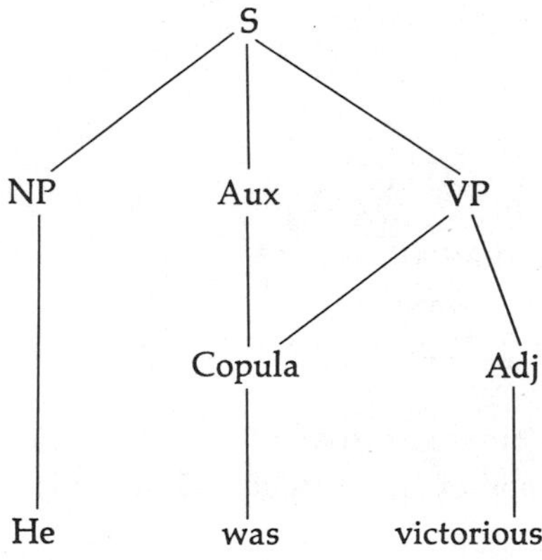

Pattern V: Glen is in the pool.

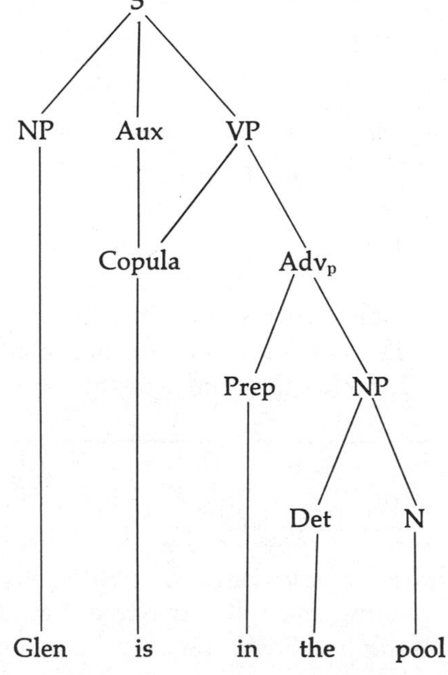

You are already familiar with all of these patterns, so you should have no difficulty in identifying verb phrases.

An infinitive can be incorporated into the verb phrases in sentence patterns I and II as a complement. For example:

Pattern I: Glen practices daily *to maintain his racing form.*
Pattern II: Roberta has a leave *to do graduate work.*

The PRO form *For that Reason* could stand in for these infinitives since they answer the question Why . . . ?

Why does Glen practice every day?
Why does Roberta have a leave of absence?

An infinitive that answers Why . . . ? questions is called an infinitive of purpose and functions as a verb phrase complement.

The infinitive is imbedded into verb phrases in the following manner:

Matrix: Glen practices daily.
Insert: He maintains his racing form. =>
T/ for . . . to; T/acc pron: for him to maintain his racing form
T/for + subj N del: Glen practices daily to maintain his racing form.

Matrix: Roberta has a leave.
Insert: She completes her graduate work. =>
T/for . . . to; T/acc pron: for her to complete her graduate work
T/for + subj N del: Roberta has a leave of absence to complete her graduate work.

The infinitive of purpose may be tested as a verb phrase complement by placing the phrase *in order* in the position occupied by *for,* in front of the infinitive:

Glen practices daily *in order* to maintain his racing form.

Roberta has a leave *in order* to complete her graduate work.

An infinitive of result bears the same relationship to the verb as does the infinitive of purpose. The number of verbs that can be used in this construction is somewhat limited. The infinitive is frequently preceded by *only* or *never:*

I arrived *only* to find him gone.

He spoke out *only* to regret it later.

They departed *never* to come back again.

She lived to be a hundred and one.

In order to clarify for yourself the difference between noun phrase complements and verb phrase complements do the exercise that follows.

EXERCISE

Underline the embedded infinitive sentences. In the space to the left, indicate whether the infinitive complements a noun or a verb.

1. _______ They hurried only to miss the boat.
2. _______ The boys decided to leave town for the holidays.
3. _______ He accepted another job to keep out of debt.
4. _______ Phil agreed to take the job for two years.
5. _______ John was waiting for her to cross the street.
6. _______ It was his only chance to see his girl.
7. _______ The best time for you to come is 3:00 p.m.
8. _______ They studied the children in order to learn their backgrounds.
9. _______ He hurried to meet his wife.
10. _______ They expected their doctor to charge less than he did.

Answers:

1. VPC, to miss the boat
2. NPC, to leave town for the holidays.
3. VPC, to keep out of debt
4. VPC, to take the job for two years
5. VPC, for her to cross the street
6. NPC, to see his girl
7. NPC, for you to come
8. VPC, in order to learn their backgrounds
9. VPC, to meet his wife
10. NPC, their doctor to charge less than he did

This lesson has gone into some detail about how infinitives become parts of the surface structure of sentences. Children with language deficiencies will need guidance in using the patterns described in this lesson and the next. Young children should be introduced first to the simplest and easiest patterns and those which are functional in their environments. It is a good idea when introducing these patterns, or any new pattern, to use familiar vocabulary. Children then have to contend with only one factor rather than several and their task of generalizing the use of the pattern is made easier.

The infinitive patterns may be associated with familiar verbs in familiar sentence patterns, as in:

I like ice cream.	I like to play ball.
I want (would like) some milk.	I want to play ball.

or presented as synonymous ways of stating an idea, as in:

I must do my homework.	I have to do my homework.
We went to the store for milk.	We went to the store to get milk.
I helped Mother with the dishes.	I helped Mother wash the dishes.
It is time for recess.	It is time to play.

The expansion of sentences using embedded infinitives takes priority over other embedding. For instance, relative clauses or noun phrase complements embedded in the subject noun can be deferred until after infinitives become established in the spoken and written expression of children.

LESSON 32

More About Infinitives

ABSTRACT

- A special feature of verbs called *catenation* allows verbs with this feature <+ catenation> to be followed by other verbal forms such as infinitives and the *-ing* forms of verbs.
- There are three patterns for embedding infinitive sentences. In these patterns:

  X → anything that precedes the infinitive in the sentence
  Y → everything that follows the infinitive
  Pattern A-1: X + V + base form + Y; A-2; X + V + NP + base form + Y
  Pattern B: X + V + to + inf + Y
  Pattern C: X + V + NP + to + inf + Y
- Some adjectives may be followed by verbal forms:
  Pattern D: NP + be + Adj + to + inf + Y
- Some verbs with the feature <+ catenation> require that they be followed by *-ing* forms (action nominals) rather than infinitives.
- Infinitives have active and passive forms.
- Aspect of infinitives is expressed by combining the infinitives of *be* and *have* with present and past participial forms.
- In the active voice the infinitive forms include the base form, the progressive, the perfect, and perfect progressive forms.
- In the passive voice the infinitive is limited to the base form preceded by *to be* and the perfect form.
- Embedded passive infinitives are transforms of passive sentences.
- An infinitive may be made negative by inserting *not* before *to.*

There is a great deal children must learn about infinitives, but it is not at all necessary that they be able to identify infinitives as noun or verb phrase complements. It is much more important that they learn how infinitives pattern with certain verbs and adjectives. We will begin this lesson with a consideration of a special feature of verbs which allows the embedding of infinitives and *-ing* forms of verbs in sentence patterns I and II and after certain adjectives in Pattern IV. Then we will look at aspect, which can be expressed by infinitives, and finally at the negative transformation for infinitives.

Children who learn language through a mode other than hearing have difficulty in remembering the proper phrasal structures that may be used after particular verbs, and thus they tend to make errors such as the following:

*The girl ran to follow baby.

*Mother let children to get good time.

*We finish to eat it.

*Father drive to go home.

*I want everyone will come to party.

*They watch the boys is play football.

*I like to skating.

Infinitives do not follow all verbs, but only those having a special feature called catenation <+ catenation>. Catenation is the characteristic that allows one verbal form to be joined with another in complex phrases. For instance, we cannot say:

*Bob fell to get hurt.

*She dreamed to have a fairy godmother.

*The balloon burst to make a loud noise.

*The meat tasted to be salty.

Verbs with the feature <+ catenation> seem to indicate the deletions required in the incorporation of embedded infinitives as well as the choice of either infinitive or *-ing* form following them. We will not go into details of the transformations producing the patterns nor discuss the constituent functions of the infinitives and action nominals in the patterns. The objective in this presentation is to point out the varieties of structures involving infinitives. Relating the patterns to specific verbs may help children to form clearer concepts of proper structuring and promote learning through meaningful associations and generalization.

There are three patterns involving intransitive and transitive verbs. Pattern A uses the simple infinitive *without its sign, to.* It involves only a few verbs: *hear, help, make, observe, see,* and *watch,* to be used in these subpatterns:

A-1: $X + V + \textit{base form} + Y$

A-2: $X + V + NP + \textit{base form} + Y$

where $X \rightarrow$ anything which precedes the infinitive in the sentence and $Y \rightarrow$ everything which follows the infinitive. For example:

Carol heard *the dog bark.* (A-2)

We helped *clean house.* (A-1)

We helped *mother clean house.* (A-2)

Daddy made *us hurry.* (A-2)

They observed *the chick hatch.* (A-2)

I saw *Phil kiss Carol.* (A-2)

Our class watched *our team win the game.* (A-2)

Pattern B involves the infinitive with its sign *to,* but does not require a subject for the infinitive. Verbs commonly used in this pattern, $X + V + to + inf + Y$, include some (in italics) which also appear in list of verbs for pattern C below.

agree	cease	expect	leap	prefer	strive
aim	choose	fail	*leave*	*prepare*	swear
appear	condescend	forget	like	*proceed*	threaten
arrange	consent	get	long	promise	try
ask	continue	happen	*love*	propose	urge
aspire	*dare*	hasten	mean	refuse	use
attempt	decide	*have*	need	remember	wait
be able	decline	hesitate	neglect	say	*want*
beg	deserve	hope	offer	shoot	wish
begin	detest	hurry	ought	start	
(don't) care	dislike	intend	plan	stop	

Notice that the examples below contain both noun phrases and verb phrase complements:

I forgot *to ask my mother.* (NPC)

He wants *to ride his bike after school.* (NPC)

We have *to go home now.* (VPC)

They stopped *to buy their tickets.* (VPC)

Pattern C, $X + V + NP + to + inf + Y$, requires that the infinitive have a subject. These are the verbs commonly found in this pattern:

advise	choose	have	remind
allow	command	lead	send
ask	compel	leave	teach
beg	dare	let	tell
bring	direct	(would) like	tempt
build	expect	love	urge
buy	forbid	prepare	want
challenge	force	promise	warn

Examples:

I want *your mother to come to school.*

Lucy brought *her sister Flora to meet us.*

Mother asked *me to go to the store.*

I would like *you to come to my party.*

Eight of the verbs in this list also appear in the list for pattern B. Children must learn to use them in both patterns. In teaching the patterns, meaning will govern their selection. A great deal of practice will help clarify their use.

Some verbs require *-ing* nouns for their completion rather than infinitives. They include *avoid, consider, deny, enjoy, mind, miss, postpone,* and *practice,* as in:

They enjoy *dancing.*

They missed *seeing* each other.

They will postpone *taking their trip.*

Other verbs, such as *attempt, begin, continue, finish, go, intend, like, remember, start, stop,* and *try,* may be completed both by an infinitive constructive and an action nominal:

I attempted *to cut out* the skirt with dull scissors.
I won't attempt *cutting out* the skirt now.

He intended *to watch the game.*
He intends *watching the game.*

Special effort must be made to help children clarify the use of infinitives versus that of action nominals early in their language learning. For instance, in talking about sports we can say:

I like to swim/skate/play ball.

I like to go swimming/fishing/hunting.

I like swimming/skating/bowling.

Meaning will determine which form is used. In the sentences:

Jeff watched the boys play tag.
Jeff watched the boys playing tag.

the distinction between them rests on whether the action was completed or whether it was in progress when Jeff left the scene.

In the first sentence the action in the embedded sentence was completed:

The boys played ball.

while in the second one the action was continuing:

The boys were playing ball.

Adjectives in sentence pattern IV may be followed by infinitives that originated as verbs in the active voice in insert sentences.

Pattern D, *NP* + *be* + *Adj* + *to* + *inf* + Y, embeds such sentences after adjectives. The sentence:

Gwen is afraid to drive.

is based on two sentences, the insert having a verb in the active voice:

Matrix: Gwen is afraid.
Insert: Gwen drives. =>
T/for . . . to: for Gwen to drive
*Gwen is afraid for Gwen to drive.
T/for + subj N del: Gwen is afraid to drive.

Infinitives may also be embedded in sentences after adjectives that follow the verbs *seem* and *appear,* as in:

He *seems* eager *to see you.*

He *appears* happy *to be of service.*

Not all adjectives may be followed directly by infinitives. For instance, we cannot say:

*The box was heavy to carry.

*The meat is tough to eat.

*The weather was cold to freeze the plants.

*The box was strong to hold its contents.

Adjectives that may be followed directly by infinitives include:

able	eager	pleased	sorry
afraid	glad	prepared	sure
certain	hard	ready	willing
delighted	happy	smart	wise
difficult	likely		

They are certain to be there.

They will be delighted to see you.

Are you prepared to go with me?

She is wise to stop smoking.

There are a great many more adjectives that may have infinitives joined to them if they are preceded by *too* or followed by *enough:*

The box was *too* heavy to carry.

The meat is *too* tough to eat.

The weather was cold *enough* to freeze the plants.

The box wasn't strong *enough* to hold its contents.

EXERCISE

Construct sentences using as many complex infinitive phrase patterns as you can for the words listed below. Identify the pattern you used by placing the appropriate letter in the left-hand blank:

A-1. X + V + inf + Y; A-2. X + V + NP + inf + Y
B. X + V + to + inf + Y
C. X + V + NP + to + inf + Y
D. NP + be + Adj + to + inf + Y

1. ______ began (V) ______________________________
____
2. ______ told (V) ______________________________
____
3. ______ (would) like (V) ______________________________
____
4. ______ refuse (V) ______________________________
____
5. ______ promise (V) ______________________________
____
6. ______ saw (V) ______________________________
____
7. ______ eager (Adj) ______________________________
____
8. ______ hard (Adj) ______________________________
____

Possible Answers:

1. (B) John began to act silly.
2. (C) John told Bill to move over.
3. (B) I like to swim. (C) I'd like you to help me.
4. (B) He refused to talk.
5. (B) She promised to go. (C) She promised me to go.
6. (A-2) I saw him catch the fish.
7. (D) He was eager to leave.
8. (D) John was hard to discipline. It was hard to discipline him.

Infinitives have an active and a passive voice. In combination with the infinitives of the verbs *be* and *have* acting as auxiliaries, progressive and perfect aspects of the two voices are created.

The phrase structure rules for aspects of infinitives are as follows:

Active Voice

Base form: (to) + base form
Progressive: to be + present participle of verb
Perfect: to have + past participle of verb
Perfect Progressive: to have + past participle of *be* + present participle of verb

Passive Voice

Simple form: to be + past participle of verb
Perfect: to have + past participle of *be* + past participle of verb

Table 12 outlines the forms for the infinitive for the verb *take*.

Table 12. The Forms of the Infinitive of the Verb *Take*

Form	*Aspect*	*Active Voice*	*Passive Voice*
Base Form		to take	
Simple Form			to be taken
	Progressive	to be taking	
	Perfect	to have taken	to have been taken
	Perfect Progressive	to have been taking	

The base form of the infinitive in the active voice usually refers to the time indicated by the main verb if no adverb of time is included:

He likes to paint pictures.

He liked to paint pictures.

All his life he has liked to paint pictures.

The active voice present progressive infinitive refers to continuing action, while the perfect generally points to a time previous to that indicated in the main verb phrase.

> They hope *to take* their vacation soon. (The adverb, *soon,* connotes future time.)
>
> They hoped *to take* their vacation last July. (Both activities occurred in past time.)
>
> They had hoped *to be taking* their vacation in July. (Remote past and continuing action in the past are indicated.)
>
> They didn't mean *to have taken* that route. (Taking the route occurred before their not meaning to take it.)
>
> They appear *to have been taking* plenty of time for the trip. (Taking time was occurring before the observation is made of what they appear to be doing.)

Hearing impaired children cannot be expected to understand or interpret passive infinitives in their reading until they are well acquainted with the passive voice itself. A passive infinitive derives from a passive insert sentence as follows:

> Matrix: They consented.
> Insert: They were questioned. (T/passive already applied.)
> T/for . . . to/T acc pro: for them to be questioned.
> *They consented for them to be questioned.
> T/for + Subj N del: They consented to be questioned.
>
> Matrix: He was known.
> Insert: He has been released. (T/passive already applied.)
> T/for . . . to/T acc pro: for him to have been released
> *He was known for him to have been released.
> T/for + N del: He was known to have been released.

EXERCISE

Underline the embedded infinitives in the sentences below and identify each according to aspect and voice.

Example:

Aspect: base form Voice: active He arrived to become my successor.

	Aspect	*Voice*	*Sentence*
1.	__________	__________	Nitchie did not claim to have discovered a new method of lipreading.

2. __________ __________ He had to pay his staff.

3. __________ __________ It is well to be reminded of our responsibilities.

4. __________ __________ In the 1920's it was not unusual for a child to have suffered a total loss of hearing.

5. __________ __________ He had prayed to be allowed to be of service.

6. __________ __________ Many children were also known to have been born deaf.

7. __________ __________ He is known to have been taking many trips abroad.

Answers:

1. perfect, active, to have discovered
2. present, active, to pay
3. present, passive, to be reminded
4. perfect, active, to have suffered
5. present, passive, to be allowed; present, active, to be
6. perfect, passive, to have been born
7. perfect progressive, active, to have been taking

EXERCISE

Make the infinitives in these sentences passive:

1. They ought to pay their bills.

____

2. The children wanted someone to praise them.

____

3. It is obligatory for you to report the accident.

____

4. Nitchie had to pay his staff.

____

Answers:

1. Their bills ought to be paid (by them).
2. The children wanted to be praised (by someone).
3. It is obligatory for the accident to be reported by you.
4. His staff had to be paid by Nitchie.

An infinitive may be positive or negative. When it is negative, *not* is inserted before the *to:*

He is known *not to have left* the country.

They decided *not to buy* a house.

The children are *not to go* outside for recess.

We asked them *not to deliver* the package.

The infinitive transformations discussed in this lesson which young children will want to incorporate in their spoken language include the following:

Beth is afraid to dive.

I am happy to see you.

This box is too heavy to carry.

This box is too heavy for me to carry.

A great deal of practice must be given in discriminating between the use of prepositional phrases beginning with *to,* infinitives, and action nominals following familiar verbs such as *went, like,* and *want:*

We went *to the pool.* (Prepositional phrase.)

We went *swimming.* (Action nominal.)

I like/to swim/swimming. (Infinitive or action nominal.)

I want *to go swimming.* (Action noun following infinitive.)

The other patterns and transformations incorporating infinitives into sentences can be introduced as needed for purposes of comprehending reading materials and for advanced written language.

LESSON 33

Embedded Questions and Indirect Discourse

ABSTRACT

- Questions may be embedded as noun phrase complements in sentences.
- The complementizers for the embedded questions are the Wh-interrogatives.
- The transformation that embeds questions restores the original order of NP + VP to the question.
- Wh- questions may be embedded as clauses with full verbs or as infinitives.
- Sentence patterns for embedding *statements, requests,* and *questions* in indirect discourse after the verbs *ask, say,* and *tell* are somewhat complicated for language-handicapped children to learn.
- Statements are embedded after the verbs *say* and *tell* using the complementizer *that.*
- Requests are embedded after the verbs *tell* and *ask* using the infinitive complementizer, with *for* deleted.
- Yes-no questions are embedded after the verb *ask* using the complementizer *if* or its alternate *whether.*
- Wh- questions are embedded as clauses or infinitives after the verbs *ask* and *tell.*

In Lessons 6 and 7 you learned how sentences could be transformed to questions. In this lesson we will discuss the embedding of questions in sentences, giving special attention to their appearance in indirect discourse. This lesson will conclude the discussion on indirect discourse by presenting the most commonly used patterns which follow the verbs *ask, say,* and *tell.*

By now you are well aware that noun phrase complements can appear in noun positions in sentences. The italicized constituents in the illustrations below are embedded questions functioning as noun phrase complements. They are introduced by the Wh- interrogatives, including *how, why, what, where, when,* and *which,* which act as complementizers in this transformation:

Subject: *How he said it* touched me deeply.

Object of NP: I remember *why he came.*

Object of Preposition: He will have to pay for *what he did.*

Object of Infinitive: He intended to show us *where they were.*

Object of VP: He doesn't know *when he lost it.*

Object of VP: He doesn't know *which he wants.*

The surface structures of these *underlined* constituents do not look like ordinary questions, but that is what they were before they became embedded in these sentences. The rationale for considering them as questions can be illustrated by paraphrasing:

I remember why he came.

in this way:

I remember the answer to the question "Why did he come?"

The next two examples involving direct and indirect discourse demonstrate even more clearly that the embedded constituents are questions:

Direct: Axel asked, "Where is Roberta?"
Indirect: Axel asked where Roberta was.

Direct: Mrs. True asked Andy, "When did you go to bed?"
Indirect: Mrs. True asked Andy when he went to bed.

The transformation that embeds questions eliminates the T/yes-no and T/do transformations which are obligatory under certain conditions for formulating ordinary questions, and, in effect, retains the natural order of noun and verb phrases as found in basic sentence patterns. The complementizer remains first in the string of words and is followed in order by the NP and then the VP. Following are the steps used for embedding a question in the subject position:

Matrix: It baffles me
Insert: Why did he write that letter? ==>
T/Wh + NP + VP: why he wrote that letter
*It why he wrote that letter baffles me. ==>
T/it del: Why he wrote that letter baffles me.

Several transformations can be applied to the last sentence to check on the verity of the embedded question as a noun phrase complement:

1. T/passive: I was baffled *by why he wrote that letter.*
2. T/extrap: It baffles me *why he wrote that letter.*
3. T/cleft sentence: *What baffles me* is *why he wrote that letter.*

Notice that there are now two embedded questions in the last sentence.

In the next example the embedded question replaces the object pronoun *it:*

Matrix: Everyone knows (it).
Insert: How long does it take to go to the moon? =>
T/Wh + NP + VP: how long it takes to go to the moon
*Everyone knows it how long it takes to go to the moon. =>
T/it del: Everyone knows how long it takes to go to the moon.

Wh- questions may also be embedded as infinitives directly following verbs having the feature <+ catenation> such as *consider, decide, discover, find out, forget, know, learn, remember,* and *wonder*. For instance the next sentence:

I wondered what to say to him.

may be paraphrased:

I wondered, "What shall I say to him?"

The process that created the infinitive is based on the now familiar *T/for . . . to* transformation. It is applied to the Wh- question as follows: The complementizer is left as the first element in the string; *to + base form of verb* replaces tense and aspect in the question; and *T/accus pron* replaces a nominative subject where it is required:

Matrix: I wondered.
Insert: What shall I say to him? =>
T/for . . . to; T/accus pron: What for me to say to him? =>
T/for + N del: What to say to him
I wondered what to say to him.

This is a very useful pattern for hearing-impaired children to learn. They will find it not too difficult to master and it can be very functional in their spoken and written expression. Here are some examples:

Bill knows how to ski.
I remembered when to go to gym.
We learned how to make brownies today.
I forgot how to spell Mississippi.

All of the noun phrase complements we have studied are involved in reporting what people ask, say, or tell. Some important aspects of indirect discourse were introduced in Lessons 16 and 22. You may wish to refresh your memory about attracted sequence of tenses and the complications of pronoun reference by rereading these lessons.

In this lesson we will concentrate on the most common patterns used for embedding *statements, requests,* and *questions* after the verbs *ask, say,* and *tell,* but we will not concern ourselves with the transformations used to create the embedding nor analyze the functions of the embedded constituents. You should recognize them for what they are and be able to identify their roles if you have thoroughly mastered the transformations discussed in the last several lessons. The teacher should be aware that these patterns may serve as an organizing principle to help the children learn to report what people have said to them.

Since we are dealing mainly with the spoken form of language in direct and indirect discourse, some liberty has been taken to state alternate ways of reporting the direct discourse in the illustrations that follow. We are not concerned with precise transformations and therefore need not adhere to the exact words in translating from direct to indirect discourse. The past tense is used in the examples in order to help isolate the generalities presented in the patterns. All rules for correct sequence of tenses are observed.

To embed statements such as:

Dad will be home soon.

Bibi can't find her kitten.

in indirect discourse, the complementizer, *that,* is used after the verbs *say* and *tell* in these patterns:

Pattern 1.1 X + *say (that)* + Y

Pattern 1.2 X + *say to N (that)* + Y

Pattern 1.3 X + *tell N (that)* + Y

where X is everything that precedes the verbs *say* and *tell,* and where Y is everything that follows the complementizer. Parentheses indicate optional constituents which may be removed from the pattern. For example:

Pattern 1.1

Direct: Mother said, "Dad will be home soon."
Indirect: Mother said that Dad would be home soon.
Mother said Dad would be home soon.

Pattern 1.2

Direct: Elvira said to me, "Bibi can't find her kitten."
Indirect: Elvira said to me that Bibi couldn't find her kitten.

Pattern 1.3

Indirect: Elvira told me that Bibi couldn't find her kitten.

To embed a request such as:

Hurry up!
Please don't be late.

in an indirect report, an infinitive sentence is used after the verbs *tell* and *ask. Ask* is used in more polite forms where *please* or a tone of voice indicates a softening of a request. The complementizer *for* is deleted in these patterns:

Pattern 2.1 X + *tell NP to* + *inf* + Y

Pattern 2.2 X + *ask NP to* + *inf* + Y

For example:

Pattern 2.1

Direct: "Hurry up!" said Bill to Flora.
Indirect: Bill told Flora to hurry up.

Pattern 2.2

Direct: Flora said to Barry, "Please don't be late."
Indirect: Flora asked Barry not to be late.

To embed a yes-no question such as:

Will Stan call for you?

the complementizer *if* or its alternate *whether* introduces the question after the verb *ask* in this pattern:

Pattern 3 X + *ask (N) if/whether NP* + *VP* + Y

The question must be retransformed to its original state as a sentence. The number of deletions in the indirect sentence depends on what the reporter wishes to include in his message. For example:

Pattern 3

Direct: Mother asked Miriam, "Will Stan call for you?"
Indirect: Mother asked Miriam if Stan would call for her.
Mother asked Miriam whether Stan would call for her.

Direct: Mother said, "Will Stan call for you?"
Indirect: Mother asked if/whether Stan would call for me/him/her.

In the last example the person spoken to would be identified by the situation in which it occurred.

Wh- questions may be embedded as clauses containing full verbs, or as infinitives after the verbs *ask* and *tell*. The complementizers *who, what, where, when, why, which,* and *how* are used to introduce the questions in these patterns:

Pattern 4.1 X + *ask N Wh- complementizer* + *clause* + Y

Pattern 4.2 X + *ask N Wh- complementizer* + *infinitive* +Y

Pattern 4.3 X + *tell N Wh- complementizer* + *clause* + Y

Pattern 4.4 X + *tell N Wh- complementizer* + *infinitive* + Y

For example:

Pattern 4.1

Direct: "Gene, where shall I meet you?" asked Eunice.
Indirect: Eunice asked Gene where she should meet him.

Pattern 4.2

Direct: "Gene, where shall I meet you?" asked Eunice.
Indirect: Eunice asked Gene where to meet him.

In Patterns 4.3 and 4.4 the indirect sentence is not a report of what the questioner *asked,* but gives the response of the person questioned. This may seem quite complicated, but it becomes relatively clear when presented in a natural and meaningful situation where an experience clarifies the interchange. For example:

Pattern 4.3

Direct: Ken to Kathy: "When shall I feed the baby?"
Indirect: Kathy to Ken: Kathy told him when he should feed the baby.

Pattern 4.4

Direct: Ken to Kathy: "When shall I feed the baby?"
Indirect: Kathy to Ken: Kathy told Ken when to feed the baby.

EXERCISE

Use the direct quotations below to create indirect discourse. Use as many different patterns for expressing the same idea as you can.

1. "I am annoyed by your antics," said Mother to John.

___

___

___

2. "Meet me at the haunted house at seven o'clock," said Dale to Bill.

___

___

___

3. "What are you chewing?" asked Bill's teacher.

___

___

___

4. "I'll call Phil later," said Mary to Jane.

___

___

___

5. "We're planning a surprise but don't tell Jane," said Dick. (Dick + Phil = we)

____

____

____

6. "When shall I meet you?" said Phil to Dick.

____

____

____

7. "Why are you so ornery?" said Mary to Phil.

____

____

____

Answers:

1. John's mother said to him that she was annoyed by his antics.
   John's mother said she was annoyed by his antics.
   John's mother told him she was annoyed by his antics.
2. Dale told Bill to meet him at the haunted house at seven o'clock.
   Dale asked Bill to meet him at the haunted house at seven o'clock.
3. Bill's teacher asked him what he was chewing.
   His teacher asked Bill what he was chewing.
4. Mary said to Jane that she'd call Phil later.
   Mary said that she'd call Phil later.·
   Mary told Jane that she'd call Phil later.
5. Dick said that he and Phil were planning a surprise party but not to tell Jane.
6. Paul asked Dick when he should meet him.
   Paul asked Dick when to meet him.
7. Mary asked Phil why he was so ornery.

Indirect discourse can become very complicated and confusing to children when they are expected to learn the many transformation rules with which it is involved. Language is not learned by learning rules about it. Children might better learn patterns under circumstances that clarify their use. If children have not derived the rules by induction, the teacher should guide them with pattern practice as the basis for learning to use indirect discourse.

LESSON 34

Pronouns Again: Indefinite Pronouns

ABSTRACT

- Indefinite pronouns are compounded with the determiners *no, any, some,* and *every* and the nouns *body, one,* and *thing,* resulting in this set: *nobody/one, nothing, anybody/one, anything, somebody/one, something, everybody/one,* and *everything.*
- The hybrid quality of these compounds is more appropriately described by the term *pronominal* than *pronoun,* since they are more like nouns than pronouns.
- Of the entire set, the words *nobody* and *nothing* deviate somewhat from the general phrase structure rules governing the indefinite pronouns. They may be preceded by another article and by adjectives, and they have a <— singular> feature.
- In general, indefinite pronouns are not preceded by determiners, cardinals, or ordinals, because they have their own built-in determiners, and because they have only the <+ singular> feature.
- Single adjectives and other noun modifiers may follow indefinite pronouns.
- The compounds containing *body* and *one* have the <+ human> feature and form their possessives by adding *-'s.* Those compounded with *thing* require the *of* + *N* phrase.
- The indefinite pronouns containing the nondefinite determiners *no, any,* and *some* may be used in the T/there transformation.
- Hearing-impaired children may find it difficult to differentiate between the meanings of the pronouns compounded with *some* and *any.*
- The compound relatives *whoever* and *whatever* are closely related in meaning to the phrase *anyone who* and *anything which.*
- The word *something* appears at early reading levels and may refer to a variety of conditions and events which must be clarified if reading matter is to be understood.

A category of words with which hearing-impaired children will come in contact are those designated, for want of a better term, as *indefinite pronouns* in most grammars. They include words compounded with the determiners *no, any, some,* and *every,* and the nouns *body, one,* and *thing,* and result in this set:

nobody	anybody	somebody	everybody
no one	anyone	someone	everyone
nothing	anything	something	everything

All are written as single words except *no one.* In their spoken form the major stress is on the first syllable.

Although the resulting set is not completely homogenous syntactically, it has many of the features of nouns. All the words may occupy noun positions in sentences, but unlike the personal pronouns, *he, she, it, we,* and *they,* and the relative pronouns, they do not have direct referents to other nouns. It would seem more appropriate to call these words *pronominals,* a term implying their hybrid noun-pronoun quality. Since they are familiarly known as *indefinite pronouns,* we shall refer to them as such, but consider their characteristics as a special category of nouns.

In the following sentence the indefinite pronouns function as subject, direct and indirect objects, and object of a preposition:

No one gives *anybody something* for *nothing* these days.

EXERCISE

To refresh your memory concerning the function of NPs in sentences, indicate the role of each of the italicized words. The italicized indefinite pronoun may be the head word in the NP or the entire noun phrase. In the space provided, write either *subject, direct object, indirect object, object or preposition,* or *complement* to indicate its function.

____________ 1. I'll leave *everything* to you.

____________ 2. He is *somebody* to be admired.

____________ 3. Give it to *someone* who cares.

____________ 4. *Everyone* ought to be notified.

____________ 5. She called Julie *something* unprintable.

____________ 6. Ruthie told Charlotte *something,* but she didn't tell me.

____________ 7. Dorothy will give *someone* her old fur coat.

____________ 8. There is *no one* here but me.

____________ 9. I don't like *anything* sour.

____________ 10. *Everything* is in an uproar now.

Answers:

1. direct object
2. complement
3. object of preposition
4. subject
5. complement
6. direct object
7. indirect object
8. subject
9. direct object
10. subject

The two words that deviate most from the general phrase structure rules for the entire set are *nobody* and *nothing*. As we go along, we will note their exceptions to the general rules.

Since indefinite pronouns have built-in determiners, they are not preceded by other determiners. However, the words *nobody* and *nothing* may sometimes appear with another determiner or predeterminer. We do not say:

> **An anybody* may apply for the job.
>
> *George gave a *something* to *that someone.*

But we can say:

> He's *a nobody.*
>
> That's *a lot of nothing.*

The indefinite pronouns may be preceded by the predeterminers *even, just,* and *only.*

> *Even nothing* would be better than that.
>
> *Just anything* will do.
>
> If *only someone* would tell the truth!

Except for *nobody* and *nothing*, this group of words has a <+ singular> feature only. None in the group may be preceded by cardinals or ordinals:

> **Several somethings* bothered Terry.
>
> *Give this to *the three everybodies.*

We do see and hear sentences like these:

> They are *nobodies* in my estimation.
>
> He whispered sweet *nothings* in her ear.

In poetic expression, which allows for all kinds of syntactic deviation, adjectives may precede these indefinite pronouns; otherwise they follow them. The exception to this rule again are *nobody* and *nothing*, which may be preceded by adjectives. Acceptable sentences include:

> A *bright something* lit up the southern sky.
>
> Here's *something* for you. It's just *a foolish little nothing.*

These sentences are not grammatically correct:

**The exact something* left him puzzled.

*Marcia likes *neat everything.*

A single adjective follows the indefinite pronoun:

. . . something old, something new, something borrowed, something blue.

All of the compounds may be followed by the usual types of post-nominal constituents which result from the transformations discussed throughout this book:

Prepositional phrase: something *of importance*

Clause: something *that Jo Ann wanted badly*

Infinitive: something *to live for*

The forms compounded with *body* and *one* have the noun feature <+ human> and the possessive feature <+ genitive>. They form their possessives like nouns by adding *-'s*. The others, compounded with *thing,* require the *of* + *N* phrase:

Everybody's business is *nobody's* business.

That is *anybody's* guess.

Jerri found *someone's (somebody's)* purse.

Carrying the burden *of everything* was too much for Don.

Irene had an attack *of something* or other.

The indefinite pronouns compounded with the nondefinite determiners *no, any,* and *some* may be used in the T/there transformation:

There is nothing here for you.

There isn't anyone at the door.

There is someone at the door.

On the whole the syntactic rules for indefinite pronouns are relatively simple. Their semantic aspects may be more difficult for children who must learn language without benefit of hearing it. Meaning will have to be taught in conjunction with syntax in situations which clarify both of these aspects.

Words compounded with *no* and *every* are relatively easy to understand since they represent the extremes of *none* and *all.* The difference in meaning between those made up with *some* and *any* is much more subtle. *Somebody, someone,* and *something* refer to unspecified generalities while the idea behind *anybody, anyone,* and *anything* implies a narrowing of the generality to involve one or each of the group referred to.

In this request:

Will *somebody* please turn off the lights?

no one of the group to which it was addressed is singled out to respond, nor is anyone obliged to respond. If someone asks:

> Has anyone seen Jim?

the implication is that at least one or each of the persons addressed is expected to respond.

The next examples should clarify the meanings of *something* and *anything*. In the next sentence, a general, unspecified thing is referred to:

> I'd like *something* to drink.

In response to the question:

> What will you have (to drink)?

the answer might be:

> *Anything* will be just fine.

implying that any one of a number of things such as coffee, tea, milk or the like would be acceptable.

The most easily taught use of *anything* is its replacement of *something* in negative statements, as in:

> Ella saw *something*.
>
> Bea didn't see *anything*.

In passing, it is interesting to note that the compounded relative pronouns *whoever* and *whatever*, have meanings closely related to the phrases *anybody, anyone/who* and *anything/which, that* as in:

> *Anybody who* is exposed to continuous loud noise may lose some of his hearing. =>
> *Whoever* is exposed to continuous loud noise may lose some of his hearing.
>
> *Anything that* you say will be held against you. =>
> *Whatever* you say will be held against you.

While it is difficult for hearing-impaired children to sense the subtleties of meanings of these compounds, they can be clarified over a period of time through constant use in meaningful situations. All of the indefinite pronouns appear in easy reading materials prepared for hearing children. The word *something* seems to be the most important of the set, for it is found even in preprimers and is widely used thereafter. The others are gradually introduced and used at all levels beyond the first grade.

The meaning of *something* in children's books may involve anything from an implied reference to an object, a physical event, an involved series of activities, or a thought. As such, it is similar to a pronoun in that its referents have to be identified through implication before a child can understand what he is reading. For instance, here are some sentences which could be encountered in readers:

> Come here and do something, Jan. (Push the swing.)
>
> I can do something. (Kick the ball.)
>
> Pete heard something behind him. (A rustle in the bushes.)
>
> We made something funny. (Hats, cookies.)
>
> I know something. (Paul hit Jerry. Jerry got a bloody nose and went home crying.)

Children will have to be exposed to the indefinite pronouns early in their language learning experiences, and should become familiar with their function and meaning through constant association with conditions and situations in which they can be naturally explained.

EXERCISE

Write out the basic sentence (or sentences) from which the following transformed sentences were constructed.

1. Everybody who reads this book will want to buy it.

 ____

 ____

2. Nothing Lola Jean could say would improve the situation.

 ____

 ____

3. Grace needs something to write with.

 ____

 ____

4. Jo Ann wants something with a long skirt.

 ____

 ____

5. Nothing was revealed by the committee.

 ____

 ____

6. Do you have something for sale?

____

____

7. Hazel couldn't find anything.

____

____

Answers:

1. Everybody will want to buy it. Everybody reads this book.
2. Nothing would improve the situation. Lola Jean could say nothing.
3. Grace needs something. She writes with something.
4. Jo Ann wants something. Something has a long skirt.
5. The committee revealed nothing.
6. You have something for sale.
7. Hazel could find something.

LESSON 35

Prepositions and Prepositional Phrases

ABSTRACT

- Prepositions are words that function to establish structural units called prepositional phrases.
- Prepositions may have as their objects nouns with their determiners, pronouns, action nominals, phrases and clauses.
- Some grammarians believe that nouns carry the feature <+ preposition> in the deep structure of a sentence, since specific nouns seems to govern specific prepositions.
- Basic sentence pattern V, $NP + be + Adv_p$, is frequently completed with an adverbial prepositional phrase.
- In conjunction with verbs expressing action, some of the prepositions of position are also used to connote movement.
- Many intransitive verbs are followed by complements. Prepositional phrases frequently function as verb phrase complements.
- The complement follows the verb and may not be shifted to the beginning of the sentence.
- Prepositional phrases that serve as sentence modifiers may be shifted to the beginning of the sentence by T/adverbial shift.
- Some prepositional phrases are merely sentence introducers and have no syntactical relation to other parts of the sentence.
- Prepositions are highly involved in idiomatic expressions in which literal meanings of the components involved are replaced by entirely new meanings.
- Two-word verbs consisting of verb and preposition are frequently involved in idiomatic usage.
- Adjectives may be followed by prepositional verb phrase complements.
- Particular adjectives pattern with particular prepositions.
- Prepositional phrases in postnominal positions are usually the result of a relative clause reduction.
- The transformation *T/with* + *NP* may be derived from an insert sentence containing the verb *have*.

Prepositions are a special kind of word which functions to establish structural units called prepositional phrases. Such phrases are composed of a preposition followed by a noun phrase. Prepositions may have as their objects not only nouns with their determiners, or pronouns, but also action nominals, phrases, and clauses:

Noun: The child ran *across the street.*

Pronoun: He talked *about himself.*

Action Nominal: She made a fortune *by modeling.*

Phrase: They liked him *in spite of his insistence on inconsequential minutiae.*

Clause: He took her *to the shows she wanted to see.*

There are about 60 simple prepositions and about 25 compound prepositions in use in English. They are listed below:

about	before	except	off of	through
above	behind	except for	on	throughout
across	below	from	on account of	together with
across from	beneath	in	on top of	toward
against	beside	in addition to	onto	under
after	between	in behalf of	opposite	underneath
along	beyond	in front of	out	unlike
along with	but	in place of	out of	up
alongside of	by	in regard to	outside of	up to
amid	by means of	inside	over	up with
among	concerning	instead of	over to	until
apart from	considering	in spite of	regarding	unto
around	despite	into	regardless of	with
away from	down	like	round	within
as	down from	near	since	without
at	due to	of	till	
back of	during	off	to	

Nine of these prepositions, according to Fries (1940) accounted for over 90 percent of the prepositions used in the large body of written materials he surveyed. He found the order of their frequency to be: *of, in, to, for, at, on, from, with,* and *by*. Unlikely as it may seem, there may be as many as 250 meanings for these nine prepositions alone. It is not surprising then to learn that children who have severe hearing deficits have considerable difficulty in learning the syntactical functions of prepositions and prepositional phrases as well as in understanding their multifaceted semantic aspects.

Some grammarians believe that nouns carry the feature <+ preposition> in the deep structure of a sentence. This is illustrated in the passive transformation where the subject of the verb in the active voice is converted to an object of the preposition *by* in the passive. It is conjectured that *by* was a part of the noun phrase in the deep structure and was retained in this instance in the surface structure. Moreover, some nouns seem to affect the choice of the prepositions used with them. This is particularly evident in prepositional phrases expressing time:

> I go to school *on* Monday/Tuesday/Wednesday.
>
> I go to school *at* night.
>
> I woke up *at* noon/midnight/dawn.
>
> I go *in* the evening/afternoon/morning.
>
> I go only *in* summer/winter/fall/spring.

If we believe that the current theorizing about prepositions is correct, nouns become the keys to the choice of prepositions. However, much is yet to be learned about the relationship of specific prepositions to specific nouns. Until linguists verify and amplify or change their theories, we can only hope to look at the surface structure of sentences containing prepositional phrases and try to pull together some salient facts which may help pupils understand the use of prepositions.

Basic sentence pattern V, NP + be + Adv_p, may be completed by the adverbs *here* and *there,* but is more frequently completed with an adverbial prepositional phrase of place. These phrases of place are introduced by prepositions which indicate position: *above, across, against, among, at, back of, behind, below, beneath, beside, between, beyond, by, inside, near, on, on top of, outside, outside of, over,* and *under:*

> My notebook is *among the others.*
>
> The newspaper is *under the table.*
>
> The mistletoe is *over the entrance.*

We should note that prepositional phrases other than those of location can also serve as the complement in the pattern, NP + be + Adv:

> The man was *up to his ears in debt.*
>
> She was *under the weather.*
>
> Bill was *onto her tricks.*
>
> They were *on trial.*

Some of the prepositions that indicate position also express movement when they appear in sentences with verbs of action. Some prepositions used with movement include: *above, across, around, away, by, down, down from, from, into, onto, off, through, to, toward, up,* and *up to. Into* and *onto* substitute for *in* and *on* in this list. Below, prepositions of position and movement are contrasted:

> Position: Marynell is across the street.
> Movement: Mary Ann ran across the room.

Position: Gloria is in the pool.
Movement: She jumped into the pool.

Position: Virginia sat under the tree.
Movement: Dennis crawled under the fence.

EXERCISE

Underline the prepositional phrases in the sentences below. In the blanks, identify them as referring to movement, place, time, or duration.

1. ____________ They stood on the steps outside.
2. ____________ They walked through the library doors.
3. ____________ All through the night they studied.
4. ____________ They have been working since seven this morning.
5. ____________ They have decided to go to the library.
6. ____________ They will study again after supper.
7. ____________ The library is way across the campus.
8. ____________ The librarian asked them to check out their books.
9. ____________ Their efforts paid off when they took their tests.
10. ____________ They went to the Union to celebrate.

Answers:

1. *on the steps outside,* place
2. *through the library doors,* movement
3. *all through the night,* duration
4. *since seven this morning,* duration
5. *to the library,* place
6. *after supper,* time
7. *across the campus,* place
8. no prepositional phrase (*to* is the sign of the infinitive)
9. no prepositional phrase (*off* is part of a two-word verb)
10. *to the Union,* movement

Many intransitive verbs like *apply, attend, glance, go, laugh, play, rely, sit, stand,* and *tend,* which generally do not occur alone, are often completed by adverbial prepositional phrases known as verb complements:

He applied *for a job.*

He attended *to his brother's affairs.*

He glanced *at the newspaper.*

He went *to the party.*

He laughed *at their jokes.*

He played *with their children.*

He relied *on his wife* for help.

The complement follows the verb and stays with it. It cannot be moved around. If it is, an ungrammatical sentence results:

*For a job he applied.

*To his brother's affairs he attended.

*At the newspaper he glanced.

*To the party he went.

Some types of prepositional phrases may be shifted by the adverbial shift transformation without disturbing the meaning of the sentence. These phrases function as adverbial sentence modifiers rather than as verb complements. The following sentences illustrate T/adv shift:

Margaret should be able to find a job with your help.
T/adv shift: With your help Margaret should be able to find a job.

Pete left the college against his better judgment.
T/adv shift: Against his better judgment Pete left the college.

Betty Jane won the first prize to her amazement.
T/adv shift: To her amazement Betty Jane won the first prize.

Prepositional phrases may also serve as sentence introducers rather than sentence modifiers. These introducers have no syntactical relationship to other parts of the sentence. Many of them are idiomatic expressions and must be learned as such:

For all I know, he has resigned.

For one thing, I know he won't be back tonight.

For example, here is a quote from his last speech.

For that matter, I'm not sure either.

Most of the common prepositions are highly involved in idiomatic language. Fifty or more idioms using the preposition *for* are listed in a dictionary of idioms (Boatner and Gates, 1966). There are few, if any, patterns that govern these idioms, and thus the whole matter of learning many additional combinations of words with their multiple meanings complicates the matter for children who must learn language without the benefit of hearing it.

The idioms in the following sentences change the literal meaning of both the verb *ran* and the prepositions involved. New linguistic units are created, but the prepositions still maintain their characteristics as prepositions:

Louise *ran for* the School Board. (sought office on)

La Verne *ran into* her friend downtown. (met)

Lorraine *ran across* some old letters. (found)

Lois *ran through her lines.* (practiced)

In Lesson 19 you learned that a preposition may be brought to the beginning of a sentence in a question transformation. Applying this test to the above sentences we see that they contain prepositions even though semantically the verb and preposition are inseparable:

For what did Louise run?

Into whom did La Verne Louise run?

Across what did Lorraine run?

Through what did Lois run?

You will recall that it is not possible to shift a particle to the first position in a sentence, but the particle may be shifted to a position after a noun phrase as this example illustrates:

The woman *ran down* her neighbors.

*Down whom did she run?

T/part shift: The woman *ran* her neighbors *down*.

The use of prepositional phrases following adjectives is fairly complex. In Lesson 32 we learned that certain adjectives could be followed by verb phrase complements, either clauses or infinitives, as in:

Lillian was afraid that Lauri had had an accident.

Claudia was glad to see Marilyn.

Many adjectives may be followed by prepositional phrases, but there are some constraints placed on the prepositions that may pattern with particular adjectives. We can say:

John was crazy about Jean.

John was good to Jean.

but not:

*John was crazy with Jean.

*John was good by Jean.

The following table contains a partial list of adjectives and prepositions that may be used together.

Table 13. Adjectives That Pattern with Prepositions

Adjectives	*Prepositions*
cheerful, clear, concerned, confused, crazy, funny, glad, happy, pleased, sad, troubled	about
confused, distracted, pleased, troubled, united	by
easy, favorable, good, great, hard, necessary, qualified, useful, wonderful	for
acceptable, applicable, attractive, cordial, courteous, equal, essential, faithful, favorable, funny, good, grateful, harmful, necessary, thankful	to
affiliated, alive, astir, careless, clumsy, contented, cross, disgusted, dissatisfied, happy, overgrown, pleased, satisfied, stiff	with

In Lesson 24 you learned how prepositional phrases became postnominal modifiers as the result of deletions applied to relative clauses:

The boys who are in the yard are his sons.
T/rel pron + be del: The boys *in the yard* are his sons.

Let's visit the girls who are across the hall.
T/rel pron + be del: Let's visit the girls *across the hall.*

Not every prepositional phrase that modifies a noun is derived from a relative clause. In particular, some phrases that begin with the preposition *with* are derived from insert sentences containing the verb *have*. The subject and *have* are deleted and replaced with a prepositional phrase, as in:

Matrix: Grace bought a dress.
Insert: The dress has a pleated skirt. =>
T/with phrase: Grace bought a dress with a pleated skirt.

It is important for children to be aware of the synonomy of these sentences.

EXERCISE

Underline the prepositional phrases, if any, in the following sentences. Indicate the function of each prepositional phrase in the sentences by checking the columns to the right of the sentences.

Key to columns:

Comp: Complement of basic sentence pattern V
Vb Comp: Complement of transitive or intransitive verb
Sent Mod: Sentence modifier
Sent I: Sentence introducer
Doub V: Part of a two-word verb
Noun Mod: Modifier of a noun

	Comp Patt V	Vb Comp	Sent Mod	Sent Intr	Doub Verb	Noun Mod
1. Ed came with Allison.	____	____	____	____	____	____
2. Betty looked critically at the proposal.	____	____	____	____	____	____
3. For that matter, Alice is very frank.	____	____	____	____	____	____
4. The children are in the yard.	____	____	____	____	____	____
5. They are playing on the swings.	____	____	____	____	____	____
6. They are in Miss V's class.	____	____	____	____	____	____
7. The children on the swings are having fun.	____	____	____	____	____	____
8. For that price, you ought to get two.	____	____	____	____	____	____
9. Please sit on the sofa.	____	____	____	____	____	____
10. Put away your books.	____	____	____	____	____	____
11. He took me for a ride.	____	____	____	____	____	____
12. She has a new car with whitewalls.	____	____	____	____	____	____
13. It doesn't seem possible to get along without a car.	____	____	____	____	____	____
14. Without thinking, she gave the plan away.	____	____	____	____	____	____

Answers:

1. *with Allison,* Vb Comp
2. *at the proposal,* Vb Comp
3. *for that matter,* Sent Intr
4. *in the yard,* Comp Patt V
5. *on the swings,* Vb Comp
6. *in Miss V's class,* Comp Patt V
7. *on the swings,* Noun Mod
8. *for that price,* Sent Mod
9. *on the sofa,* Vb Comp
10. no prepositional phrase (particle)
11. *for a ride,* Vb Comp
12. *with white walls,* Noun Mod
13. *without a car,* Vb Comp
14. *without thinking,* Sent Mod

LESSON 36

Adverbials

ABSTRACT

- A few adverbs have the same form as adjectives.
- Most adverbs of manner are derived from adjectives.
- *-ly* adverbs may be preceded by the same qualifiers as are used with adjectives.
- Polysyllabic adverbs ending in *-ly* are compared with the function words *more* and *most*.
- Monosyllabic adverbs, like adjectives, are compared by adding the inflectional endings *-er* and *-est*.
- Some adverbs have special distributional characteristics which allow them to be placed at the beginning of a sentence, before a finite verb or auxiliary, between an auxiliary and a following verbal form, and at the end of the sentence.
- An adverb with negative connotations cannot be used with another negative qualifier in the verb phrase.
- Adverbials can be shifted to positions away from the final one, if they are not complements of the verb.
- Adverbs of time and place generally have little relationship to the verb itself, but instead modify the whole VP or even the whole sentence, thus making a shift possible.
- Adverbs of place resist shift a bit more than do adverbs of time and manner.
- An adverbial clause may be created from any English sentence by adding an introductory word to the sentence and then embedding it in a matrix without changing its word order.
- There are many introductory adverbs or subordinators that introduce clauses of cause, condition, concession, comparison, location, manner, purpose, and time.

A quick summary of what we have learned thus far about adverbs and adverbial constituents in sentences should set the stage for a more detailed study of adverbial elements in this lesson. We know that:

(1) The order of adverbs in a series generally places the adverb of place first in the series, the adverb of manner second, and the adverb of time the last, as in:

They performed *here magnificently yesterday.*

However, the order is not inviolable, for we could say:

They performed *here yesterday magnificently.*

(2) Some adverbs are closely identified with a verb and become an integral part of the verb phrase, as in:

Sit down/Stand up/Go away/Look out.

(3) Prepositional phrases may occupy the regular adverbial positions after the verb or at the end of a sentence. Prepositional phrases that serve as complements are not shifted to the beginning of a sentence, whereas adverbial phrases that modify the entire sentence may be moved. For example, we ordinarily do not shift an adverbial complement as in:

The boys *ran down the street.* =>
Down the street the boys ran.

but in the next sentence, it is entirely feasible to shift the adverbial modifier:

The children played tag *during recess time.* =>
During recess time the children played tag.

(4) An infinitive sentence may serve as an adverbial complement of a verb, as in:

The children hurried *to get their prizes.*

(5) The interrogatives, *where, when, why,* and *how,* introduce questions whose answers are adverbial elements in sentences.

In this lesson we will look at the creation of adverbs from other classes of words, the transformation that moves adverbs around in sentence patterns, and the function of adverbial clauses as modifiers.

A few adverbs such as *cheap, early, fast, hard, near, slow,* and *straight* have the same form as adjectives. Adjectives are generally distinguished from adverbs by their positions before nouns. Adverbs, on the other hand, usually, but not always, follow verbs:

That's *hard* work. (Adj)

Elaine *works hard.* (Adv)

Most adverbs of manner, those answering the question *how,* are derived from adjectives. The derivational suffix *-ly* is added to an adjective to form the adverb, as in:

creative, creatively

contented, contentedly

logical, logically

The *-ly* ending is also a feature of adjectives, but their base is usually a noun as in:

body, bodily

hour, hourly

Other derivational affixes which mark small groups of adverbs are *-ward(s)* and *-wise* as in *backwards* and *lengthwise*. The prefix *a-* is the marker of quite a number of adverbs derived from nouns, verbs, or adjectives as *ahead, apart, around, afire, adrift, afloat, aglow, astir, anew, aboard, aloud, aloft and alone.*

Generally, intransitive verbs, transitive verbs that can be passivized, and the linking verbs *become, stay, remain, grow* and *turn* may be followed by adverbs of manner. The copula *be* or the verb *have* cannot be followed by an adverb of manner:

He went *quietly*.

The storm battered the coastline *mercilessly*.

*They were tired *logically*.

*The dog has a bone *eagerly*.

Adverbs ending in *-ly* may be preceded by the same qualifiers as are used with adjectives. They are: *a bit, a little, somewhat, pretty, quite, rather, too, very, mighty,* as in:

a bit/noisy/noisily

quite/harsh/harshly

mighty/spasmodic/spasmodically

Polysyllabic adverbs ending in *-ly* are used in structures of comparison with the function words *more* and *most,* while monosyllabic adverbs are compared by adding the inflectional endings *-er* and *est:*

She accepted her status *more* complacent*ly* than I did.

He works hard*er* than most men.

In the comparative degree the following qualifiers may be used: *no, a bit, a little, somewhat, a lot, a whole lot, much, very much, even,* and *still,* as in:

. . . no more spiritedly than his sire.

. . . even more dejectedly than predicted.

. . . still more triumphantly than they had anticipated.

An outstanding characteristic of adverbs is their movability within the sentence. Normally they occur at the end of a sentence, but they may also be found in these positions:

At the beginning of the sentence.

Before a finite verb.

Before an auxiliary.

Between an auxiliary and the following verbal form. (If the negative transformation has been applied, the adverb follows the word *not.)*

A simple adverbial shift transformation moves adverbs of manner, time, and frequency from the end of the sentence to the other positions. The following examples illustrate this shift (T/adv shift):

Adverb of Manner

Martha has discharged her duties faithfully.

Faithfully, Martha has discharged her duties.

Martha faithfully has discharged her duties.

Martha has faithfully discharged her duties.

Adverb of Time

Charlotte is making her decision now.

Now she is making her decision.

She now is making her decision.

She is now making her decision.

Adverb of Frequency

A rather large subset of adverbs answering the question *How often?* has the special distributional characteristics outlined above. Organized according to their lexical meanings from lowest to highest frequency, they include, *never, rarely, seldom, occasionally, sometimes, frequently, often,* and *always.* These adverbs can be used with the past and present tenses and with the present perfect aspect in the active and passive voices. Not all of them may be used in all of the four positions suggested above, so special guidance must be given children as they learn the positions allowed for each word. Because *sometimes* can fill the four positions, it will be used in the illustrations in the present tense and the present perfect aspect.

Active Voice:

Present tense:

Sheila shows flashes of brilliance *sometimes.*
Sometimes Sheila shows flashes of brilliance.
Sheila *sometimes* shows flashes of brilliance.

Present perfect aspect:

Joyce has surprised her friends by her wit *sometimes.*
Sometimes Joyce has surprised her friends by her wit.
Joyce *sometimes* has surprised her friends by her wit.
Joyce has *sometimes* surprised her friends by her wit.

Passive Voice:

Present tense:

Events are reported incorrectly *sometimes.*
Sometimes events are reported incorrectly.
Events *sometimes* are reported incorrectly.
Events are *sometimes* reported incorrectly.

Present perfect aspect:

Burt has been mistaken for a movie actor *sometimes.*
Sometimes Burt has been mistaken for a movie actor.
Burt *sometimes* has been mistaken for a movie actor.
Burt has *sometimes* been mistaken for a movie actor.

Those adverbs which can appear at the beginning of the sentence before the NP include *sometimes, occasionally,* and *frequently.* Those which ordinarily appear directly before a finite verb or the first auxiliary and after the auxiliary are: *never, rarely, seldom, sometimes, occasionally, frequently, often,* and *always.* Those which ordinarily appear at the end of the sentence are: *sometimes, occasionally, frequently,* and *often.* Table 14 shows the usual distribution of this subset of adverbs.

Table 14. Distribution of Adverbs of Frequency in Sentences

At the beginning of a sentence	*Before a finite verb or auxiliary and between the auxiliary and a verbal form*	*At the end of a sentence*
	never	
	rarely	
	seldom	
sometimes	sometimes	sometimes
occasionally	occasionally	occasionally
frequently	frequently	frequently
	often	often
	always	

Since *never* has a negative connotation, it cannot be used with a VP containing another negative element. We cannot say:

*The girl has never not made the Honor Roll.

However, when *rarely* and *seldom* are used in negative statements, as in:

The girl has rarely not made the Honor Roll.

The girl has seldom not made the Honor Roll.

the meaning of the sentence is so modified as to mean that the girl has very often or almost always made the Honor Roll. The semantic aspects of this special set of words must be carefully considered as they are presented to children with language problems.

When *never, rarely,* and *seldom* occur first in a sentence, the T/yes-no transformation is necessary to make the sentence correct after the adverb shift has been applied.

I have never seen such diligence. =>
T/adv shift: *Never I have seen such diligence. =>
T/yes-no: Never have I seen such diligence.

Sue has rarely been late. =>
Rarely has Sue been late.

Pat was seldom challenged to do her best. =>
Seldom was Pat challenged to do her best.

Other adverbs that may be distributed throughout the sentence include: *conceivably, fortunately, frankly, generally, luckily, normally, obviously, possibly, probably, regrettably, theoretically, understandingly, undoubtedly,* and *usually.* Placing adverbs in different positions may or may not influence meaning. For instance, in the following sets of sentences, meaning is changed by the adverb shift in the first set but not in the second. The intonation and stress pattern influences the meaning of the second sentence.

Possibly I won't be able to go.
I won't possibly be able to go.

Usually Carol doesn't nap after dinner.
Carol usually doesn't nap after dinner.
Carol doesn't usually nap after dinner.

When position influences meaning, it should be brought to the attention of children with language problems.

EXERCISE

Use the adverb suggested in as many positions as possible:

1. *occasionally:* Barbara has missed her exams.

____

____

____

____

2. *frequently:* Jerri visits her parents in Wisconsin.

3. *often:* Janet has been commended for her skill in teaching.

4. *always:* Kathleen is expected to come through with an idea.

5. *rarely:* Sally has not cried at a sad movie.

Answers:

1. Occasionally Barbara has missed her exams.
   Barbara occasionally has missed her exams.
   Barbara has occasionally missed her exams.
   Barbara has missed her exams occasionally.
2. Frequently Jerri visits her parents in Wisconsin.
   Jerri frequently visits her parents in Wisconsin.
   Jerri visits her parents in Wisconsin frequently.
3. Janet often has been commended for her skill in teaching.
   Janet has often been commended for her skill in teaching.
   Janet has been commended for her skill in teaching often.
4. Kathleen always is expected to come through with an idea.
   Kathleen is always expected to come through with an idea.
5. Sally rarely has not cried at a sad movie.
   Sally has rarely not cried at a sad movie.
   Rarely has Sally not cried at a sad movie.

Adverbs of place resist shifting a bit more than adverbs of manner, frequency, and time, but they too may be moved. We find sentences such as these in children's literature:

Away she ran.

There they are.

Here he comes.

Up, up went the balloon. (Shift of NP and VP obligatory here.)

When we are dealing with adverbial prepositional phrases of place, the shift depends on whether the constituent is a complement or a sentence modifier. The complement is retained in the post-verbal position.

They live in New York.

*In New York they live.

In the following sentence there are two prepositional phrases. The first is a complement and the second an adjective prepositional phrase derived from a deleted relative clause:

They live in a high-rise apartment in New York.

The sentence was transformed as follows:

Matrix: They live in a high-rise apartment.
Insert: The apartment is in New York.
T/rel: They live in a high-rise apartment which is in New York.
T/rel + be del: They live in a high-rise apartment in New York.

It would not be possible to shift the complement *in a high-rise apartment in New York* to the beginning of the sentence:

*In a high-rise apartment in New York they live.

However, if we wished to contrast two sentences containing adverbial sentence modifiers we could say:

In New York they live in an apartment but in Florida they live in a house-trailer.

Children with language handicaps sometimes find it difficult to master even one of four possible patterns, but when they are learning to use adverbs they must become aware of the several options available for placing adverbs in sentences. After one pattern is learned it may be contrasted with others until all have become familiar. This requires a good deal of pattern practice.

An adverbial clause may be created from any English sentence by preceding it with an introductory word and embedding it in a matrix without further transformation. There are dozens of such introductory words called *subordinators* or *subordinating conjunctions*. Some of these words are used infrequently but they are included in Table 15 to emphasize the length of the list. Some subordinators introduce clauses of time or place, others introduce clauses of duration, purpose, cause, condition, location, comparison, or concession. Some of them introduce several types of clauses. Table 15 lists the subordinators for the various kinds of clauses.

Table 15. Subordinators Used to Introduce Adverbial Clauses

	KINDS OF CLAUSES							
Subordinator	*Cause*	*Condition*	*Concession*	*Comparison*	*Location*	*Manner*	*Purpose*	*Time*
as	x			x		x		x
as — as				x		x		x
as if						x		
as soon as								x
as though						x		
although			x					
after								x
before								x
because	x							
despite the fact that			x					
for	x							
for the purpose that							x	
for the reason that	x							
if		x						
inasmuch as	x							
in that						x		
in spite of the fact that			x					
in the way that						x		
in order that							x	
now that								x
notwithstanding that			x					
once								x
provided		x						
provided that		x						
since	x							x
so	x							
so as				x		x		
so long as		x					x	
so that							x	
than				x		x		

that						x	
the — the			x		x		
though		x					
unless	x						
until							x
when							x
whence				x			
whenever							x
where				x			
whereas		x					
wherever				x			
wheresoever				x			
whether	x						
while		x					x
whither				x			

Children with hearing impairments are not expected to learn the names of the categories of clauses nor even to use the less commonly encountered subordinators. First they learn the most useful introductory words in relation to their meaning in the context of a particular sentence. For instance, inspection of Table 15 reveals that there are seven subordinators that may be used to introduce casual clauses, the most common of which is *because*. In order to use *because* in a sentence children must first understand the relationship of cause and effect. When they are able to include *because* in a sentence correctly, they may then be introduced to other subordinators in the set, especially when they need to understand reading passages containing them.

Adverbial clauses, such as clauses of cause, condition, frequency, and time, may be shifted from the end to the beginning of sentences just as adverbs and prepositional phrases may be moved, when they modify the entire sentence. In the following sets of sentences a slight adjustment was made in the noun-pronoun sequence to make the second sentence sound more natural. Notice that the introductory clause is set off with a comma:

> Pete and Lydia were married *soon after he finished college.*
>
> *Soon after Pete finished college,* he and Lydia were married.
> Charles will drive you to the airport *if you ask him.*
> *If you ask Charles,* he will drive you to the airport.

Adverbial clauses may also also serve as complements of those intransitive verbs which generally require an additional constituent to complete the verb phrase. While a shift of the complement does not necessarily result in a completely ungrammatical sentence, the end product is usually an awkward sentence. This should be avoided.

> Estelle and Lois lived *where the road turns.*
> **Where the road* turns Estelle and Lois live.

The syntactical aspects of adverbial clauses are rather simple but the semantic relationships of two or more sentences involved in a transformation that embeds sentences can be quite complicated. For instance, temporal and causal relationships may become very subtly intertwined in sentences containing several adverbial clauses, especially if the clauses also contain prepositional phrases and if there are clauses within clauses. These relationships may be expressed in alternate ways, depending on the emphasis one wishes to place on the several constituents. For example:

> Mr. Smith killed his engine when he suddenly stepped on the brakes because he saw a squad car behind him.
> Because he saw a squad car behind him, Mr. Smith suddenly stepped on the brakes and killed his engine.
> Mr. Smith killed his engine because he stepped on the brakes suddenly when he saw a squad car behind him.

Therefore, teachers must keep in mind that meaning relationships are equally as important as syntactic ones when they are teaching children to interpret and use adverbial clauses.

EXERCISE

Underline the largest adverbial constituents contained in the sentences below and identify them in the space provided. You need not underline a phrase within a phrase, or a phrase within a clause, or a clause within a phrase. However, there may be more than one adverbial element in a sentence you will want to underline. Use the following key for your answers:

Adv: adverb IC: adverbial infinitive complement
PP: adverbial prepositional phrase AC: adverbial clause

Example:

AC Please come as soon as you can.

1. ______ The school is situated in the center of the city.
2. ______ The excellence of the school's program is determined by the people who teach the children.
3. ______ As the school began its second century, its goals were reaffirmed.
4. ______ Mrs. Smith has recently been granted a one year's leave of absence.
5. ______ Her grandfather was president of the board of trustees until his death.
6. ______ Gradually, the school has grown in size.
7. ______ In spring arrangements were made for her to go to England.
8. ______ At the Board's request, they visited many foreign schools.
9. ______ As they visited schools, they sent back many interesting letters.
10. ______ They will make a full report to the Board when they return.
11. ______ They will bring with them the slides they took.
12. ______ By action of the Board of Trustees, admission to the program is limited.
13. ______ After the testing is completed, the guidance counselor interviews each student individually.
14. ______ Whenever it is possible, visits are made to the homes of former students.
15. ______ Graduates may expect assistance when it is needed.

Answers:

1. in the center of the city, PP
2. by the people who teach the children, PP
3. As the school began its second century, AC
4. recently, Adv
5. until his death, PP
6. Gradually, Adv; in size, PP
7. in spring, PP; to England PP
8. At the Board's request, PP
9. As they visited schools, AC
10. to the Board, PP; when they return, AC
11. with them, PP
12. By action of the Board of Trustees, PP
13. After the testing is completed, AC; individually, Adv
14. Whenever it is possible, AC; to the homes of former students, PP
15. when it is needed, AC

There are a few rules that we should review about embedding clauses:

1. Generally, the tenses used in clauses follow a normal pattern, but there are conditions under which the tense in the clause is attracted to and changed according to the tense used in the matrix sentence. Refer to Lesson 16 if you have forgotten the rules for attracted sequence.

Normal sequence:

> The children *may go* to town whenever they wish.
> They *will leave* soon despite the fact that it *is* drizzling now.

Attracted sequence:

> They *decided* that they *would return* if it *rained* too hard.
> It *had begun* to pour before they *started.*

2. Deletions of repetious items from clauses are necessary when an identical item appears. Reference to Lesson 17 on modals will help you recall this rule:

> John stayed out as late as he could (stay out).
> John hurried home as fast as he could (hurry home).

EXERCISE

Underline only those subordinators introducing adverbial clauses. Indicate the category of the clause by writing its name, such as *cause, condition,* etc., in the space provided.

1. ______ After he had inspected all the hearing aid equipment, he conferred with the administrators.
2. ______ The hearing aids were antique and had been purchased before modern equipment was available.
3. ______ The experiment was less than earth shaking despite the fact that he had a carefully prepared hypothesis.
4. ______ Since the teachers had failed to carry out instructions, the tests had to begin again.
5. ______ Once they learned the directions, the tests proceeded on schedule.
6. ______ They put the data through the computer.
7. ______ Will you please send in your data so that we can complete our computer run?
8. ______ If a child failed to pass the test, he was eliminated from the list.
9. ______ We have tested 700 children since we began our testing.

Answers:

1. after, time
2. before, time
3. despite the fact that, concession
4. since, cause
5. once, time
6. no clause
7. so that, purpose
8. if, condition
9. since, time

It is possible for you to help children with language and hearing impairments to become better consumers of written materials and better users of the English language, if they become aware of the movability of adverbial elements in sentences.

EXERCISE

Move the adverbial elements in the following sentences to as many positions as you can.

1. Stand up, children.

______

______

______

2. Honestly, I think he's too smart for his own good.

3. They prepared for the exam by studying all night.

4. I would never have consented had I known it would turn out so dismally.

5. He took Spanish as his major in his undergraduate program.

6. For that matter, you needn't report again.

7. I'd rather not go, to be honest.

8. Unless he returns the books at once, he will lose his library privileges.

9. He must return the books immediately.

10. You will have completed the last exercise of the last lesson when you finish this sentence.

Answers:

1. not movable.
2. I honestly think he's too smart for his own good.
   I think honestly he's too smart for his own good.
   I think he's too smart for his own good, honestly.
   Honestly, I think he's too smart for his own good.
3. By studying all night, they prepared for the exam.
   They prepared, by studying all night, for the exam.
4. Had I known it would turn out so dismally, I would never have consented.
5. As his major, he took Spanish in his undergraduate program.
   In his undergraduate program, he took Spanish as his major.
6. You needn't report again, for that matter.
   You needn't, for that matter, report again.
7. To be honest, I'd rather not go.
8. He will lose his library privileges unless he returns the books at once.
9. He must immediately return the books.
10. When you finish this sentence, you will have completed the last exercise of the last lesson.

References

Boatner, M. T. and Gates, J. E., Eds.: *A Dictionary of Idioms for the Deaf.* West Hartford, Conn.: American School for the Deaf, 1966.

Chomsky, N.: *Syntactic Structures.* The Hague: Mouton, 1957.

Fitzgerald, E.: *Straight Language for the Deaf.* Washington, D.C.: Volta Bureau, 1926 (reprinted, 1956).

Francis, W. N.: *The Structure of American English.* New York: The Ronald Press, 1958.

Fries, C.: *American English Grammar.* New York: Appleton-Century-Crofts, Inc., 1940.

Krug, R. F.: *Teaching Syntax to Deaf Children.* Boulder, Colo.: Edumat Associates, 1968.

Loban, W.: *The Language of Elementary School Children.* Champaign, Ill.: National Council of Teachers of English, 1963.

Loban, W.: *Problems in Oral English.* Champaign, Ill.: National Council of Teachers of English, 1966.

Palmer, F. R.: *A Linguistic Study of the English Verb.* Coral Gables, Fla.: University of Florida Press, 1968.

APPENDIX A

Forms of the Past Tense of Regular and Irregular Verbs

This list of verbs is by no means comprehensive, but it may be used as a basis for adding other verbs in the categories suggested.

REGULAR VERBS

Regular verbs add *-ed* (or *-d* if the verb ends with the vowel *-e*) to the present tense form. Most verbs in English form the past tense in this manner. In speech, the pronunciation of *-ed* is dependent on the sound preceding the suffix.

1. *-ed* → [t] after *p, k, f, s, sh,* and *ch*

hel*p*/help*ed*; jum*p*/jump*ed*	mi*ss*/miss*ed*; for*ce*/forc*ed*
as*k*/ask*ed*; loo*k*/look*ed*	fi*sh*/fish*ed*; wa*sh*/wash*ed*
cou*gh*/cough*ed*; lau*gh*/laugh*ed*	rea*ch*/reach*ed*; wat*ch*/watch*ed*

2. *-ed* → [d] after voiced consonants and vowels

ro*b*/robb*ed*	admir*e*/admir*ed*
dra*g*/dragg*ed*	ai*m*/aim*ed*
lov*e*/lov*ed*	bur*n*/burn*ed*
graz*e*/graz*ed*	cr*y*/cri*ed*
judg*e*/judg*ed*	hurr*y*/hurri*ed*
ca*ll*/call*ed*	li*e*/li*ed*

3. *ed* → [ed] after *t* or *d*

collec*t*/collected	nee*d*/needed
consen*t*/consented	lan*d*/landed

IRREGULAR VERBS

Irregular verbs form the past tense by: (1) changing the vowel sound and adding *t* or *d*; (2) changing the vowel sound and not adding *t* or *d*; (3) changing a final *d* to *t*; (4) omitting a final consonant before adding *t* or *d*; and (5) retaining the present tense form in the past.

1. Verbs that change the vowel sound and add *t* or *d*.

buy/bought	do/did
lose/lost	hear/heard
may/might	say/said
sweep/swept	tell/told

2. Verbs that change the vowel sound, but do not add *t* or *d*. Many verbs fall into this category.

bite/bit	hold/held
bleed/bled	know/knew
blow/blew	lie/lay
break/broke	meet/met
draw/drew	read/read
choose/chose	ring/rang
dig/dug	run/ran
drink/drank	see/saw
eat/ate	shake/shook
fall/fell	sit/sat
feed/fed	slide/sled
fight/fought	speak/spoke
forget/forgot	swim/swam
find/found	take/took
fly/flew	tear/tore
get/got	throw/threw
give/gave	wear/wore
grow/grew	win/won
hang/hung	write/wrote

3. Verbs that change a final *d* to *t*.

bend/bent	send/sent
build/built	spend/spent
lend/lent	

4. Verbs that omit a final consonant before adding *t* or *d*. The vowel sound may also change.

bring/brought	shall/should
can/could	teach/taught
catch/caught	think/thought
have/had	will/would
make/made	

5. Verbs that have identical present and past tense forms.

cast	burst	spit
broadcast	hurt	split
forecast	shut	let
cost	cut	shed
bid	quit	set

APPENDIX B

Grammar I

Grammar I is a minimal grammar with which hearing-impaired children should be able to express their actions and thoughts with sufficient clarity to make their needs and wants known.

I. BASIC SENTENCE PATTERNS

I. NP + V_i (+ $Adv_{p, m, t}$)
II. NP + V_t + NP (+ $Adv_{p, m, t}$)
III. NP + be + N (+ $Adv_{p, t}$)
IV. NP + be + Adj (+ $Adv_{p, t}$)
V. NP + be + Adv_p (+ Adv_t)

II. TRANSFORMATIONS

1. T/yes-no
2. T/negative
   includes T/*any* replacement for *some*
3. T/do
4. T/request
5. T/contraction
6. T/particle shift
7. T/adj shift
8. T/adv shift
9. T/Wh- question
10. T/coordinating conjunction
    and, but, or
11. T/deletion
    Pronoun, N
12. T/reflexive
13. T/factive clause
    that deletion
14. T/there
15. T/adverbial clause
    time, cause
16. T/for-to (+ deletions)
    NP complement of object, infinitive of purpose, complement of adjective
17. T/rel clause
    who or *that* embedded in object
    or last noun in sentence
18. T/rel pro (+ *be*) deletion
19. T/comparative
    Adj, Adv
20. T/passive substitute
    got
21. NP complement following verbs of *know, think, forget, hope*

III. PHASE STRUCTURE RULES

1. *Noun Phrases*
   - 1.1a. Det + N
   - 1.1b. Det → reg art
     - [*a, an, the*]
     - [gen]
     - [dem]
   - 1.1c. Det → <± def>
   - 1.1d. Det → Ø
   - 1.1e. Det → dem
     - *this, that, these, those*
   - 1.2. Det + card + N
   - 1.3. Det + N + Modifier (prep phrase from del rel clause)
   - 1.4. Predet + Det + N
     - *all of, some of*
   - 1.5. Poss →
     - [N's, -s']
     - [of phrase]

2. *Verb Phrases*
   - 2.1. VP → t + V
     - [past]
   - 2.2. VP → t + M
     - [pres]
     - [past]
     - [*can*]
     - [*will*]
   - 2.3. VP → t+*be* + *-ing* + *V*
     - [pres]
     - [past]
   - 2.4. VP → t + V
     - [pres]

3. *Adjectives*
   - 3.1. Adj + N
   - 3.2. Adj + N adjunct + N

4. *Adverbs*
   - 4.1. Order → place, manner, time

IV. FEATURES OF LEXICON

1. *Nouns*
   - 1.1 <± common>
   - 1.2 <± count>
   - 1.3 <± singular>
   - 1.4 <± possessive>
   - 1.5 <± abstract>
   - 1.6 <± animate>
   - 1.7 <± human>

2. *Pronouns*
   - 2.1 <± personal>
     - 1st, 2nd, 3rd
   - 2.2 <± singular>
   - 2.3 <± gender>
     - M, F, N
   - 2.4 <± case>
     - nom, poss, accus
   - 2.5 reflexive
   - 2.6 indefinite

3. *Verbs*
   - 3.1 <± transitive>
   - 3.2 <± progressive>
   - 3.3 <± catenation>
   - 3.4 v + particle
     - v + complement
   - 3.5 inflec suffixes
   - 3.5a. pres 3rd pers sing. (*-s*)
   - 3.5b. past (-ed) regular and irregular
   - 3.5c. pres part (*-ing*)
   - 3.5d. past part (*-en*)

4. *Adjectives*
   - 4.1 <± comparative>
     - *-er, -est, more, most*
   - 4.2 <± catenation>

5. *Adverbs*
   - 5.1 <± preverbs>

6. *Prepositions*
   - 6.1 <+ movement>
     - <+ time>
     - <+ place>

EXAMPLES OF EXPRESSIVE LANGUAGE BASED ON GRAMMAR I

The examples of written language that follow are based on the concept of expansions of basic sentences through application of transformations, additions to phrase structure rules, and features of the lexicon. At each step only new expansions are listed. Each set of paragraphs generally incorporates the language aspects suggested in the previous examples. The last essay contains almost all of the items listed in Grammar I.

This series of examples is not intended to imply developmental growth in language usage but to illustrate the range and depth with which expression of ideas can be stated using minimal patterns and a limited number of expansions. Two examples at each step are given to encompass ideas congenial to both younger and older children.

	Elementary Level	Upper Level	I *Basic Sentence Patterns*	II *Transformations*	III *Phrase Structure Rules*	IV *Features of Lexicon*
1.	We ran. We played. We laughed.	I goofed. I stumbled. I fell.	I		$VP \rightarrow t + V_i$ (past)	<± singular> (1st pers Pro) < + nom> Pro
2.	I fed Fluffy. He ate some lettuce. Fluffy likes lettuce.	We lost the game. We had bad luck. We need some breaks.	II	T/adj shift (prenom adj)	Det → <± def art> $VP \rightarrow t + V_t$ (pres) (past) Det → Ø	<± common> N <± count> N <± masc> Pro <± sing> Pro (3rd pers)
3.	My father is home today. He's sick. I'm sorry.	My car is in the garage today. It's out of order. I'm disgusted.	V $(+ Adv_p + Adv_t)$ IV	T/contraction (1st, 3rd pers Pro + be)		<± possessive> (1st pers Pro) <+ nom + singular neuter> (3rd pers Pro)
4.	Dear Mother: Come to Room 26 on Friday. We will have a show. Your daughter, Alice	Dear Dan: On Friday, October 16, we will have a Fall Dance at the Hearing Center. Please come and	II	T/request T/coordinating conjunction (V_1 *and* V_2)	$VP \rightarrow t + M + V$ (pres) (*will* + *have*)	<+ singular> (N)

		bring a friend. Admission is 50 cents. Sincerely, Duffy	III			
5.	*My New Brace* Yesterday I went to the dentist. He put a brace on my teeth. I can't chew now. My mouth is sore.	*Bowling on TV* Yesterday afternoon I watched the bowling championships. Jack Doll made seven strikes in a row.	(+Adv prep phrase_p)	T/adv shift (time) T/negative T/contraction (*can't*)	Det + N (*-ing* modifier) Det → card + N VP → t + M + *not* + V (pres + *can*)	$\left\langle \begin{matrix} -\text{ singular} \\ +\text{ abstract} \end{matrix} \right\rangle$N
		His score was 296. He can't lose now. I'm betting on him.	(+ Adv_t)		VP → + be — *-ing* + V	
6.	*To the Zoo* We are going to go to the zoo in the school bus tomorrow. We are going to take our lunch. I want to watch the monkeys. They're funny animals.	*Notice* The Nature Club will have its first meeting September 25 at 7:00 p.m. We are going to discuss our next program. We want everyone to be on time. We need you. Please come.	(+ Adv prep $\text{phrase}_{t,m,p}$) III	T/for-to (*for* + N deletion) T/for-to (*for* deletion) T/contr (3rd pers + *be*)	Order → Adv_p + Adv_m + Adv_t VP → t + *be* + *going* + inf (future aspect) Det → gen + ordinal	<possessive, neuter> (3rd pers Pro) <possessive, –singular> (1st person Pro) <nom, –singular> (3rd pers Pro) <–sing> 2nd pers Pro

	Elementary Level	Upper Level	I Patterns Basic Sentence	II Transformations	III Phrase Structure Rules	IV Features of Lexicon
7.	*No Bus*	*Wating for the Bus*			Det → dem + N	
	This morning the	This morning I	IV		(this)	
	bus was late. I	had to wait a long				
	waited a long time	time for the bus		T/coordinating		
	on the corner and	because an accident		conjunction		
	then I went back	happened on 20th		(S_1 *and* S_2)		
	home because I	Street.		T/adverbial clause		
	was cold. My	All of the traffic		(cause)	Predet + Det + N	
	mother took me to	had to stop for half			(*all of*)	
	school in the car.	an hour. Then six				
	Maybe the bus	busses came at one				
	will break down	time.				
	again. Next time	It was late for		T/coordinating		
	I would like a	school but it wasn't		conjunction	VP → t + M + V	
	vacation.	my fault.		(S_1 *but* S_2)	(past + will + like)	
8.	*Feeding Monkeys*	*Fight! Fight!*				
	There were lots of	After the game		T/there		
	monkeys on	some kids were			(past) T/V → t + *be* +	
	Monkey Island.	having a fight			*ing* + v	<accusative,
	Some of them were	because East lost the			Det + Predet + Pro	—singular>
	swinging on ropes.	game. Some of them			∅ Det	(3rd pers Pro)
	Some were watching	were kicking, some		T/deletion		<indefinite Pro>
	us.	were pushing and		of N		<accusative
	I threw a peanut	some were punching				—singular>
	to a monkey.	pretty hard. A			Intensifier + adj	(1st pers Pro)

	He shelled it and ate it. Some other monkeys wanted a treat but I didn't have any more peanuts. Too bad!	couple of cops came and stopped the fight. There were a few bloody noses and black eyes in the crowd but nobody got hurt badly. I was lucky!	T/do T/negative contraction T/ *any* in negative statement T/passive substitute: *(got)*		
9a.	*A Fire near School* Two fire engines stopped near school at recess time. All of of us were excited and curious. There was a big fire in a house down the street. We saw the flames and the smoke. The flames were higher than our school. We all wanted to go to the fire but we had to go back to our rooms. I am going to look in the paper and maybe I can read about it tonight.	*Moon Landing No 3* The next moon landing will be tricky. It will be riskier than the last one because the astronauts will land in a deep crater. The astronauts are ready for all kinds of dangerous maneuvers. They will drill three holes ten feet deep and hike two miles to get ninety-five pounds of moon rocks. They will try to walk up the hill to look down into the crater. Good luck, Astronauts!	T/comparative of adjective (*-er* + *than*) T/rel clause deletion: (embedded postnominal phrase) T/infinitive (noun complement) T/infinitive of purpose T/infinitive (verbal complement)	Det $\rightarrow$ card + N adjunct Predet $\rightarrow$ N of quantity	<+ catenation> (*ready* + *for*)

	Elementary Level	Upper Level	I Basic Sentence Patterns	II Transformations	III Phrase Structure Rules	IV Features of Lexicon
9b.	*What Happened at the Fire* There was a picture of the fire in the paper. A fireman rescued an old woman who lived on the second floor. He climbed a ladder and carried her down safely. Nobody was hurt but the fire almost destroyed the house. The fire started in the basement in some trash.			T/rel clause (embedded after object)		
10.	*Robin Red Breast* Robins spend the winter in Florida, Mexico and Guatemala.	*Signs of Spring* This morning, February 28, I saw my first robin.				
		"Where did he come from?" I wondered.		T/Wh- question		
	In summer they live in the northern part of the United States, in Canada and in	Did he live in Florida or Mexico or Central		T/yes-no T/coord conj (*or*)		

Alaska. About a million robins fly up the Mississippi flyway every year. Some follow the Missouri River and others follow the Ohio River to their summer home.

The male robins return first and the females arrive later, when the weather is warmer. The male selects a site for the nest but his mate builds it. She lines a mud bowl with grass and usually lays four light blue spotted eggs in the nest.

The female sits on the eggs except when she goes out to eat. Then the male keeps the eggs warm.

The eggs hatch after two weeks but the babies stay for two more weeks.

America during the cold winter? Robins are good navigators because they can fly thousands of miles and they don't get lost. Most robins return to a place near their old homes. Some come back year after year.

The American robin is really a kind of thrush. His food consists mainly of small insects and small fruits like cherries and mountain ash berries. He is an excellent worm and grub hunter.

Robins are friendly birds and I am always happy to welcome back my friends, the robins, every spring.

Art + N mod + N

Gen + N mod + N

T/rel clause del postnominal prep phrase)

T/adverbial clause (*when*)

Preverb + v
card + color + past
part + N

T/embedded inf sent after adj
T/rel clause deletion

APPENDIX C

Grammar II

Grammar II is an advanced grammar which can be used basically for expanding the written expressive language of older children who are college bound or who show evidence of mastering Grammar I at an early age. Selections of items from Grammar II will be dependent on a pupil's need for expressing himself more clearly and more succinctly. Undoubtedly a more complex semantic component would accompany the development of Grammar II. This grammar requires considerable control over embedded noun phrase and verb phrase complements including all types of infinitive and question embedding. Grammar II, while encompassing a great many more transformations and phrase structure rules than Grammar I, is still a rather limited base for sophisticated writing since it does not deal with idiomatic or poetic expression. These aspects must be dealt with concurrently with growing syntactic competence.

II. TRANSFORMATIONS

1. T/nominalization
   - 1.1a. poss + *-ing (his talking)*
   - 1.1b. N's derived from N, V, Adj + derivational suffix
2. T/indirect object
3. T/rel
   - 3.1. T/rel (introduced by *who, whose, whom, which*) embedded in subject, object and object of preposition as restrictive clause
   - 3.2. T/rel pro shift (when rel pro is object of embedded sentence)
   - 3.3. T/prep + rel pro shift
   - 3.4. T/rel pro deletion (when rel pro is not subject of embedded sentence)
   - 3.5. T/rel pro + *be* deletion
   - 3.6. T/rel (nonrestrictive clause)
   - 3.7. T/rel adv (introduced by *where, when)*
   - 3.8. T/rel pro replacement (for *that which, to that place, in that way,* and *at that time* with *whatever, wherever, however* and *whenever)*

4. T/embedded questions (introduced by *who, what, where, when)*
5. T/extraposition
6. T/*it* replacement
7. T/wh- article replacement (as in *which* boy, *what* number)
8. T/question tag
9. T/neg (*much* replacement for *lots of)*
10. T/subord conj *(if unless, in order that,* etc. as needed for introducing adverbial clauses)
11. T/preverb shift (intensifier)
12. T/passive
13. T/indirect discourse
    - 13.1. T/embedded NC (*that* after verbs such as *say, tell, declare, inform)*
    - 13.2. T/embeded inf (after verbs *tell* and *ask)*
    - 13.3. T/embedded NC (*if* after verb *ask*)
14. T/verb agreement (tense sequence)
15. T/deletion
    - 15.1. T/complementizer deletion
    - 15.2. T/conjunction deletion (in series)
    - 15.3. T/*it* deletion (from factive clause)
    - 15.4. T/pronoun deletion
    - 15.5. T/verb deletion (following modal or aux)
    - 15.6. T/*for* + N + *to* (from embedded sentence)

III. PHRASE STRUCTURE RULES

1. *Noun Phrases*
    - 1.1. Determiners
    - 1.1a. Preart + art + N
    - 1.1b. Preart + predet + art + N
    - 1.1c. Det + modifiers in series
    - 1.1d. Det + N + deleted rel clause appearing as prep phrase
    - 1.1e. Det +N + deleted rel clause appearing as *-ing* or *-en* verbal
    - 1.1f. Det art + N + of + N (poss)
2. *Verb Phrases*
    - 2.1. Active
    - 2.1a. VP → t(pres/past) + M + *be* + *-ing* + V
    - 2.1b. VP → t(pres/past) + *have* + *-en* + V
    - 2.1c. VP → t(pres/past) + *have* + *-en* + be + *-ing* + V
    - 2.1d. VP → t(pres/past) + M + *have* + *-en* + *be* + *-ing* + V
    - 2.2. Passive
    - 2.2a. VP + t(pres/past) + *be* + *-en* + V
VP → t(pres/past) + *have* + *been* + *-en* + V
VP → t(pres/past) + *be* + *being* + *-en* + V

3. *Infinitive phrases*
   3.1. positive active (*to say*)
   3.2. *to* + *be* + *-ing* + base form (*to be saying*)
   3.3. *to* + *have* + *-en* + V (*to have said*)
   3.4. *to* + *have* + *been* + *-ing* + base form (*to have been saying*)
   3.5. passive-positive
   3.6. *to* + *be* + *-en* + V (*to be said*)
   3.7. *to* + *have* + *-en* + *be* *-en* + V (*to have been said*)
   3.8. negative active: *not* + *to* + base form (*not to say*)
   3.9. negative passive: *not* + *to be* + *-en* + V (*not to be said*)
4. *Adjectives:* superlative followed by clause
5. *Adverbs:* comparison of all adverbs
   5.1. Preverb + V
   5.2. aux + preverb + V

FEATURES OF THE LEXICON

<+ derivational suffices>
(added to N's, V's, and Adj's to produce new N's, V's, and Adj's)
<+ prefixes>
(aded to N's, V's, and Adj's)

EXAMPLE OF EXPRESSIVE LANGUAGE BASED ON GRAMMAR II

This essay is an adaptation of a book report written by a student in a high school program in a school for the deaf. It does not include all of the transformations or phrase structure rules listed in Grammar II, but it shows the type of writing which uses many of its features. The complexity of sentences is achieved by conjunction and multiple embeddings in NP's and VP's. Notice the extensive use of embedded infinitive sentences. Deletions also play a large role in the production of complex sentences in this example.

Book Report: Frederick Douglass	II *Transformations*	III *Phrase Structure Rules*	IV *Features of the Lexicon*
Frederick Bailey, born a slave in 1817 on a planta-	T/rel pro + be deletion (resulting in postnominal modifier)		
tion in Maryland, barely knew his mother from whom he was separated at an early age. He never found out	T/rel; T/prep shift	passive: t(past) + *be* + —*en* + V	
who his father was. Frederick lived with his grandmother, but when he was seven, he was taken away to live with other slave children on the big plantation of his master. It made him sad to leave his grand-	T/rel T/extraposition T/inf (as VP compl after adj)	Def art + N + *of* + N (poss)	
mother for now he had no one to love him; he had no	T/adv clause (cause introduced by *for* T/conj		
bed nor blanket; and he had no clothes except two	*nor*) T/conjunction deletion		
rough, handwoven shirts. He was often very cold and always very hungry. He did not like being a slave	(in series) T/adv shift (*often, always*)	Det → card + adj + verbal + N	action nominal (*being*)
child.			

After a few years, Frederick was lucky enough	T/inf (after adj *enough*)		
to be sent to Baltimore where he was to take care of	T/inf (after *be* implying the past of future time) T/rel (intro by rel adv *where*)	passive inf: to + be + —*en* + V (*to be sent*)	
little Thomas Auld, the son of his master. Every evening, they would listen to Thomas' mother read the Bible. Frederick wanted very much to learn to read, so he asked Mrs. Auld if she would teach him.	T/adv *so* clause T/embedded NC (after *ask*, indirect discourse)		
Mrs. Auld was happy to give him some lessons and	T/indirect obj (*him*)		
she enjoyed helping him because he was an intelligent boy and a good pupil.			action nominal (*helping*)
In a short time, Frederick learned the alphabet and could spell. When Mr. Auld, Thomas' father, found out that Frederick was learning to read, he		active: t(past) + *be* + *ing* + V	
became exceedingly angry. He said none of his	T/NP comp (after *say*, indirect discourse		
slaves were to be taught to read. He knew they would become dissatisfied with their life of slavery.	T/compl deletion (*that*)		prefix + V (*dissatisfied*)
Frederick was very unhappy and so he decided that		intensifier + adj	

	II *Transformations*	III *Phrase Structure Rules*	IV *Features of the Lexicon*
some day he would be a free man. But first he had to learn to read. It was very hard to learn without a teacher, but Frederick found some books and studied by himself until he could read.	T/*for* + N deletion		
Frederick stayed with the Aulds a long time. He and some of his slave friends had met secretly and decided to escape to the North. Their plans	T/aux deletion	active: t(past) + *have* + —*en* (*had met*)	
were discovered so Frederick was sent away to a		passive: t(past) + *be* + —*en* (*were discovered*)	
cruel master who beat and starved him. He became more and more determined to run away in order to get his freedom. Finally, in 1838, when Frederick	T/infinitive of purpose (embedded as VC)		
was 21 years old, a chance came for him to escape. He had been working as a slave in a shipyard where	T/*for* + *to* + inf (embedded as NPC)	active: t(past) + *have* + —*en* + *be* + *ing* (*had been working*)	
he had learned the trade of caulker. His master had let him keep some of his small earnings. What little money Frederick saved, he used for train fare. One	T/wh- article replacement (*what little money*)		action nominal (*earnings*)

Sunday, he got onto a northbound train and left for New York. At last he was free. He was very lucky not to be caught this time.

onto for *on* with verb of action

negative passive infinitive: not + to + be + V (*not to be caught*)

After Frederick escaped, he changed his name to Frederick Douglass so people would not know

where to find him. All his life he worked for equal justice for black men. You can read his entire story in his interesting autobiography, *Life and Times of Frederick Douglass* (adapted by Barbara Ritchie, New York, Thomas Y. Crowell Co. 1966).

T/question embedded as infinitive

Index

4 5 6 7 8 9 0 1 8 2
c d e f g h i j